AFGHANISTAN

CHINA

JAMMU AND KASHMIR

PAKISTAN

My dad was born in
Buttar Sivia Village,
District Amritsar

Rice

My mom was born in Jalandhar

HIMACHAL
PRADESH

PUNJAB

I was born here

Chandigarh

UTTARAKHAND

NEPAL

Mount Everest
29,029 ft
(8,848 m)

SIKKIM

BHUTAN

ARUNACHAL
PRADESH

Wheat

HARYANA

DELHI

Taj Mahal

RAJASTHAN

Jaipur

UTTAR PRADESH

BIHAR

ASSAM   Tea

NAGALAND

MEGHALAYA

MANIPUR

BANGLADESH

TRIPURA

MIZORAM

MYANMAR

GUJARAT

MADHYA PRADESH

CHHATTISGARH

JHARKHAND

WEST
BENGAL

Kolkata
(Calcutta)

MAHARASHTRA

ORISSA

Fish

Bay of
Bengal

Mumbai
(Bombay)

India Gate

Pune

Prawn

My husband's birthplace

Hyderabad

Coconut

My father-in-law was born in Pasumarru Village,
District Krishna

Arabian Sea

ANDHRA PRADESH

Chili peppers

My mother-in-law was born
in Repalli

Panaji
GOA

Fish

KARNATAKA

Banana

Rice

Fish

Chennai
(Madras)

Bangalore

LAKSHADWEEP

Fish

TAMIL
NADU

Coffee

ANDAMAN & NICOBAR ISLANDS

N

W   E

S

KERALA

Coconut

Coconut

MALDIVES

SRI LANKA

INDIAN OCEAN

0   300km

scale 1 : 12 300 000

Entice with Spice

Easy Indian Recipes for Busy People

Shubhra Ramineni

Photography by Masano Kawana

Styling by Christina Ong and Magdalene Ong

TUTTLE PUBLISHING
Tokyo • Rutland, Vermont • Singapore

Note to reader: The vast majority of Indian names for recipes, specialized cookware, etc. are in Hindi, which is the most common Indian language spoken and written in India. However, the names for some regional dishes from the state of Andhra Pradesh are given in the local Telugu language.

Published by Tuttle Publishing, an imprint of Periplus Editions (HK) Ltd

www.tuttlepublishing.com

Text copyright © 2010 Shubhra Ramineni
Map and photos copyright © 2010 Periplus Editions (HK) Ltd except: Page 9 and author's photo on front cover by Bruce Bennett, © Shubhra Ramineni and also all of the following: Endpaper photos (except photos of food); pages 11; 12; 13; 16; 17; 18; 22; 23; 24; 30 (middle column left photo); 32 (bottom right); 35 (middle column); 41 (bottom right); 42 (bottom row); 44 (bottom); 51 (right row); 53 (bottom row); 56; 57 (right row); 65 (bottom and right row); 69; 71; 73; 75; 77

ISBN: 978-0-8048-4029-3

Distributed by
North America, Latin America & Europe
Tuttle Publishing
364 Innovation Drive, North Clarendon, VT 05759-9436 U.S.A.
Tel: 1 (802) 773-8930; Fax: 1 (802) 773-6993
info@tuttlepublishing.com; www.tuttlepublishing.com

Japan
Tuttle Publishing
Yaekari Building, 3rd Floor, 5-4-12 Osaki,
Shinagawa-ku, Tokyo 141 0032
Tel: (81) 3 5437-0171; Fax: (81) 3 5437-0755
tuttle-sales@gol.com

Asia Pacific
Berkeley Books Pte. Ltd.
61 Tai Seng Avenue #02-12, Singapore 534167
Tel: (65) 6280-1330; Fax: (65) 6280-6290
inquiries@periplus.com.sg; www.periplus.com

13 12 11 10   5 4 3 2 1
Printed in Singapoe

TUTTLE PUBLISHING® is a registered trademark of Tuttle Publishing, a division of Periplus Editions (HK) Ltd.

To my dear, dear husband, Naveen. From the beginning, he encouraged me to develop and write this cookbook, and he supported me through the entire process of creating it. I vividly remember when he brought home a slice of cake to celebrate the day I found out I had a book deal. He was there when recipes needed to be retested—trying out the food and all the while helping to keep the kitchen clean by washing the never-ending pile of dishes. I hope he still likes Indian food despite being overloaded with it for more than a year of recipe testing!

Acknowledgments

I would like to thank my mother, Neelam Verma. This book definitely would not have been possible without her help and contributions. She spent many a day and night tirelessly helping me cook and test the recipes. She always cooks by sight, feel and taste rather than with exact measuring tools, so it was tricky and frustrating at times for us to standardize the recipes. However, she patiently answered every question, and we did it! She also offered and provided much advice and guidance on different aspects of Indian cuisine and as it relates to the culture. I would also like to thank her for providing me with nutritional guidance throughout my life and for teaching me a healthy eating lifestyle.

I am also grateful for the contribution my mother-in-law, Rajani Ramineni, made to the book. She taught me how to cook dishes from a different Indian regional cuisine and helped me develop and test those recipes. Whenever my in-laws came to visit us this past year from out of town, I would put her to work and she and I would work on those recipes during her entire short stay. On her last visit, after a long day of standing, cooking and cleaning, she joked that she was not going to come visit anymore! She was always willing to help and I thank her for that and her patience.

Also thanks to D.G.K. Varma for his input and culinary expertise and to Sonia Yadav for sharing her wealth of knowledge on Indian cuisine.

The following business deserve a word of thanks: Black Diamond Builders (Bonner S. Ball and Thomas H. Zenner), for providing the photo shoot location; and Sur la Table, for providing the kitchenware for the photo shoot.

Finally, I would like to thank my editors, Holly Jennings and June Chong, and my designer, Chan Sow Yun, for working with me through the different stages of the development of this book. Their advice and suggestions were always helpful and supportive.

Contents

Preparing Home-style Recipes for Family and Friends

Having grown up in an Indian home in the suburbs of Houston, Texas, with immigrant parents, I certainly have had a diverse food experience. This includes home-style Indian meals prepared by my mother, eating out at Mexican and Italian restaurants (my parents' favorite when not eating at home), ordering pizza at home, and traditional American food from school and college cafeterias, as well as in the homes of my American

friends. We spent many summers in India visiting our family and touring the country. While there, I enjoyed Indian street food and watching and helping my relatives prepare meals. I was intrigued by the efforts and techniques involved in making a traditional meal in India. Cooking three meals for a family seemed to be an all-day, labor-intensive event, but it did seem interesting—especially when I got to help my grandmother make bread in her *tandoor,* an Indian oven. When we returned home to the United States, I noticed that my mom's quicker and easier cooking methods resulted in the same great-tasting food. Of course my mom had more modern conveniences, but as a career woman she was also pressed for time and did not have all day to prepare a meal.

Once I became a working professional, I realized that I did not know how to cook efficiently—a necessity for enjoying a wholesome homemade meal after a tiring day at the office. Following graduate school, I re-entered corporate America and became Manager of my department. I found myself coming home late, tired and hungry after a long day's work. At first, I would simply pick up a quick take-out dinner on the way home or resort to a frozen meal, but, as time went by, this was becoming more unhealthy and less satisfying. It was time to learn how to quickly make delicious and healthy home-cooked Indian meals!

I began by utilizing two of the most expert Indian home cooks I know—my mom, who is from the northern region of India and my mother-in-law, who is from the southern region of India. I called them when I wanted one of their recipes and would quickly jot down the verbal recipe on a handy piece of scrap paper. To these "scribbles" I added my own personal touches—all for the purpose of being able to make a traditional Indian meal as efficiently as possible. In time, after honing and developing the recipes, I was able to come home after an exhausting day at work and have a satisfying and delicious Indian home-cooked meal in minutes! Eventually I decided to collect all of my scraps of sloppy handwritten recipes and neatly type and compile them into binder to make my own personal Indian "cookbook." One day, as I was browsing the cookbooks at a local bookstore, I noticed that there weren't any Indian cookbooks that had clear and easy home-style recipes that are commonly made in Indian homes and are from the diverse regions in India. At that moment I realized that my "binder" was a unique recipe collection that could be of use and interest to Indians and non-Indians alike.

I am very excited to share my recipes and techniques with you! If you love Indian food but think it must be too time consuming for a busy person like you to make, especially for a weekday meal, I hope you will pick up this book and give it a try. It was with you in mind that this book was written! You will be amazed at the simplicity of my recipes, which use easy-to-find ingredients and everyday cookware—all without sacrificing the authenticity of the taste.

I certainly did not get it perfect the first time I tried cooking Indian food at home, but I do hope my simplified recipes with clear step-by-step instructions will help you get it perfect or very close to perfect the first time you try. Don't be scared, don't get frustrated, but do have fun. Practice makes perfect. And remember, it's always nice when you entice with spice!

Shubhra Ramineni

Sautéed Okra with Onions

Indian Cooking Made Easy

Namaste! I am delighted to share my easy Indian recipes with you. I have just a few helpful words before I start you off making fabulous quick, Indian home-style meals that will have you and anyone that is lucky enough to savor a bite simply wowed.

Indian food is flavorful food that is cooked with a mixture of exotic spices. The recipes in this book, which I have learned from my mother and mother-in-law, and a few I have learned and created on my own, are from all over India. My mother is originally from the northern Indian state of Punjab and my mother-in-law is from the southern Indian state of Andhra Pradesh, each of which has distinct dishes, flavors and cooking styles. The southern part has rice as a main staple, and very spicy foods, since rice and hot chili peppers are grown abundantly in this region. The northern part has richer foods with butter and cheeses. There wheat grows plentifully and so bread is the main staple. Food from this region is not as spicy as the food from the southern part of India, but you can always increase the heat by adding more chili peppers or ground red pepper (cayenne). Traditional home-cooked Indian dishes are passed down from generations: Both my mother and my mother-in-law learned to cook from their mothers, who in turn learned from their mothers. My version of these classic recipes uses easy-to-find ingredients and basic cookware and, more importantly, I have standardized them with actual measurements—rather than just adding ingredients based on sight, feel and taste as traditional Indian cooks do! In fact, the only reason my mother has a set of measuring cups is because she bought them for me when I was younger. She simply uses a coffee cup as her one-cup measurement and can estimate one-quarter or one-half cup from it.

The ABCs of Indian Cooking

Here in the United States, and in other Western countries, when we think of Indian food, the word *curry* most often comes to mind. In fact, in Britain, where Chicken Tikka Masala is now as popular as fish and chips, curry is synonymous with Indian food (a Brit will say, "I'm in

Below: *Dried red chili peppers for sale at an open street market in India.*

the mood to eat curry tonight," meaning Indian food in general). Curry powder, a Western invention that is not used in traditional Indian cooking, is a convenient readymade blend of various Indian spices. Indians typically use the word *curry* to simply mean "sauce" or "gravy" (either thin or thick), and thus all dishes that have a saucy or gravy consistency are called "curries." In this book I use the term in the same way. When I refer to "curried vegetables" or "curried meats," I mean that those dishes have a "wet" curried base—that is, a gravy or saucy (sometimes near soupy) consistency instead of a "dry" sautéed style dish. There are some exceptions to this rule—for example, even though lentils are typically cooked in a liquid base, they are not called "curries." Then there is the curry leaf—an aromatic leaf from the curry tree that is used as an herb in cooking. Many Indian homes around the world grow a curry tree in their backyards so they will have fresh curry leaves on hand. (I use fresh curry leaves in some recipes, but have made their use optional because they are one of the few ingredients I use that do require a trip to an Indian market.)

After curry, the term *masala*, which is the Hindi word for "spice," is probably the second most commonly used word when discussing Indian food. Masalas can be "dry" or "wet," but in either case they form the flavor base of a dish and are a key component in Indian cooking.

Dry masalas may consist of individual spices, such as turmeric, red pepper (cayenne), and coriander, or be a special blend of spices that have been roasted and ground together. Garam Masala (page 44), Biryani Masala (page 80), Rasam Masala (page 90) and Sambar Masala (page 92) are all examples of the latter type of dry masala. These roasted spice blends can be stored up to three months in an airtight container, but after that they lose potency.

Wet masalas are both a flavor base and

Below: *Tomato and onion masala before adding the spices.*

a cooking method that consists of cooked and spiced onions and/or tomatoes. The "wet" masala cooking technique is common in the northern region of India, especially in the state of Punjab, and is used in many of the dishes from this region. It is the base that adds flavor to the fish, meat or vegetable. First, onions, if used, are shredded or finely cut and browned in oil until golden so that they no longer have a raw taste. Then tomatoes, if used, are added and cooked until they are completely mashed, and then the dry spices are added. When making a masala with tomatoes, the end result looks like a coarse paste. The longer the tomatoes and onions cook with the dry spices, the darker the masala will become, resulting in a darker base or "curry" for the dish, and the more the flavor of the spices will develop. When I was little I used to watch my mom make a masala and, before she would add the vegetables, I would ask her to save a small amount of the masala for me to enjoy with a slice of plain white bread!

Wet masalas are customized based on the amount of onions, tomatoes and combination of dry spices that are added. Some are made with just tomatoes and dry spices, some are made with just onions and dry spices and some are made with both tomatoes and onions and dry spices. There is not a definite ratio of the amount of onions to tomatoes—it depends on whether you like the taste of less or more onions or tomatoes. You will see that in my recipes the amount of onions and tomatoes varies a bit, but you can adjust if you like.

My mom usually just adds ground turmeric, ground red pepper (cayenne), salt and ground black pepper to most of her masalas. Even though she often uses the same combination of spices, each dish has a unique flavor that comes from the main ingredients that are added to the masala. If she is really feeling fancy, she will add spices such as cardamom or carom seeds to the masala for added flavor. Once you become comfortable cooking masalas, you can make the un-spiced onion and/or tomato paste in bulk and refrigerate or freeze it until ready to make a dish. When you are ready to cook a dish, lightly oil your saucepan or skillet, add the desired amount of refrigerated or defrosted masala, and then add the specific spices. This way, you can make it in advance, and then simply add the desired spices when you are ready to make the dish. With practice, you will get a feel for how much masala to use for a dish, and also if you want your dish to have more onions or tomatoes in the masala. You can also then customize what spices you want to add to the masala. You can even make the spiced masala for a specific recipe and then refrigerate or freeze it.

Some recipes for wet masalas call for garlic or ginger. If you plan on making either a spiced or un-spiced masala in bulk, leave out the garlic and ginger. Instead, for better flavor, when you are ready to make a dish that calls for garlic or ginger, cook them in oil first before adding the refrigerated or defrosted masala and any needed spices.

Enjoying Indian Food with Family and Friends

Whether a formal or casual meal, Indian food is typically served family-style—meaning everyone gathers around the table, the dishes are placed in the center, and everyone helps themselves to a bit of each dish. In India, modern homes have dining tables but many families still sit on the floor, gathered around the food. A sheet, large cloth or thin bamboo mat is spread out on the floor and the food is placed in the center. Everyone sits on the sheet, or on small floor stools or cushions, with their plates in front of them on the ground. Small bowls may be given to everyone to put yogurt or any dish with a liquid or curried base. In the southern part of India, giant fresh banana leaves are sometimes used as plates, since bananas are abundantly grown there. When visiting my paternal grandparents in their village, I remember having delicious, fun and intimate meals with relatives in their open veranda on the ground while sitting on floor cushions. Sometimes we would place the food on large tweed cots, and sit outdoors on the cots and eat. It was a like a fun family picnic right at home!

There are no special rules for eating an Indian meal, except usually the food is only eaten with your right hand, while your left hand is placed in your lap, but you can use it if needed. Since much of Indian food is eaten with your hands, washing your hands before eating (and of course after!) is essential. In the southern part of India, rice is traditionally eaten and mixed with other dishes with your hands. In the northern part of India, where breads are a common part of the daily diet, a piece of bread is torn off and then used to grab or scoop up the sautéed or curried dish. Other than that, basic table manners apply. If your guests can't help but exhibit a burp after the meal, consider that the ultimate compliment . . . at least that is what they do in India!

What's for dinner?

The easy-to-make yet elegant dishes in this cookbook are perfect for both casual meals or for special occasions. You can make just one or two recipes of your choice for a quick snack or simple week-day meal, or you can go all out and serve a formal Indian meal, beginning with appetizers and ending with dessert and an after-dinner Indian cappuccino or tea. If you're new to Indian cooking, the myriad of recipes and possible combinations may seem daunting. Don't worry—there was rhyme and reason to the way I organized the chapters in this book. If you follow the simple blueprint (page 14) and select your favorite dishes from the relevant chapters, you can feel confident about serving a delicious Indian meal when you want to impress family and friends.

Below: *1981 India: Our family friend, Hardwari Sharma, cooking chapati with ghee in her home near my dad's childhood village.*

In daily home cooking in India, appetizers, soups and salads are not separate courses. Traditional Indian cuisine does not feature soups as they are thought of in the West—rather, we have soupy dishes, such as lentils, that are served with the main meal. A simple salad of sliced cucumbers, tomatoes and raw onions is typically eaten along with dinner to provide a refreshing crunch during the meal. You do not have to stick to this . . . if you enjoy lentils as a soup course or if you'd like to have a salad course—go for it! Though appetizers are not part of a typical, everyday home-style meal in India, I enjoy serving an appetizer or two when entertaining guests, which are always a big hit.

If a formal Indian meal, complete with appetizer and dessert, seems too elaborate for a hectic weeknight, you can still enjoy a quick but well-balanced and satisfying Indian meal by serving just plain yogurt, rice or bread, a vegetable dish, and a meat, chicken, fish or seafood dish (or a lentil or legume dish for a vegetarian meal), which is how my mom puts together a weeknight Indian meal for us. I will indicate when dishes, such as Dosa and Uttapam, do not neatly fit into the blueprint and will provide other suggestions instead. I understand that making traditional Indian breads can get a bit messy, so you can save that for weekend meals or special occasions. Or you can use the shortcut that I use, and that my mother also uses now: Simply buy Mexican wheat tortillas and heat them up on a gas stove or skillet. You can use this in place of homemade Indian bread or even rice. The whole idea is to make it easy to prepare and serve delicious and nutritious meals.

Throughout the book I suggest traditional pairings for each dish. When choosing which vegetables and meat, chicken, fish or seafood dishes to serve together, keep in mind the colors and consistencies of the dishes for variety in taste and texture, and for beautiful presentation. Along with pairing complementary flavors, and spicy hot dishes with cooling plain yogurt or raita, Indians enjoy pairing contrasting textures at the table. Ideally, try to have both a sautéed dish and a curried dish at the table to balance out the "dry" and "wet" dishes—for example, a sautéed vegetable and a curried meat, fish or seafood, or vice versa, or a sautéed vegetable and a "soupy" lentil dish. In general, I prefer to eat sautéed dishes with breads since they are easy to grab with a small piece of bread, and I like a side of raita to eat between bites in order to provide a fluid consistency that goes down smoothly. I enjoy curried dishes with rice since the fluid consistency mixes and absorbs well with the rice. This is not a hard and fast rule, since I prefer to eat the "gravylike" lentil dishes with breads such as chapati—here a part of the bread is torn off and sort of folded to scoop up the lentils.

Using the "blueprint" and the several serving suggestions sprinkled throughout this book, you will be able to invite friends and family over and amaze them with traditional home-style Indian meals, made quickly and easily by you. To help you along every step of the way, I share time-saving methods I've learned and developed over the years in "Tips & Techniques," including guidance on how to best reheat refrigerated or frozen Indian food (for the quickest possible meal!).

Before you know it, you will be making homemade yogurt and stocking it in your refrigerator just like in a typical Indian home. And once you get a good feel for the recipes, you may even start eyeballing measurements like a real Indian cook and wean yourself off from strict measuring!

BLUEPRINT FOR A FORMAL INDIAN MEAL	
1 or 2 Appetizers, depending on how elaborate you want to be	**Chapter 1**
Salad (Tomato, Cucumber and Onion Salad)	**The Basics**
Pappadum (omit this and still look like a master!)	**Chapter 1**
Pickled Condiment (Mango Pickle) (this is not an absolute necessity)	**The Basics**
1 Yogurt (plain yogurt or salted and spiced Raita)	**The Basics**
1 Bread (Chapati or Naan)	**Chapter 2**
1 Rice Dish (Plain Rice or Cumin and Peas Rice)	**Chapter 2**
1 Lentil or Legume Dish	**Chapter 3**
1 Vegetable Dish (sautéed or curried)	**Chapter 6**
1 Chicken, Lamb, Fish, Seafood, Egg or Cheese Dish (sautéed or curried)	**Chapters 4 or 5 or 6**
1 Dessert	**Chapter 7**
Tea or Cappuccino	**Chapter 7**
Mixture of half fennel seeds and half sugar to chew on as breath freshener	**(no chapter)**

Sautéed Potatoes with Onion

Cookware and Tools

I always enjoy strolling through kitchen specialty stores looking for interesting new kitchen tools and cookware, while my husband impatiently reminds me that I already have this or that, or that I do not have room for more things, or that I simply don't need it! I tell him to relax and that I am just looking for fun, although sometimes I do find an irresistible serving platter or interesting gadget that I must take home with me—much to my husband's chagrin!

Even though I enjoy browsing fancy kitchen gadgets, I keep to the basics at home with easy-to-use and -clean kitchen cookware and tools. My cooking style does not require any fancy or specialized Indian cookware, but instead just basic items that you probably already have or are easy to find. Naturally, there is specialized Indian cookware that is used in traditional Indian homes, such as the *tandoor, karahi,* and *tawa,* but I have developed ways to prepare delicious Indian food using common everyday cookware.

I prefer to use heavy bottom cookware—it gives me more control than thin pans do because food does not heat up too quickly, which will cause food to burn if you do not keep an eagle eye on it. I use stainless-steel pots and pans for the majority of my cooking, but I also sometimes use nonstick skillets. Stainless-steel is durable, dishwasher safe and nonreactive to acidic ingredients such as tomatoes. If you prefer to use nonstick stockpots and saucepans for easy cleanup and for healthier cooking (less fat will be required), that is perfectly fine. Lids for cookware are useful, but if you do not have one, you can use a plate instead. In the entries that follow, you'll find useful information about the cookware and tools I use to make the recipes in this book.

Box Grater This tool is used to grate (shred) food. A typical box grater has at least four different sides, each with a different purpose. I use the side with the largest round grooves to grate onions and the side with the smaller grooves to grate ginger, carrots and pickling mangoes. Then you might see some other prickly holes that look like small pointed rasps, which I use to grate whole nutmeg. You can even zest lemons, limes and oranges on this side. Some box grates also have raised, sharp horizontal slits that are used to get shavings of food, such as cheese and vegetables. To use a box grater, stand it on a plate or cutting board, hold the handle with one hand, and grate the food by holding it in the other hand and moving it up and down across the surface. Be careful not to scrape your knuckles!

Cast-iron skllet When making Indian crepes (*Dosa*), pancakes (*Uttapam*) and flatbreads, a cast-iron skillet works best. You need a surface that gets quite hot and that retains heat well. (You can also use an Indian *tawa* for this purpose, see page 18.) A cast-iron skillet can be seasoned (to create a smooth and safe nonstick surface) by repeatedly heating up the skillet and coating it with vegetable or other cooking oil. A cast-iron skillet should be gently scrubbed with water only and immediately dried to prevent rusting.

Cheesecloth This is a light-weight, cotton gauze that is traditionally used in cheese making. The cloth allows the whey to quickly drain out, while retaining the curds, creating the Indian cheese *paneer*. You can also use it to strain tamarind pulp and coconut milk if you want to extract them from whole tamarind and fresh coconuts. If you do not have cheesecloth, you may use a thin muslin cloth instead. The size of your cloth does not matter—as long as you can fold it at least four times so none of the curds slip through. After using a cheesecloth, wash it by rinsing any food products off it, and then use a few drops of dishwashing liquid and rub it in the cheesecloth. Rinse thoroughly and hang outside on a line to dry, or drape it over a dish rack on your counter, or in an empty rack in your dishwasher. My husband did not know what a cheesecloth was until he saw mine. Once, after using the cheesecloth, I had washed it and placed it to dry over my counter dish rack. He saw it and thought it was a worn-out old rag, and was going to throw it, but I caught him just in time!

Citrus Squeezer Small-sized citrus squeezers, also called a citrus press, are used to squeeze lemons and limes, and sometimes they are big enough to handle oranges too. My mother uses an old wooden citrus press she brought from India years ago, but I use a study metal one. If you do not have a citrus squeezer, you can squeeze citrus fruits by hand over a small strainer to catch the seeds.

Cutting Board My mother does not use a cutting board because she cuts and chops food quickly and skillfully by holding the fruit or vegetable and knife in her hand, but I prefer to use a cutting board. It is best to get one that is made with smooth plastic or composite material such as polypropylene rather than the glass ones with a grooved surface. The latter are bad for knives and can dull them quickly. A wooden board is also good to use, but it is not ideal to cut meat on because you would have to thoroughly immerse it in water to wash away the bacteria, and this is damaging for the board. Wooden boards should be wiped clean with a damp cloth. That is why I stick to a multipurpose composite board that can be washed by hand or in the dishwasher and is also easy on knives.

Food Processor, mini This compact version of a big food processor is small and simple, with just a basic two- prong blade. I can easily shred onions with it and make Mint Chutney (page 40) in a flash. Although some foods can be similarly processed in a blender, a blender is typically used to purée liquids or items with a soupy consistency. A food processor allows for more options of cuts than a blender, depending on the blade used. For the recipes in this book, a simple, mini food processor with just the basic blade and a low and high speed button will do just fine.

Garlic Press This tool makes fast work of mincing garlic. It is usually made of metal and presses peeled or unpeeled garlic cloves through small holes, creating a close substitute for hand-minced garlic. Although this tool saves time, I have found the downside it that it can be hard to clean out, since garlic can get stuck in the grooves. After using it, be sure to pry out any garlic stuck in the press so it does not go to waste.

Immersion blender This handy tool is also called a hand blender. It has a stick handle and a small metal blade at the bottom. It is called an immersion hand blender because you hold it in your hand and immerse it directly in the food to be blended. This works great for puréeing soups and sambar because you do not have to wait for the hot food to cool and you can avoid the step of transferring the hot food to a blender. Instead, you simply immerse the hand blender directly into the hot pot and blend until smooth. To avoid splattering, try to keep the blender deep in the pot, fully immersed in the food while using it.

Indian Spice Box In Hindi, this common Indian spice box is called a *masala dabba*, with the word *masala* meaning "spice," and *dabba* meaning "box." I think almost every Indian home around the world has one of these! A spice box is a round stainless-steel container with a lid, and inside are about seven smaller containers for you to keep your most frequently used spices right at your fingertips. Spice boxes are very convenient and time saving, especially if you cook frequently and use a certain combination of spices repeatedly.

Karahi A *karahi* is an Indian wok that is used to deep-fry foods. The bottom of a karahi is not as rounded as a Chinese wok, but it is still an efficient utensil to deep-fry foods. If you prefer to get an Indian wok, they are sometimes available at Indian grocery stores, or you can order them online. A Chinese wok or deep stockpot both make excellent substitutes. Also see Wok (page 18).

Microplane A Microplane is a very handy kitchen tool that I use for grating nutmeg and fresh ginger. It is a rectangular flat metal grater with sharp grooves throughout. They come in different sizes, but I prefer to use one with small, fine blades to get a very fine grating of ginger. I often use my Microplane because it is small and easy to clean, but you can use a box grater instead for the same purpose.

Mortar and Pestle A mortar and pestle is the traditional Indian tool used to crush and grind spices. It has a bowl-shaped base (the mortar) and a small bat-shaped stick (the pestle) that is used to crush the spices by repeatedly and forcefully pressing down on spices with the pestle and rotating it. A mortar and pestle come in different sizes and materials, from marble or other stone, to wood, porcelain or metals. I personally prefer to use an electric coffee/spice grinder because it is faster, but a mortar and pestle is ideal for small amounts of spices or nuts—amounts that will not grind properly in a coffee grinder or spice grinder. You could also crush small amounts of spices or nuts by placing them in plastic bag and, with the bag on a cutting board, tapping it with a rolling pin.

Parchment Paper This is a nonstick paper that is used in baking. I place a small piece between hot breads before freezing them so they will not stick to each other and tear or break when separating them for thawing and reheating. Even if the breads are very hot, they will not stick to the parchment when frozen. Parchment paper can be found in the same section of the grocery store where aluminum foil is found.

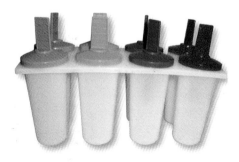

Popsicle Molds Popsicle molds are fun to use to make Indian ice cream (*kulfi*). You can get different mold shapes, such as ice cream bar molds or rocket shapes, but I prefer the basic popsicle shape because it is similar to the kufli in India, although the Indian kulfi mold is much longer. After the kulfi is frozen, turn over the molds and run them under hot water for about thirty seconds, or until you can feel that you can easily pull out the pops. Just make sure they do not fall out when you have them turned over!

Rolling Pin Rolling pins are used to roll out dough, but I also use mine to crush nuts, cardamom seeds and roasted cumin seeds. Rolling pins come in different material, such as metals, marble, silicon and plastic. I prefer to use a wooden one because they are easy to find, relatively lightweight, and easy to clean. It is best to wipe wooden rolling pins clean with a wet cloth instead of submerging them in water, and then wipe them dry with a kitchen towel. Rolling pins vary in thickness and some have handles, and some do not. I use a medium-thick tapered rolling pin that is about 1 1/2 inches (3.75 cm) around at the center. Tapered rolling pins can be pivoted and rotated while rolling out dough, which is very helpful when trying to roll out a perfect circle of dough. They are also very lightweight, which allows me to get a good feel for the dough when I am using it. The style and thickness of rolling pins is a matter of personal choice—you should use what feels most comfortable to you—some people prefer to use the thicker, heavier ones and some people use very thin ones.

Spice Grinder This handy gadget, also called a coffee grinder, can be used to grind spices, and definitely beats using a mortar and pestle—the traditional tool for grinding spices. If you use a spice grinder for grinding coffee, it is best to have a separate one for spices, unless you like cumin-flavored coffee! From my experience, I have seen the motor can burn out if you overload the spice grinder, or run it for a long time at one stretch. It is best to grind spices in small batches, and frequently rest the motor for a few seconds while operating it.

Tandoor A *tandoor* is an outdoor cylindrical clay oven resembling a pit, either above or underground, that can be found in backyards or verandas of homes in India. It is fired with wood or coal and the open flames give excellent heat and smoky flavor to foods cooked in it. Both sets of my grandparents had a clay tandoor in their backyards in which they made delicious Indian breads. A tandoor reaches much higher temperatures than a western oven and is good for making breads and cooking skewered meats and fish. Breads, such as Oven Baked White Bread (page 66) and Oven Baked Wheat Bread (page 68) are slapped against the inside wall of a tandoor, while meats and seafood are skewered and placed inside the tandoor. Indian restaurants around the world have professional metal-exterior and clay-interior tandoors installed in their kitchens that are either coal fired, gas fired, or even electric, but none of these are not practical to have in a western home kitchen.

Tawa A *tawa*, also spelled *tava* or *tawah*, is a cast-iron rimless skillet used to make various types of Indian flatbreads as well as Crispy Rice and Lentil Crepes (page 56) and Vegetable Pancakes (page 53). I find that using my large low-rimmed American cast-iron skillet works just as well. A tawa is commonly around 10 or 12 inches (25 to 30.5 cm) in diameter. If you feel this size is too small, you can use a cast-iron griddle pan and make several breads at a time! Also see cast-iron skillet (page 16).

Wok A wok is a round-bottomed cooking utensil popular in Asian cooking for stir-frying. It can also be used to efficiently deep-fry, since the round-bottom shape creates a deeper frying area that requires less oil than a flat-bottomed pot with straight sides does. Also see *karahi* (page 17).

Easy Shrimp Curry

Roasted Lentil Wafers

Tips and Techniques

After compiling, perfecting and tweaking the recipes in this book for nearly a decade, I have accumulated lots of cooking tricks and shorts cuts from trained cooks in India and America and, of course, my family. These basic techniques and cooking tips will be of use to you time and time again, and particularly if you haven't spent a lot of time in a kitchen. For those busy and hectic days when you want to skip the cooking part and get right to the eating part, I give you time-saving tips to prepare the food days in advance and use freezing, refrigeration and reheating techniques without compromising the taste and texture.

Over the years, I've noticed that my cooking students often ask the same questions or run into the same problems when preparing a dish. This list of tips is meant to answer those questions and, I hope, keep you running smoothly in the kitchen without any snags.

- It is a good idea to be prepared at each step—so I recommend reading the entire recipe beforehand to make sure you have the right ingredients, cookware, lids and utensils close at hand before you get started, rather than frantically searching for something in the middle of a recipe.
- Compared to typical American portions, you might think that the serving sizes in this book are small, but since a well-balanced Indian meal is comprised of a variety of condiments and dishes, including bread and/or rice, the serving sizes should be adequate. If you are in a rush and only have time to prepare one main dish and plain rice or bread, you may want to double the recipe depending on the number of people you are serving.
- For convenience and to save time, I recommend getting an Indian spice box (*masala dabba)* and keeping it filled with your most frequently used spices so you can have them at your fingertips.
- If you are using raw meat, chicken, fish or seafood that is chilled in the refrigerator, remove it from the refrigerator to allow it to come to room temperature or at least warm

up a bit for faster and even cooking. This is most important for big, thick cuts of meat such as lamb rib chops or chicken thighs and drumsticks.

- When heating oil in a saucepan or skillet, heat it until it is hot, but not overheated and smoking. You can test the heat of the oil by adding a very small amount of the first ingredient to be added—for example, a pinch of chopped onions or a few cumin seeds. If the oil starts bubbling in tiny bubbles around the food, the oil is sufficiently heated. If nothing happens, the oil is not yet heated.
- To check the heat of a dry pan or skillet, hold your palm directly above the pan. You should be able to feel the heat.
- If you accidentally add cumin seeds to an overheated pan or if you cook them too long in oil and they burn and turn black, simply discard them along with the oil and start again. Burnt cumin seeds will ruin the taste of your dish and they are unsightly.
- When adding liquid ingredients or ingredients that have a lot of moisture in them to hot oil, be careful of splatters. Food such as onions, tomatoes, washed and drained rice, or washed fresh coriander leaves or curry leaves will cause the oil to splatter, so do not stand too close or bend close to the pan when adding these ingredients to hot oil.
- When roasting or tempering (frying in oil) mustard seeds, do not lower your face near the pan because the hot mustard seeds may pop out of the pan and can hit your face or

eyes. To be on the safe side, you can use a splatter screen, especially if you think the oil has been overheated.

- For quicker cooking times, the best flavor and their beautiful deep red color, always use fully ripe, soft, red tomatoes. In the cooking process, tomato skins usually separate from the flesh. For better presentation, I often remove the loose tomato skins before serving the dish.
- You will notice that I use onions a lot in my cooking, and in different recipes they are cooked to different degrees of doneness. I cook with yellow onions simply because they are readily available, well-priced, and give good flavor to the dishes. However, based on your personal preference, you may use either yellow, white or red onions. There are different stages of cooking onions, from becoming translucent to a golden brown, brown, dark brown, and finally to the point of caramelizing them, when the natural sugars cook and lend a sweet taste. When sautéing onions to make a *masala*, it is important to golden brown them so they do not give a raw onion taste to the final dish. Always cut or shred onions just before you are ready to cook them so they do not sit for a while and start smelling off.
- I have provided measurements in both American and metric units. Measurements do not have to be exact so do not stress about measuring ingredients precisely. Just try to get them close to the indicated amount, especially when making rice dishes and dough for the breads. Do note that the metric measurements are rounded so you can easily measure the ingredients; also note that I use a standard 250-milliliter equivalent when using cup measurements.
- My cooking times are based on using heavy cookware on a gas stove. Light cookware can be used, and is beneficial in the sense the food will cook faster, but you have to keep a sharp eye on it and stir the food more frequently because it can easily burn.

- If the recipe calls for a nonstick skillet, but you prefer to use a skillet without a non-stick surface, simply add an additional tablespoon of oil and stir the food more frequently. If your skillet is not heavy bottomed, you may also need to lower the heat to keep the food from burning. If I do not specify in a recipe that a non-stick skillet should be used, such as when roasting or tempering spices, then you can use either a non-stick or stainless-steel (or other metal) skillet without increasing amount of the oil, if any, that is called for.
- I use plain iodized table salt in all of my recipes. You may adjust the salt to taste by adding a bit more or less than the amount indicated in each recipe. You may also use kosher salt or sea salt if you prefer. Both are coarser than table salt, so you will need to add a bit more that what is indicated in the recipes for equal seasoning. Finely ground sea salt can be used in equal amounts to that of table salt.
- You can control the fiery spice level in dishes by decreasing or increasing the amount of ground red pepper (cayenne), dried red chili peppers, or fresh green chili peppers used in the recipes. In general, the spice level in the recipes is moderate.
- If you make a recipe that calls for deep-frying, you can save the oil to use again, but it is generally not recommended to use oil for deep-frying more than twice because the smoking point is altered and harmful gases are released. After the first use, I just leave the oil in the wok, cover the wok, and store it in an unwarmed oven until I am ready to use again. Before heating the oil again, if you see too many burnt particles in the bottom of the wok, you can strain them out with a slotted spoon. When you are ready to discard the oil, first let it cool. Then pour it into a sealed non-recyclable container and throw it in the trash. Do not pour the oil down the sink, as it may clog it.

Basic Techniques

If you run across a recipe and wonder how to cut a carrot into matchsticks, deal with a whole garlic bulb, roast spices, or even the difference between cubing, dicing, chopping and mincing, this section is the place to find the answers! The basic methods that follow are what I personally use, although if you run across another technique that you prefer that gives the same results, feel free to use that.

Cutting matchsticks

Vegetables such as carrots and potatoes are commonly cut into thin strips called matchsticks, but usually not as thin as an actual matchstick! This cut is also known as "julienne." The vegetable is first cut into thin slices, and then the slices are cut across to the desired length, resulting in a short or long "matchstick." I like to use this attractive cut when preparing the carrots for Vegetable Pilaf (page 83) and Vegetables with Coconut Curry (page 134).

1 Cut off the both ends of the carrot and discard.
2 Peel off the outer skin and discard. Wash the carrot with cold water.
3 Cut the carrot in half crosswise to make it an easier size to work with.
4 Cut each half lengthwise down the middle.
5 Cut each piece in half lengthwise again. For the thicker part of a carrot, you might want to make another lengthwise cut to create strips of even size.
6 Stack the strips and cut them crosswise into approximately 2-inch (5-cm)-long matchsticks.

Cutting a Carrot into Matchsticks

1. Peel away skin and discard. Wash the carrot.
2. Cut each half again lengthwise down the middle.
3. Line up the strips and cut into matchsticks.

Cutting cubes and dices

Cubing means to cut into desired-size cubes—the standard size being 1/2-inch (1.25-cm) or larger. Meats, fruits, cheese and vegetables such as potatoes can be cubed. It is okay if all of the cubes are not exact squares, or if they have some rounded sides, but try to cut almost equal-size pieces so that the food cooks at an even rate. When a recipe calls for an ingredient to be diced, cut it into small cubes, or "dice," that are approximately 1/4-inch (6-mm) or smaller.

1 To cube a potato (or other food), cut the potato crosswise into 1/2-inch (1.25-cm)-thick or larger circles for cubes, or about 1/4-inch (6-mm)-thick circles or smaller for dice.
2 Work with 1 circle at a time. Lay it flat and cut across it into 1/2-inch (1.25-cm) strips (or whatever size cube or dice you will be making).
3 Gather the strips and turn them 90° and cut across them into 1/2-inch (1.25-cm) increments (or whatever size cubes or dice you will be making) to create cubes.
4 Repeat this process with the remaining potato circles. Once you feel comfortable using this technique, you may even stack the circles to cube or dice multiple circles at one go.

Chopping and mincing

Chopping and mincing are cuts in which you do not have to be so precise, especially when a recipe calls for something to be coarsely chopped. Chopped food is bite-size or smaller pieces, "finely chopped" is chopping food even smaller, and minced food is cut into very small pieces (smaller than dice), almost to the point where the food seems crushed, such as minced garlic. Mincing food is handy when you do not want to bite into a big piece of garlic, but you would still like your dish to have the flavor of garlic evenly dispersed throughout.

Cutting half moons

Sometimes I specify a "half moon" cut for onions, which is a semi-circle. This can be done by slicing an onion crosswise into rings, and then cut the rings in half to create half moons.

Mashing potatoes by hand

In some recipes, I call for potatoes to be mashed with a potato masher or by hand. The latter may sound unusual to Americans, but it's a common Indian practice. To mash a boiled and peeled potato by hand, place it in a bowl and, using one hand, mash or squeeze the potato between your fingers until it is soft and smooth.

How to wash rice and dried legumes

It is always a good idea to thoroughly wash rice and dried legumes to make sure you are cooking with clean food. Thoroughly washing the rice before cooking also removes any starchy residue, resulting in less sticky rice. Lentils are known to have small pieces of stone and grit from the packaging process, so sorting though them and then washing will ensure your cooked dish will be clean and delicious.

1 Place dried legumes—such as lentils or peas—on a plate and pick through them, removing any grit and blemished or wrinkled legumes that you find.
2 Place the rice or dried legumes in a bowl. Cover the rice or legumes with water.
3 Swish the rice or legumes around in the water a few times, while rubbing them between your fingers to thoroughly clean them.
4 Drain off the water, being careful not to pour out the rice or legumes. Repeat with three or four changes of fresh water. The rice water will become clearer with each rinsing. The clearer you can get the water, the better. (*Note*: The water may become cloudy and frothy when rinsing split lentils, which is okay, so you do not need to worry about washing away all of the cloudiness and froth.)
5 Pour the rice or legumes into a large fine-meshed strainer and allow to thoroughly drain.

Washing Lentils

1. *Sorting through grit.*
2. *Rubbing clean the lentils under water.*
3. *Pouring through a sieve to drain.*

Grating an Onion

1. Hold the peeled onion against the grater and move up and down.
2. Finished grated onion.

Grating

Grating means to shred. To grate an onion, unripe mango, carrot or piece of ginger, first peel the vegetable or fruit. Use the largest holes on a box grater for onions, and the smaller holes for unripe mangoes, carrots and ginger. Firmly hold the peeled onion, or other food, and grate on the holes, pressing down with some force, while making sure you don't scrape your knuckles! A Mircoplane can be used for ginger as well.

Roasting and grinding whole spices

Roasting spices is a common Indian technique used to deepen the flavors of the spices. Whole spices, such as coriander seeds, cumin seeds and cloves, may be roasted in a dry skillet and then ground into a fine powder that is added to dishes during cooking. The intense aroma given off by the spices while roasting and grinding them is amazing! It is best to roast and grind spices just when you plan to use them, since they lose their potency over time, though you can keep them in an airtight container at room temperature for up to three months.

1 Place a small, heavy bottomed skillet over medium heat. When the skillet is heated, add the whole spices. (You can check to see if the skillet is heated by holding your palm directly above the skillet. You should be able to feel the heat.)
2 Roast the spices until they are fragrant, stirring frequently, about 1 to 2 minutes. Some spices will turn a darker shade as they roast. Do not let the cumin seeds or any spices turn black and burn. Immediately remove the spices from the skillet and place in a bowl. Let cool before grinding.
3 In a coffee or spice grinder, or using a mortar and pestle, grind the roasted spices to a fine powder.

Boiling potatoes

Boiling potatoes are an easy task, but you do have to factor in the half hour it will take when making a recipe that will use them. If my mom plans to make Potato Stuffed Wheat Breads (page 72) for a delicious breakfast, she boils the potatoes the night before, which is a useful tip that I also follow.

1 Wash the unpeeled potatoes with cold water. In a large pot, add the potato(es). Cover them with about 1 inch (2.5 cm) of water, making sure that the level of the water is at least 2 inches (5 cm) from the top of the pot so that the water does not boil over.
2 Cover the pot. Bring to a rolling boil over high heat. Reduce the heat to medium-high and continue boiling for about 30 minutes, or until you can easily insert a knife into the potato. (Make sure you do not boil them to the point when they become too tender and easily fall apart, especially if you are going to cube or dice them.)
3 Drain the potatoes in a colander and let the potatoes cool slightly so you can handle them, or you can run cold water over them to cool them faster.
4 Using your fingers or a small knife, peel the skin off the potato and discard. The potatoes are now ready to be used in a recipe.

> **TIP:** You may boil the potatoes up to one day in advance. They may be refrigerated already peeled or with the peels on, though it is easier to peel the skin off potatoes when they're still warm.

Shelling and parboiling fresh peas

Fresh raw peas take longer to cook than frozen peas because frozen peas are already blanched. If you'd like to use fresh peas in my recipes, adjust the time to fully cook the peas, or you could parboil them first in order to follow my recipe as if you were using frozen peas. I prefer to use frozen peas since they are already shelled, easily available, and I do not even have to thaw them. The frozen peas found in stores are the garden pea variety, also known as "green peas" or "English peas." They grow in plump pods, from which the peas are removed, or "shelled." The pods are discarded. **To shell peas,** pry open the pod at the seam with your fingers and remove the peas out of the pod. Wash the peas before using them. **To parboil peas,** place them in boiling water for about 4 minutes, until they start to just soften, drain them, and then add them to the dish at the same time frozen peas would be added.

Cutting a cauliflower head

The first time I prepared fresh cauliflower at home, without my mother by my side, I wasn't sure how to cut it. For those new to using fresh cauliflower, here are instructions for preparing it for use in the recipes in this book.

1 Pull away the green leaves and discard. Using a small knife, gently scrape away any brown marks on the cauliflower head.
2 Slice off the stem at the bottom of the cauliflower head and discard (see "Tip" below).
3 Turn the head upside down so that is stem-side up. Insert a small knife inside the head to cut loosen the florets from all around the internal stem (core).
4 Cut all the loose florets into bite-size pieces.
5 Place the florets in a colander and wash with cold water.

> **TIP:** If you're averse to wasting any part of an ingredient, as my Mom is, don't discard the cauliflower stems. If you're cooking 3 or 4 heads of cauliflower, you can peel them, slice them and sauté them for a "cauliflower stem" dish. Or, if you're preparing just one head, you can peel the stem, dice it and cook it along with the cauliflower florets in the same dish. You can even munch on peeled cauliflower stem matchsticks as a raw vegetable crudité. The outside stem (which looks like a thick stump and has thick skin) should be peeled and chopped, but the internal stem (core) does not need to be peeled before chopping and eating.

Peeling and chopping or mincing garlic

To chop or mince fresh garlic, first pry off a clove with your finger or by carefully using the tip of a small knife. Place the clove on a cutting board and lay the side of a chef's knife flat on a clove with the blade facing away from you. Then firmly push down on the knife to smash the clove, which makes it easy to remove the papery white peel. After removing the peel, mince or chop the clove with a chef's knife. Or, you can use a garlic press, which is quick (and with some presses you don't even need to take the peel off!), but the downside is that it is hard to clean since the garlic gets stuck in it. Or, you can keep the cloves whole and slice into them to help release their flavor (this technique is used in the recipe for Whole Green Lentil Stew (page 99), but it can be used in other recipes as well). My mother actually just coarsely chops the cloves since that is quicker, but then you run the risk of biting into a piece of garlic, so I prefer to mince it instead. Wash your hands after working with garlic, as they will be sticky and have a garlic aroma.

Peeling and grating ginger

I find grating ginger to be faster than mincing it and it provides fine shreds that evenly disperse flavor in a dish. Using the sharp edge of a small knife, or even the edge of a small spoon, scrape off the thin tan skin from just the amount you want to grate. Grate it using a Microplane or the small holes on a box grater. Sometimes my mother chops ginger into small pieces instead of grating it, but I prefer to always grate it because I do not like to bite into a piece of ginger, although some people may enjoy its strong taste straight up!

Blanching almonds

Blanching almonds is the process of removing their brown skin. To blanch almonds, place them in a small bowl of water and microwave them on normal level for 30 seconds. Let them cool and then remove the skin with your fingers (the skin should slip off easily). You can also boil them on the stovetop for two minutes, let them cool and then peel off the skin. Alternatively, let the almonds sit overnight in small bowl with water. In the morning the almonds will be puffed up and tender and the skin can easily be removed. To sliver the blanched almonds, carefully use a paring knife and thinly slice the almonds lengthwise. The almonds will split apart as you sliver them. My mother tells me eating almonds improves your memory, and that it is good to eat a few daily.

Peeling and deveining shrimp

If the head is not already removed, using your fingers, hold the head in one hand, and the body in the other and gently twist off the head and discard.

1 Remove the shell and legs from the body by grabbing a part of the shell at the bottom side of the body by the head end of the shrimp. Pull up and lift it up and away towards the tail end and discard.
2 If you are removing the tail, hold the body of the shrimp with one hand, and grab the tip of the tail with your fingers and gently squeeze it as you pull it off. Discard the tail shell.
3 To expose the vein (the digestive tract which also may have sand and grit in it), using a small knife, make a shallow cut on the topside of the body from the head end to the tail end. The vein will look like a thin dark tube running the length of the body of the shrimp.
4 Using the tip of a small knife or your fingers, lift out the vein and discard. Make sure to scrape out any remaining parts of it the vein if it breaks.

Freezing, Refrigerating, and Reheating Methods

Once you get the hang of cooking Indian food, you can quickly prepare many of the appetizers, main dishes and desserts days, or even a month, in advance! Yes, a month! The trick is either freezing or refrigerating the food and then reheating it so it will taste just like it was freshly made. Some foods, like rice, reheat great in the microwave without altering taste or texture. Reheating food is a great way to save time and reduce stress on a hectic day, or simply during the busy work week. My mom usually does most of the week's cooking on Sunday and refrigerates the food, so dinner simply needs to be heated up after she comes home from work. It also works great when you are having a party or a get-together, so on the day your guests arrive all you have to do is reheat the food you already cooked days in advance, and you can spend more time getting yourself ready for the party!

For each recipe, I have indicated whether it can be made in advance, refrigerated or frozen, along with tips on how to reheat the food. I have also indicated when prep work such as boiling a potato or making dough for breads can be done in advance, which leaves you more time to get straight to the cooking and eating part when ready.

Refrigerating and reheating

Most of the dishes in this book will stay fresh in the refrigerator for at least up to three days. However, there are some dishes that taste best when cooked and served immediately and are not recommended for reheating. When you're ready to refrigerate a dish, allow the freshly cooked food to cool to room temperature and then place in a covered container in the refrigerator. When you are ready to eat the refrigerated food, you can heat up the food in a saucepan or skillet on the stovetop over medium-low heat, stirring occasionally until the food is warmed up. You can also use a microwave to reheat food, but I find it alters the taste and texture for certain foods such as meat, fish, seafood and egg dishes, so I prefer the stovetop for these. For recipes that suggest reheating in an oven, you can use a toaster oven to reheat small quantities of food to save energy.

However, for some rice and vegetable dishes, the microwave is actually the best and easiest way to reheat the food without altering the taste, and I will specify that in those recipes. You may notice that some of the curried dishes, once refrigerated, become thicker than when they were first cooked and still hot. Usually curried food will thicken when chilled, but when reheated, it will return to its original consistency. If the food is still thicker after being reheated, simply add some water to thin it out. When reheating the drier sautéed (versus curry style) dishes or rice, it's best to sprinkle a few drops of water on the food before reheating it so it does not dry out.

Freezing and reheating

With the exception of fish and seafood, freezing works great for most dishes. For each recipe I will specify whether it is okay to freeze it. When you're ready to freeze a dish, make sure the hot food has cooled to room temperature, especially before putting them in plastic containers or in freezer-safe plastic bags, and place in the freezer for up to a month. Make sure the container is well covered or airtight so that ice crystals won't form on the food. The easiest way to reheat frozen food is to first thaw it by placing it in the refrigerator. For example, if it is Monday morning and you know after a long day at work you will want to enjoy the Chicken Tikka Masala (page 105) and Creamed Spinach with Cheese Cubes (page 140) that are in your freezer, place the frozen dishes in your refrigerator before heading off to work to thaw. Then, when you come home, you can quickly warm up the thawed food and some rice or Mexican wheat tortillas (the latter is a great substitute for *chapati*, the daily homemade bread eaten in Indian homes). If you have some plain yogurt to enjoy along with the meal—you are all set! Some rice dishes freeze well, so you can freeze them into individual or family size containers or plastic bags and let them thaw in the refrigerator while you are away. If you forget to thaw the food during the day, you can use a microwave to defrost it and then finish reheating it on the stovetop, in the microwave, or in the oven, depending on how the dish reheats bests without altering its taste and texture. (I specify in each recipe the ideal way to reheat food.) Or, you may also reheat the frozen food directly without thawing by heating it in a saucepan or skillet on the stovetop over medium-low heat, stirring occasionally, until the food is thawed and warmed up. Normally, food will thicken when chilled, but when reheated it will return to its original consistency. If the food is still thicker after being reheated, simply add some water to thin it out.

Clockwise from top: coriander seeds, cinnamon stick, cumin seeds, cardamom pods, black peppercorns, and cloves.

Essential Indian Ingredients

In this section, I explain the basics of the frequently used ingredients in this book—how and where to buy items, how to store them and more. I have made every effort to use easy-to-find spices and ingredients so that you do not have to make special trips to ethnic markets, but there are a few ingredients such as fresh curry leaves and the different varieties of Indian lentils that might be hard to find at your local grocery store. Start by checking the international section in your grocery store for a greater selection and better prices. Natural foods stores and gourmet grocery stores can also be good places to look for Indian ingredients. You can even purchase items on-line or from Indian stores that will ship to your door. (See Resource Guide, page 156, for a listing of such stores). If you're lucky enough to have an Indian market nearby, shop there for one-stop economical shopping.

Basmati rice (*Basmati* chawval) Basmati rice is long-grained, fragrant rice used in Indian cooking. It is now commonly available in most grocery stores in small packages, or you can buy big burlap sacks of Basmati rice at ethnic stores, which is more economical if you cook rice often. Rice can be stored in a jar, plastic bag, or in the burlap bag it came in for at least six months in your pantry. It is a good idea to thoroughly wash the rice before cooking it to clean it and remove any starchy residue so that the final result is less sticky. In general, the rule of thumb to cook Basmati rice is to use twice the amount of water to rice. One cup of uncooked rice yields about three cups of cooked rice.

Bay leaf (*tej patta*) Bay leaves come fresh or dried, but it is common to use dried bay leaves in Indian cooking, especially if one does not cook with them too often. I use the dried leaf to add a sweet and woody scent to rice dishes such as Vegetable Pilaf (page 83) and Chicken Biryani (page 80). When cooking, the leaf is added to heated oil or butter to release its aromas. You may leave the bay leaf in your dish for presentation purposes, but with its sharp dried edges, it is best to avoid eating it.

Black pepper, (ground and whole peppercorns) (*kali mirch*) Pepper is a berry that grows in grapelike clusters on the pepper plant. The berries can become green, black or white peppercorns, depending on how ripe the berry is when it is plucked and how it is processed. The black peppercorns have the strongest flavor whereas the white ones are milder and are used when you do not want the black pepper to show in food, such as a white sauce. The green berries are unripe when plucked and are commonly preserved in brine or pickled for a fresh taste. It is common in India to buy whole black peppercorns and then to crush them using a mortar and pestle. For everyday cooking, I use the finely ground black pepper that comes in a tin, but for some dishes, like Vegetable Pilaf (page 83), I prefer to use whole black peppercorns so that I do not give the rice dish a black tinge from finely ground pepper. If you prefer to use freshly ground whole peppercorns rather than the pre-ground pepper, you can do this throughout the book whenever ground black pepper is called for.

Cardamoms (*elaichi*) Cardamom pods are the aromatic fruit of the cardamom plant, and they are plucked when they are still unripe and then dried. Cardamom are available in small green pods with intensely flavored small back seeds inside, which is what I use, and there are big black pods, which I used to call a "roach" when I was a kid! If you shop in ethnic markets, you may also see small white cardamoms, which are simply the green ones that have been bleached for aesthetic purposes and result in a milder flavor. Cardamoms are used to flavor Garam Masala (page 44), rice and meat dishes, and add a special touch to tea and desserts. **To open a pod to release the flavorful seeds,** place it on a cutting board. Place a small knife on its side over the top of the cardamom and press on the knife to crack it open. You can also tap on the pod with a rolling pin to break it open and then pry it apart with your fingers. If I am just cooking for my family, I simply bite the cardamom pods between my teeth until it cracks open, and then I pry it apart with my finger. Cardamom pods also make good breath fresheners. Simply pop a whole pod in your mouth and chew on it and eventually you can swallow everything.

Carom seeds (*ajwain*) Also called "bishop's weed," these tiny brown seeds are a great natural remedy for an upset, gassy tummy. Even till this day, when I complain of an upset tummy, my mother will tell me to take a teaspoon full of carom seeds with water. I like to use carom seeds when cooking seafood dishes. The seeds look small and harmless, but if you bite into them, they release a peppery punch, though they are not spicy. Carom seeds can be found at Indian markets, and are more commonly known by their Hindi name, *ajwain*. If you cannot find them, you can use dried thyme leaves as a substitute, but it will not have the exact sharp flavor of carom seeds. Do not confuse it with caraway seeds.

Chapati flour (*chapati ka aata*) This is a whole wheat flour with a bit of all-purpose flour (white flour that is non self-rising, called *maida* in Hindi) added to it to lighten the color for aesthetic purposes. There is no set proportion of whole wheat to white flour, as each brand has a different proportion. If you do not have *chapati* flour, in general, you can use a 1:1 whole wheat to white flour ratio, although sometimes I use a 3:1 ratio of whole wheat to white if that is easier to measure for a recipe. Some bags of Indian chapati flour say "100% whole wheat flour" on them, but if you compare that flour to American whole wheat flour, you might notice the American one is darker. This is due either to different crops of harvested wheat that have slight variations in color, or the Indian chapati flour may indeed have some all-purpose flour added to it. Store in an airtight jar in your pantry up to three months. Because chapati flour has natural oil in it, it can go rancid if kept over three months, but keeping it in the freezer can prolong the life of the flour for at least up to six months.

Chili peppers, green (fresh, whole) (*sabut hari mirch*) There are hundreds of varieties of chili peppers, varying in length, thickness and spice level. Generally, the smaller a pepper, the hotter it is because there are more seeds proportionally, and the seeds are where the heat is. In Indian cooking, many types of chili peppers are used, but I use the spicy hot bird's-eye chili pepper (also sometimes referred to as the "Thai chili pepper"). The bird's-eye chili pepper is thin and can be found in ethnic markets and some American grocery stores. You can also use fresh chili de arbol, Serrano chili pepper or the easy-to-find jalapeño pepper. Slicing or halving the

chili pepper exposes the seeds and allows it to release more flavor and heat. When green chili peppers are left on the plant long enough to fully ripen, they turn red and are then plucked and dried for use in cooking. Wash your hands thoroughly after handling a chili pepper so you do not irritate your eyes, nose or lips if you touch them afterwards.

Dried red chili peppers

Fresh green bird's-eye chili pepper

Fresh finger-length red and green chili peppers

Dried red bird's-eye chili pepper

Chili peppers, red (dried, whole) (*sabut laal mirch*) Red chili peppers are green chili peppers that have been allowed to fully ripen and turn red on the plant, after which they are plucked and dried. Because the dried bird's-eye chili pepper is not typically available in regular grocery stores, I use the easy-to-find dried red chili peppers of the chili de arbol variety, which are usually found in small clear bags in the spice section or the Mexican international section of a regular grocery store. Sometimes these dried peppers are even found in the fresh produce section. When cooking with dried red chili peppers, I sometimes first dry roast them (see page 24) to release their flavors. I also sometimes tear these chili peppers before tossing them in the hot pan to expose the seeds, which releases more heat into the dish. Usually dried red chili peppers come with the stems removed, but if they are not, just tear them off. Different types of dried red chili peppers are also ground into a fine red pepper and used frequently in Indian cooking. In American grocery stores, the closet substitute is ground red pepper (cayenne). Dried red chili peppers can be stored for at least up to six months in an airtight jar in your pantry.

Cilantro *See* Coriander leaves

Cinnamon (*dalchini*) Cinnamon sticks are intensely flavored woody rolls of bark from the cinnamon plant. When using cinnamon sticks, it is important to use just a small piece because it gives a very strong flavor. You can break a cinnamon stick with your hands, but to get smaller pieces, lay the stick on a cutting board and hit it with a rolling pin to break it up. Ground cinnamon is also used in Indian cooking—from meat dishes to spiced teas and in vegetable pickles. When making Garam Masala (page 44), I first dry roast the cinnamon stick to develop its flavor more and then grind it.

STORAGE AND FOOD HANDLING TIPS
When purchasing ingredients, try to buy the smallest packages available so items can be used quickly and stay fresh. You can store all of your individual spices and rice in airtight jars in a cool, dry place and out of direct sun, such as your kitchen pantry, for up to at least six months. However, lentils and flours are best kept up to three months in the pantry to ensure they are in their optimal state. Flours may also be frozen up to six months. Roasted and ground spice blends, such as Biryani Masala (page 80), lose their flavors more quickly and are also best if kept up to three months only. When handling spices, rice, lentils and flour, always use dry hands and utensils when removing them from or adding them to storage containers.

Citrus (*nimbu*) Citrus fruit, such as green limes and yellow lemons, are used commonly in Indian cooking to add zing dishes, and also to make *paneer*, a homemade Indian cheese. Limes tend to be less expensive than lemons, and they are easily found, so I use them, but if you have lemons on hand, you can use them instead. Limes come in different varieties and sizes from the small key lime to the common lime, and all are usually smaller than lemons. If limes are left on the tree long enough, they will eventually turn from green to yellow (but they are still limes!), but they are usually plucked before this happens. To add confusion to the lime/lemon discussion, limes are sometimes called "lemons" in India, but in the end it does not matter if you use a lemon or lime when making the recipes, or what variety you use. If a recipe calls for the juice of one lime, and you'd like to substitute lemon juice, use the juice of one-half lemon. And if you use key limes, you can use two of them to equal one lime. Before cutting open a lemon or lime, if you press on it while rolling it back and forth a few times on the counter, it will loosen the fibers inside and allow the juice to come out easier and in greater quantity. Then cut the citrus in half crosswise and squeeze it over a small sieve to catch the seeds, or use a citrus squeezer to squeeze out the juice. You can keep citrus fruits in your refrigerator for up to two weeks. Unused portions of lemons or limes should be wrapped tightly in plastic wrap and stored in the refrigerator for up to three days.

Cloves (*long*) Cloves have a very distinct flavor and aroma and should be used sparingly so as not to overpower a dish. A clove is a small brown woody piece with a pronged, rounded

tip, which almost resembles a tiny nail. Cloves are grown on tropical evergreen clove trees, and are actually the unopened flower buds that grow in clusters. After the green buds are fully grown and just about to open, they are picked off the tree and sun dried until they become dark brown and woody. Cloves are sold whole or ground, but I prefer to buy the whole cloves so that I can grind them when I need to make Garam Masala (page 44). I use whole cloves to flavor Vegetable Pilaf (page 83).

Coconut milk (*nariyal ka dood*) Coconut milk is extracted from the pulp of coconuts. It is not the coconut water or "juice," which is the liquid that you can hear when shaking a coconut and that leaks out when you crack it. Coconut water is clear and thin and should be quite sweet. The milk, instead, is white and creamy and makes an excellent rich base for coconut curry dishes, providing a hint of sweetness. In India, people traditionally extract coconut milk from fresh coconuts, but this can be a lengthy process. I simply buy canned coconut milk, which is available in the Thai international section of grocery stores. Coconut milk is somewhat fattening; a light version is available, which I personally think is a suitable substitute. Coconut milk curries are common in the southern coastal regions of India, where coconut trees are commonly grown in people's backyards. Unopened canned coconut milk can be kept for months in your panty—though do keep an eye on the expiration date. If you open a can and have leftover coconut milk, transfer it to a glass or plastic container, cover it, and refrigerate it for no more than three days.

Coriander leaves (cilantro) (*dhania ka patta*) Fresh coriander leaves, commonly referred to as "cilantro" in America, are used in Indian cooking both as a garnish and as an ingredient. Bunches of fresh coriander leaves are easy to find in the produce section of grocery stores. It keeps just about a week in the refrigerator before it starts discoloring and wilting. I store the bunch in a plastic bag in the refrigerator and tear off a handful or chop off a small quantity when I need to use some. Since there is no need to destem the leaves, you may chop the leaves and stems together. Coriander leaves should be thoroughly washed before being chopped.

Coriander seeds (*dhania*) (ground and whole seeds) These are the seeds that grow into the coriander plant, which gives us the fragrant coriander leaves, also known as "cilantro." The seeds have a light and sweet citrus, almost orange-like, undertone that comes out more when they are roasted and ground. I use ground coriander and the whole seeds, both of which are available in the spice section of grocery stores. You may grind whole seeds as needed for a fresher and stronger flavor, but to make things easy, I simply use pre-ground coriander. Whole roasted coriander seeds are one of the main spices in my mother-in-law's Garam Masala (page 44). (See page 24 for instructions on roasting and grinding whole spices such as coriander seeds.)

Cumin seeds (*jeera*) These tiny brown-colored oval seeds are a must-have in my spice box. Cumin flavors rice and many other dishes amazingly well. To release their flavor, cumin seeds are often added to heated oil and incorporated directly into a dish or they are dry roasted and then ground. When they're added to heated oil, they will quickly darken. To keep the seeds from burning and turning black, you must quickly add the next ingredient. Luckily, since cumin seeds are usually introduced in the first steps of cooking a dish, if you do burn them you can just discard them along with the oil and try again. This spice provides a whole different level of flavor when it is roasted and crushed, and can be added to meat marinades as well as to Three Vegetable Raita (page 37). (See page 24 for instructions on roasting and grinding whole spices such as cumin seeds.)

Curry leaves (*kari patta*) Fresh curry leaves have a distinct fragrance and are frequently used in southern Indian cooking. Though adding curry leaves to a dish will add another level of exotic flavor, the recipes in this book are still delicious

without them. Because curry leaves are typically only found in ethnic grocery stores, I have made them an optional ingredient in my recipes. Many Indians who cook with curry leaves have a curry tree in their garden, so fresh fragrant leaves are always on hand! Curry leaves can be left in the cooked dish and may be eaten, if desired. If you do buy fresh curry leaves, put them in a plastic bag and refrigerate them for up to one week, or until they start to dry up, whichever comes first. Wash and pat them dry before adding to hot oil to prevent splatters.

Essences, rose and pandanus (*gulab and kewra*) Essences are concentrated liquid extracts derived from various foods or plants that add magic to desserts, and can be thought of as flavorful, edible perfumes for food. They are similar to other common extracts such as almond or vanilla. When using an essence, it is important not to add too much of it because you do not want it to overpower the dish, or make it bitter. Some essences are more potent than others, but usually just two or three drops sprinkled over the dish or mixed in with the sugar syrup or milky syrup used in a dessert will do the trick. I use rose essence (more concentrated than rose water) and pandanus essence, which is commonly labeled with its Hindi name, *kewra*. Rose essence is extracted from fragrant rose petals and is clear in color. Pandanus essence is made from pandanus leaves and is light yellow to clear in color. Essences are found in small glass bottles in ethnic markets or the international section of some grocery stores. If you don't have an essence for a dessert recipe, the dessert will still be excellent. I've stored my essence bottles in the refrigerator for two years, but they can be stored indefinitely in a cool dark place, or until their potency lessens.

Fennel seeds (*sanf*) Fennel seeds are small light-green seeds that come from the fennel plant. Sometimes the use and name of fennel seeds is incorrectly interchanged with anise seeds, which have a somewhat similar flavor and appearance. A common way to use fennel seeds is as a breath freshener: It is chewed thoroughly and then swallowed. You may notice that in many Indian restaurants, near the door, there is a bowl with fennel seeds mixed with sugar to sweeten and freshen your mouth. I use fennel seeds to flavor Tamarind Chutney (page 39). On my summer trips to India as a child, one of my maternal aunts, Kamlesh Aunty, would always put together little plastic baggies of fennel candy, which was fennel seeds coated in a brightly colored, hardened sugar coating. I loved to visit her because she would always have the baggies ready to hand out to all of us cousins.

Garam Masala In Hindi, *garam* means "hot" and *masala* means "spices," so Garam Masala can be translated as "hot spices." In fact, this spice mixture is not as spicy as it is warming and aromatic. Garam masala is a roasted spice mix that is commonly used in cooking throughout India. A combination of select whole spices is dry roasted and then ground to release amazing aromas. Although this spice mix is commonly available in most grocery stores, each brand will have a slightly different flavor because there is really no set proportion or combination of spices to use. In general, most garam masala mixes will contain coriander seeds, cardamom, black peppercorns, cloves, cumin seeds and cinnamon, but some brands of spice mixes may leave out or add certain spices, such as bay leaves, nutmeg and black cardamoms. For convenience, you can use the pre-blended mixes available in stores, but for the best flavor I recommend you make your own homemade batch with freshly roasted and ground spices (see page 44 for a recipe).

Garlic (*lasan***)** The assertive flavor of garlic makes it one of my favorite cooking ingredients. Garlic bulbs are the underground root part of the plant, and are made up of several cloves (small wedges of garlic) that are held together by a flaky skin that can be white, purple or pink (but I use the white skinned variety). Though mincing garlic may seem tedious, it's definitely worth it for the flavor it adds to a dish. (See page 25 for instructions on peeling and chopping garlic.) I have found that pre-minced bottled garlic doesn't come close to the strong aroma and flavor of fresh garlic, so do try to avoid to using the pre-minced garlic. Garlic should be stored loosely covered (a paper bag is ideal) in a cool dark place away from direct sun or heat. I like to keep mine no longer than three to four weeks, but you can store it longer (just discard it when it has started to dry out). You can store the unused peeled cloves in an airtight container in the refrigerator for up to a week. Don't forget to chew on some fennel seeds after eating a dish that has a lot of garlic in it!

Ghee Ghee, a cooking fat made from clarifying butter, is used in traditional Indian kitchens. To make ghee, butter is melted to remove the water and separate off the milk solids, leaving pure butterfat. Once cow or buffalo milk is churned to make butter, the butter is then separated by slowly melting and simmering it until the milk solids settle at the bottom, the water boils off, and golden liquid floats on top. The golden liquid may be collected and heated again so any remaining water boils off, resulting in pure, creamy clarified butterfat. As it cools, ghee will solidify and become smooth and creamy.

Because the water and moisture are removed, ghee can be kept much longer than butter—up to at least six months in an airtight jar in your refrigerator or pantry. Today, health-conscious people avoid the use of ghee in daily cooking, but it is still used in Indian cooking, and especially to make rich desserts. Ghee does have a unique smell and taste to it that may not be pleasant to some. To make things quick, easy, and relatively healthy, I suggest sticking to vegetable or canola oil when cooking Indian food, although if you would like to use melted ghee, it can substituted in equal amounts for oil or butter throughout the recipes in this book.

Ginger (*adrak***)** Ginger is a root with a unique flavor and aroma, and is a must-have in my mother's refrigerator. It is sold in the fresh produce section of grocery stores. If the root pieces are too big, you can snap off the desired size you want to buy. (See page 25 for instructions on peeling and grating ginger.) Ginger keeps for two to three weeks when put in a paper bag and stored in the crisper drawer of the refrigerator. The exposed cut end of a partially used piece of ginger root should be tightly wrapped with plastic wrap before placing it back in the refrigerator.

Gram flour (*besan***)** Gram flour, also known as chickpea flour, is made from a dried, split and skinned legume called Bengal gram. Bengal gram is a small dark brown chickpea (*kala channa*). The small dark brown chickpea is different from the bigger cream-colored chickpea known as the "garbanzo." When Bengal gram is split and skinned, a yellow lentil called *channa daal* is revealed. This is crushed to make gram flour, which is pale yellow in color. You may find this flour in the international section of grocery stores, or you

may find it at an organic store. I use gram flour to make the batter for Vegetable Fritters (page 61), and also to make Gram Flour and Onion Breads (page 69). You can also use gram flour to make a natural face mask, as my mother has recommended to me. If you have oily skin, mix gram flour with water until you get a pasty consistency; if you have dry skin, use milk instead of water. Spread the paste on your face, and let the mask dry. When it is dry, wash off to reveal beautiful skin! You can make and use the face mask as often as you like. Store gram flour in an airtight jar in your pantry for up to three months, or up to six months in your freezer.

Ground red pepper (cayenne) (*laal mirch***)** In Indian cooking, ground red pepper is practically a must-have. This spice adds fire to a dish. If you feel a dish is too spicy or not spicy enough based on the amount of ground red pepper indicated in one of my recipes, you can simply add more or less to meet your personal preference. Ground red pepper is made from various red chili peppers, such as bird's-eye chili pepper, that have been dried and ground. You can find ground red pepper of different varieties and heat intensities in ethnic markets, but you can also use ground cayenne pepper, which is readily available in the spice section of grocery stores. Ground cayenne pepper is a blend of various tropical chili peppers, including the cayenne chili. If you happen to get any of it on your hands, be sure to thoroughly wash them so you do not touch your lips, nose, or rub your eyes and cause irritation.

Mangoes ("green" pickling and "yellow" eating varieties) (***aam***) Mangoes come in many different varieties, shapes, colors and sizes, and are enjoyed throughout India many differ-

Channa daal | Whole masoor daal | Whole moong daal | Toor daal

Skinned/split Masoor daal | Skinned/split Moong daal | Skinned/split Urad daal

Lentils (whole and skinned/split) **(sabut** and ***dhuli daal)** Lentils, called *daal* in Hindi, are a type of legume, which are various bean or pea plants that have seed pods. When the seeds are removed from the pods and dried, they are called lentils or pulses. Lentils are either whole *(sabut)* or hulled (skin/shell removed) and split *(dhuli)*. Sometimes lentils are split with the skin still on. When whole lentils are skinned and split, they reveal a different color and taste. Lentils can be kept for three months in an airtight jar in your pantry. Lentils should be picked over and washed before being used (see "How to Wash Rice and Dried Legumes," page 23).

Channa daal (skinned/split) When the tiny dark brown chickpea *(kala channa)*, also known as "Bengal gram," is skinned and split , a bright yellow lentil is revealed, which is called channa daal in Hindi. This lentil is tempered in oil to provide flavor and crunch to a dish, such as Tamarind Rice (page 82). This lentil is also ground into gram flour *(besan)* for use in breads and the batter to make Vegetable Fritters (page 61). *Note*: Channa daal is not the same as skinned and split yellow peas (field peas), which can be easily found in American stores, nor is it the same as skinned and split pigeon peas *(toor daal)*, although all three varieties look similar.

Masoor daal (whole and skinned/split) Whole red lentils *(sabut masoor daal)* are disc-shaped with a flat base and reddish-tan to light brown in color. In the United States, whole red lentils are commonly used to make lentil soup and can readily be found in American grocery stores. I have noticed that the ones in American stores are slightly larger and lighter in color and more tan, whereas the ones at the Indian stores are the smaller and redder Indian variety, but either will do fine. When these lentils are skinned and split *(dhuli masoor daal)*, a beautiful orange color comes through and, surprisingly, when they are cooked, they turn yellow.

Moong daal (whole and skinned/split) Whole green lentils *(sabut moong daal)* look like tiny dark green ovals. In addition to cooking these lentils, they may also be sprouted and tossed with fresh vegetables to make a lovely salad (see Fresh Lentil Sprout Salad, page 95). When these lentils are skinned and split *(dhuli moong daal)*, they reveal a yellow color, and can quickly be made into my favorite lentil dish, Stewed Split Green Lentils (page 101)! The split and skinned lentils are also used to make Creamy Mulligatawny Soup (page 91).

Toor daal (skinned/split pigeon peas) Whole greenish tan–colored pigeon peas reveal a yellow interior *(toor daal)* when they are skinned and split. Toor daal is used to make *sambar*, Split Pea and Vegetable Stew (page 92). In Indian grocery stores, you might also see toor daal that is oiled, but I use the matte ones. The peas are sometimes oiled to increase shelf life, especially before exporting, but people usually wash the oil off in hot water before using. Toor daal resembles *channa daal*, but toor daal is slightly smaller. Also, do not confuse toor daal with split yellow peas (field peas) that are commonly found in American stores.

Urad daal (skinned/split) When whole, these tiny lentils are black and are called "black gram" or *sabut urad daal*. When they are skinned and split, they are white. The skinned and split lentil *(dhuli urad daal)* is soaked and ground to make the Dosa and Uttapam Batter (page 45), and it is also tempered in oil to add flavor to rice and other dishes.

ent ways—from pickles, chutneys, drinks, and of course eaten as a fresh fruit. I use big ripe yellow mangoes to make Mango Lassi (page 147) and green, unripe "pickling" mangoes to make Mango Pickle (page 41) and Sweet and Spicy Mango Chutney (page 38). When buying ripe mangoes for lassis or fruit salad, or just eating as is, look for mangos that yield slightly to the touch and have a sweet fragrance. The skin of ripe mangoes will be yellow-orange with red blushing, although there are also some varieties of eating mangoes that have green skin with some red blushing even when they are fully ripe. When unripe, they will be hard to the touch and the skin will be green. Though the skin color of this variety of mango may differ, the flesh of ripe eating mangoes is bright yellow, and hopefully sweet and fragrant. Pickling mangoes are green on the outside and firm to the touch, and hard and white on the inside. These are a special variety of mangoes that are plucked when they are still unripe. Eventually, these mangoes will soften and ripen, but they will remain tart. Pickling mangoes can be found in various sizes at ethnic markets and at some American grocery stores. If you do not find a specific pickling variety mango, an unripe eating variety that is very firm and has green skin can be used instead. You may notice that the inside of an unripe eating mango is not white, but instead a pale yellow, which is okay. Perfectly ripe yellow mangoes should be kept in the refrigerator up to one week after they are bought. If you happen to buy some that are hard and not quite ripe, you may put them in a paper bag for a few days until they soften, and then refrigerate them, but do not do this with green pickling mangoes since you do not want them to ripen. Pickling mangoes should be immediately refrigerated after purchasing them to stall ripening.

Mustard seeds (*sarson ka beej,* also called *rai*) Mustard seeds come in two types: white, which are really yellowish-tan in color, and black, which are actually dark brown in color, and are the ones I use. The white seeds are larger and not as pungent as the darker seeds, and are used to make American mustards. Mustard seeds are used in the tempering process of cooking, in which spices are introduced to heated oil, causing the flavors to release. When tempering mustard seeds, you can see and hear them crackle and pop, but be careful—if you put them in oil that is too hot, they might wildly fly around as they pop and hit your face or eyes. Some people believe that mustard seeds ward off evil and negative forces, so if you feel things are not going well, try sprinkling some mustard seeds around the outside of your home to see if your luck changes! If anything, you might get pretty yellow mustard plants growing around your house.

Nutmeg (*jaiphal*) Nutmeg is the light brown seed of a fruit from an evergreen tree. It is best to buy it whole and grate it on the prickly side of a box grater or a Microplane when ready to use to get the maximum flavor. The unused portion should be kept in your pantry in an airtight bottle. You can also simply buy a small amount of pre-ground nutmeg, but do keep in mind that ground nutmeg soon loses its flavor. Nutmeg has a flavor that is similar to but different from cinnamon. I use nutmeg to flavor meats, but you could also sprinkle some on Indian cappuccino and see how you like that.

Oil (*vanaspati tail*) Oil is an important part of cooking Indian food because it allows food to delicately brown and also adds fat, which of course means adding flavor! Oil also prevents food from sticking to the bottom of cookware, especially if you are not using nonstick cookware. I usually cook Indian food with either vegetable oil or canola oil, which is a specific type of vegetable oil that is expressed from the seeds of the rapeseed plant. For simplicity, I call for vegetable oil in the recipes throughout this book, but you can certainly use canola oil instead, which is healthier, although a bit pricier. Vegetable oil is a category of cooking oils that are made from plant sources, such as vegetable, nuts or seeds. When I buy vegetable oil, I buy the bottle that says "vegetable oil," which may be soybean, corn, or other vegetable-derived oils that are mixed together. Olive oil, a type of vegetable oil, is not traditionally used to cook Indian food, but now some are starting to use it for health reasons. Once opened, store oil tightly closed in a cabinet for up to six months.

Paneer is a fresh homemade cheese that is un-ripened—meaning, it has not been aged. It is a mild, versatile cheese that does not melt when heated due to its chemical structure, and can be used to make appetizers, main dishes and a variety of Indian desserts. This cheese is simply made by separating boiling milk into curds (solid clumps) and whey (watery liquid) by using lime juice. The whey is then drained by passing it through cheesecloth, leaving the moist, soft and crumbly curds, which is the Indian cheese, paneer. Depending on what you want to make with the paneer, it can be used as is in its soft, crumbled form or it may be shaped into a square and pressed under a heavy weight so the remaining whey is pressed out, leaving a firm cheese block that can be cut into pieces and fried or sautéed. I always prefer to use whole milk instead of reduced fat milk when making paneer so that

I can get the maximum yield of paneer that is rich and creamy with a beautiful texture. Paneer is usually made from cow or buffalo milk, and should be used immediately, or kept in the refrigerator only one day so it does not dry out. Paneer blocks can be found in the refrigerated and frozen sections of Indian grocery stores, and even fried paneer cubes can be found in the frozen section. But because fresh paneer is so easy to make, I prefer to make it at home.

Paprika (*degi mirch*) is made from sweet peppers (usually bell peppers) that have been allowed to turn red on the plant before being plucked, set to dry, and ground. Paprika is usually not hot, and might even have a sweet taste to it, depending on the crop of the bell peppers used. I use paprika as a natural food coloring in dishes such as Chicken Tikka Masala (page 105) and Lamb or Chicken Vindaloo Curry (pages 108 and 109), so I like to buy the brightest red paprika I can find. The colors vary from dark orange to a deep red based on the color of the red peppers that were dried. Don't be afraid to add an extra teaspoon of paprika to the dish you are cooking if you prefer a deeper color. After all, it does come from a sweet pepper, so it can't spice up your dish too much!

Pistachios (*pista*) are great nuts, either when used in a dish or simply eaten on its own. For desserts, I like to use unsalted pistachios, but for snacking, I like salted pistachios. I think pistachios are an elegant nut, and I like to place a bowl of them out when we have guests over. These nuts can be coarsely crushed by using a mortar and pestle, or simply putting them in a small plastic bag, placing the bag on a cutting board, and gently tapping the bag with a rolling pin until the nuts break

into pieces. Pistachio nuts grow on a tree in clusters. The nuts are actually the fruit of the tree and when the fruit is ripe, the shell pops open. They are then plucked and ready to eat, or some are roasted and salted. If you come across one that is not cracked open or is only slightly open, do not bother trying to open it— the nut will not be good because it did not fully ripen. Sometimes you may see pistachio nuts with red shells, which are colored with dye for aesthetic purposes, but the taste is the same. I prefer the natural pistachios with the light tan shell and green nut. You may store pistachios in an airtight container for three months.

Tamarind concentrate (*imlee*) Tamarind is the fruit pod of the tamarind tree that grows around the world, though it is especially abundant in Asia. When the ripe pods are plucked from the trees, they have a thin tan-colored shell. When the pod is opened, there is fruit pulp and seeds held together by a fibrous husk. The reddish-brown pulp is what is used in cooking, while the pod, fibers and seeds are discarded. Tamarind provides a sour tinge to food. The easiest way to use tamarind is to buy pre-extracted tamarind pulp, which is also called "tamarind concentrate", "tamarind paste" or "tamarind extract." It is thick and pasty, and typically comes in a small jar and usually can be found at natural foods stores and at ethnic markets. The older the extracted pulp, the darker it turns, to eventually black. Because tamarind has natural preservative properties, it will keep for one year in your pantry. When the concentrate is heated, it thins out. Fresh, ripe tamarind pods are also plucked, shelled, and then pressed into square blocks. Even though the pressed pods have not been dried, they may seem dried out depending on how old they are. To

extract the pulp, pull off the desired amount from the block and soak it in warm water until it is soft, about 15 minutes. Then strain it through a sieve to separate the seeds and fibrous husk. You are left with the usable pulp. You may even buy fresh whole tamarind pods and extract the (pulp) concentrate in a similar way after shelling it. Extracting the pulp from tamarind blocks or whole pods can be a messy and tedious process, so that is why I prefer to buy the tamarind concentrate. Note that I buy the tamarind concentrate in a black paste form instead of the brown liquid concentrate.

Turmeric, ground (*haldi*) This beautiful bright yellow, almost mustard color, spice is made from the turmeric root, which is dried and ground into a powder. Turmeric root, which is from the same family as ginger root, grows best in a tropical climate, making India a top producer, consumer and exporter of this spice. This spice is one of the most common spices in India cooking; and is a must-have in my Indian spice box. It imparts both color and a mild earthy flavor to a dish, but if you use too much, it can lend a bitter taste to the dish. Turmeric is used as a natural beauty product in India for soft and beautiful skin. Turmeric is also known to have antiseptic properties. Some people even use it as a household remedy for minor cuts and burns. There is one thing to be careful of when using this spice—it stains quite easily, so if you get it on your kitchen counter or your nails, be sure to wash up quickly! Turmeric is also the spice that is put in American mustard to make it bright yellow. Turmeric is available at the spice aisle of grocery stores.

The Basics
Curds, Chutneys and Relishes

An Indian meal usually always has some basic accompaniment, such as yogurt, a chutney, a fruit or vegetable pickle, and perhaps a simple salad. Yogurt is must-have at most Indian meals, and can be offered plain, or it may be spiced and salted and mixed with tomatoes, cucumbers and onions. Chutney is the Hindi word for a relish that is made from either crushed herbs or mashed fruits, to which spices and seasoning are added. If I misbehaved as a child, my mom would jokingly say that I if I don't behave, she would make a chutney out of me, meaning I would get beaten as one would crush and grind herbs and fruit when making an actual chutney! Chutneys can be spicy, sweet, or sour or have a combination of these taste components. You can treat chutney as you would ketchup, and use it as a dipping sauce for appetizers and snacks such as Vegetable Fritters (page 61), Roasted Lentil Wafers (page 55) and Potato Turnovers (page 50). You can also use chutney as you use a spread or jam, spreading it on Indian or American breads. Here we will make an assortment of chutneys made from fresh mint, tamarind, ginger, coconut and green unripe pickling mangoes.

Pickled fruits and vegetables, called *aachar* in Hindi, are another condiment typically offered with an Indian meal. They can taste tart, tangy, slightly bitter and spicy. Aachar is commonly made with ginger, fruits, such as lemons, limes or green unripe pickling mangoes, or vegetables, such as carrots or cauliflower. A small amount of aachar can be put on your plate so you take small bites of it throughout your meal, or you may sweep a piece of Indian bread over the aachar before scooping up other food with the bread.

Along with including recipes for popular accompaniments, this chapter also includes recipes for frequently used ingredients or recipe components, such as *paneer* (pages 42 and 43), a fresh cheese used in appetizers, main dishes and desserts; Garam Masala (page 44), a popular roasted spice blend; and the batter for delicious Crispy Rice and Lentil Crepes (page 56) and Savory Vegetable Pancakes (page 53), popular breakfast or lunch items in the southern states of India.

Homemade Plain Yogurt

You can bet on always finding yogurt in any Indian home, since it is served in some form with almost every meal. It is a cooling condiment that soothes your stomach if eating spicy foods. Making homemade yogurt (*dahi*) is easier than you would think, and there is no need for any fancy kitchen gadgets or appliances, since all you have to do is boil milk, let it cool to lukewarm, mix in a bit of "starter" (bacterial culture), and let it set! For your very first batch of homemade yogurt, simply buy a small carton of plain yogurt that has "live and active cultures" in it (this will be stated on the carton). Once you have a batch of homemade yogurt, it can be used to make Three Vegetable Raita (page 37), Yogurt Rice (page 86) and a variety of refreshing yogurt-based drinks known as lassi. Yogurt may be served on your plate or in small individual bowls and can be eaten between bites, or mixed with rice.

Makes 3 cups (750 g)
Prep time: 25 minutes sitting
Cook time: 5 minutes + 6 hours sitting
Refrigerator life: 1 week
Reheating method: None! Simply serve or use to make a yogurt-based dish.

3 cups (750 ml) milk (whole, reduced fat or fat free)
1 tablespoon store-bought or homemade Plain Yogurt (whole, reduced fat or fat free)

1 Pour the milk into a microwave safe container, cover and heat in a microwave until the milk comes to a rolling boil. (To bring the milk to a boil more quickly in the microwave, heat it in two batches.) Alternatively, pour the milk into a heavy bottomed, medium-sized stockpot and bring to a rolling boil over high heat, stirring frequently as it comes to a boil. Don't let the milk boil over and out of the pot! Remove from the heat.
2 Choose a steel, glass or plastic container in which you want the yogurt to set. Pour the milk into the container. Set aside to cool until the milk

is lukewarm (about 105 to 110°F/41 to 43C°) and you can dip your fingertip in it, about 25 minutes.

3 Add the yogurt and stir. Cover the container and place in an un-warmed oven to avoid any cool drafts, or by a warm and sunny window. Let sit undisturbed (do not move the container or stir it) until the yogurt sets to a firm consistency, instead of being liquidy or runny, about 6 hours.

4 Place the set yogurt in the refrigerator to chill before serving, or to use later. Remember to save the last tablespoon of yogurt so you can make the next batch!

> **Troubleshooting Tips for Yogurt:** If the yogurt does not set after six hours and it still seems runny, there is hope! This is a temperature dependant process, so first make sure that the milk had initially come to a rolling boil. Also make sure the milk is indeed lukewarm, and not too cool or hot, when putting the culture in. If it is too cool, the bacteria will not be able to multiply. If it is too hot, the bacteria will die and not multiply. When choosing a container for the yogurt to set in, do not choose one that is too wide, since it will cool down the milk faster than the bacteria will be able to multiply. If you've done all these things, and it still does not set, then preheat the oven to 100°F (38°C) and turn it off. Put the milk container in the warmed oven for it to set, and check back after three hours. Also, note that the longer you leave the yogurt out to set, the more tart and firm it will become. Once refrigerated, it stops the bacteria from multiplying, so the taste and consistency will not change.

Three Vegetable Raita

Raita is a fancier alternative to Homemade Plain Yogurt (page 36) and is traditionally served as a condiment in place of Plain Yogurt with any meal. Even though raita has a bit of spice to it, it is a cooling complement to the spicier foods at the table. A few spoons of raita taken from a small bowl can be eaten between spicier bites, or it can be drizzled over rice.

Serves 4 to 6
Prep time: 10 minutes
Refrigerator life: 1 day (best when freshly prepared)
Reheating method: None! Simply stir and serve!

1 cup (250 g) store-bought or Homemade Plain Yogurt (page 37)
1/4 cup (65 ml) water
1/4 teaspoon cumin seeds, roasted and ground (see page 24)
2 pinches ground red pepper (cayenne)
1/4 heaping teaspoon salt
2 tablespoons minced onion
1 small fully ripe tomato, such as plum (Roma), diced
4 tablespoons peeled and diced cucumber (any variety) (see below)

1 Whisk the yogurt in a large bowl until it is smooth and there are no lumps. Add the water, cumin, red pepper and salt. Mix well.

2 Add the onion, tomato and cucumber. Mix together. Enjoy now or refrigerate for later!

Peeling and Dicing the Cucumber

1 Peel the skin off half of a smaller variety cucumber (such as a Japanese cucumber) or about one-quarter of an average-size slicing cucumber. Cut off the peeled part and keep the remaining unpeeled cucumber wrapped in plastic wrap, refrigerated up to 3 days, for use in other recipes.

2 Slice the peeled cucumber in half lengthwise. (If you feel there are too many seeds for your personal preference, you may scoop them out using a small spoon, but this is optional.)

3 Cut each cucumber half lengthwise into thin strips, about 1/4-inch (6-mm) wide.

4 Line up the strips and cut them crosswise to create equal-sized tiny 1/4-inch (6-mm) dice.

Sweet and Spicy Mango Chutney

Mango chutney is a wonderful condiment that is made from pickling mangoes, which is a unique variety of mangoes that are plucked early from the tree while they are still unripe and firm, and green on the outside. These unripe mangoes, also sometimes called "green mangoes" are used for pickles and chutneys. This mango chutney makes a lovely jam to spread on toast, bagels or English muffins. It also goes well when spread on crostini (little toasts), and paired with wine and cheese. This chutney can also be spread on a soft and buttery Indian bread, Flaky Wheat Breads (page 70). Roll up the paratha for an easy way to eat breakfast on the go! Or, enjoy it Paddington bear style and spread between two slices of white bread to make a "marmalade" sandwich! I call this chutney "sweet and spicy" because at first it seems sweet, but then you can feel the heat in the back of your throat build for a spicy kick.

Makes 1 cup (300 g)
Prep time: 10 minutes + overnight sitting (12 hours)   **Cook time:** 10 minutes
Refrigerator life: 1 month
Reheating method: None! Simply serve!

1 large pickling mango or very green and firm, unripe eating mango (about 1 lb/500 g)
1 cup (200 g) sugar
1 teaspoon ground red pepper (cayenne)
1¼ teaspoons salt

1   Wash and peel the mango with a vegetable peeler. Grate the mango on the small grating holes on a box grater. You should get 1 cup (225 g) of grated mango.
2   Place the grated mango and sugar in a medium bowl. Mix well. Cover and let sit for 12 hours at room temperature.
3   Simmer the grated mango and sugar mixture, and the red pepper in a medium saucepan over medium heat, stirring frequently, until the chutney becomes sticky and turns a deep orange color with a beautiful glisten, about 6 minutes.
4   Add the salt and stir. Cook for 1 minute and remove from the heat. The chutney should have the consistency of a thin and runny jam. Do not overcook, as it will then harden after it is refrigerated, and not be spreadable. The chutney will thicken to the consistency of a spreadable jam as it cools to room temperature.
5   Enjoy now or refrigerate for later!

Ginger Chutney

This chutney is a bit on the fiery side due to the red chili peppers. But if you are like me, you may choose to reduce the amount of red chili peppers to make it a bit milder, which is perfectly okay! Ginger Chutney is traditionally made from jaggery, which is unrefined sugar made from sugar cane, commonly available in India. Light brown sugar is an easily available substitute for jaggery. Ginger Chutney can be eaten along with Crispy Rice and Lentil Crepes (page 56), Potato Stuffed Crepes (page 56), Savory Vegetable Pancakes (page 53) or simply along with Plain Boiled Rice (page 79). Due to the natural preservative properties of the tamarind in this chutney, it keeps for an entire month in the refrigerator.

Makes 3/4 cup (200 g)
Prep time: 15 minutes
Cook time: 5 minutes
Refrigerator life: 1 month
Reheating method: None! Stir the refrigerated chutney and serve either chilled or at room temperature.

6 dried finger-length red chili peppers
1 whole bulb garlic, cloves separated
   and peel removed
1/2 cup (60 g) peeled and coarsely
   chopped fresh ginger
3/4 cup (100 g) light brown sugar
1 tablespoon tamarind concentrate
1/2 teaspoon salt
4 tablespoons water
1 tablespoon vegetable oil
3/4 teaspoon cumin seeds
3/4 teaspoon mustard seeds
1 sprig fresh curry leaves, rinsed
   and destemmed (about 15 leaves)
   (optional)

1 Place a medium skillet over medium
heat. When the skillet is heated, roast 5 of
the red chili peppers until they slightly puff
up, stirring frequently, about 2 minutes.
2 Place the 5 roasted red chili peppers,
garlic, ginger, brown sugar, tamarind, salt
and water in a blender and process until
smooth.
3 In the same skillet, pour in the oil and
place over medium heat. When the oil is
heated, tear the remaining 1 red chili pepper in half and add to the skillet. Add the
cumin seeds and mustard seeds. Cook until
the cumin seeds turn brown and you hear
the mustard seeds pop, about 10 seconds.
Do not let the cumin seeds burn and turn
black. Turn off the heat.
4 Add the curry leaves, if using. Stir to
combine. Add the contents from the
blender. Stir to combine.
5 Enjoy now or refrigerate for later!

Tamarind Chutney

Tamarind Chutney is a popular Indian condiment with both a sweet and sour taste. This chutney can be eaten with Potato Turnovers (page 50) or Vegetable Fritters (page 61). I have even seen people dipping Roasted Lentil Wafers (page 55) in this chutney at restaurants. Tamarind Chutney is made from the pulp that is squeezed out of whole tamarind pods, but luckily we can avoid this messy task and instead buy ready-to-use tamarind concentrate. For a contrast in flavor and color, this dark brown, smooth chutney can be served alongside bright green Mint Chutney (page 40). Due to the natural preservative properties in tamarind, it keeps for an entire month in the refrigerator.

Makes 1/4 cup (65 ml)
Cook time: 15 minutes
Refrigerator life: 1 month
Reheating method: None. Stir the refrigerated chutney and serve either chilled or at room temperature. If you feel the chutney has gotten too thick after refrigerating, you may thin it out by slightly warming in the microwave or on the stovetop in a saucepan over medium-low heat.

1 tablespoon tamarind concentrate (paste)
6 tablespoons sugar
1/4 teaspoon ground red pepper
   (cayenne)
1/2 teaspoon salt
1/4 teaspoon ground black pepper
1/2 cup (125 ml) water
1/4 teaspoon fennel seeds

1 Place all the ingredients, except the fennel seeds, in a small saucepan. Mix well. Bring to a rolling boil over high heat. Reduce the heat to medium-low. Simmer for 10 minutes, stirring occasionally. Add the fennel seeds and stir.
2 Remove from the heat and let cool to room temperature to thicken. At this point, the chutney will be quite thin, but it will thicken to the ideal consistency as it cools, which is about the thickness of pancake syrup, or a little thinner, and it will thicken even more when chilled in the refrigerator. (You do not want the chutney to be too thin and runny, as it won't stick to the food that is being dipped into it, and you do not want it so thick that becomes gloppy). Enjoy now or let cool to room temperature and refrigerate for later!

Mint Chutney

Mint Chutney is a popular Indian condiment that can be eaten with Potato Turnovers (page 50), Vegetable Fritters (page 61), Chicken Kebabs (page 60) or anything you wish to dip in it! Making a chutney usually involves crushing something, and here we crush the mint leaves and onion together in a food processor to create a fresh and bright tasting no-fuss chutney. Traditionally crushed dried pomegranate seeds or dried mango powder (*amchoor*) are added for tart flavor, but I add lime juice instead since it is easily available. I remember as a child having the tedious job of picking mint leaves from my mom's garden when she was going to make this chutney, and now I pick the leaves from my own garden!

Makes 1/2 cup (100 g)
Prep time: 10 minutes
Refrigerator life: 5 days   **Freezer life:** 1 month
Defrosting method: Stir the refrigerated or defrosted chutney and serve either chilled or at room temperature.

1/2 small onion, coarsely chopped
1 1/2 cups (30 g) packed fresh mint leaves, rinsed
Juice of 1/2 lime
1/4 teaspoon ground red pepper (cayenne)
1/2 teaspoon salt
1/4 teaspoon ground black pepper

1 Rinse the chopped onion with cold water to reduce the bitterness.
2 Process all the ingredients in a mini food processor until almost smooth, but do not purée it because some texture looks nice.
3 Enjoy now or refrigerate or freeze for later!

Coconut Chutney

Coconuts are used throughout India in religious rituals as well as in celebrations, such as grand openings of businesses at which a coconut is cracked open. Traditionally this chutney is made from fresh coconut, but cracking open a coconut and prying out the flesh can be quite a task. To make things easy, I simply use dried and shredded unsweetened coconut that is found in the baking section at any grocery store. To bring out the flavor and aroma of the dried coconut, I quickly dry roast it. You can serve this chutney along with Crispy Rice and Lentil Crepes (page 56), Potato Stuffed Crepes (page 56) and Savory Vegetable Pancakes (page 53).

Makes 1 cup (200 g)
Prep time: 10 minutes
Cook time: 5 minutes
Refrigerator life: 3 days
Reheating method: None! Stir the refrigerated chutney and serve either chilled or at room temperature. If it is too thick after being refrigerated, simply stir in plain yogurt one-half teaspoon at a time until desired consistency is reached.

1 cup (50 g) dried, unsweetened coconut (shredded or flakes)
1 teaspoon vegetable oil
3 fresh finger-length green chili peppers
Juice of 1 lime
1/4 teaspoon salt
4 tablespoons store-bought or Homemade Plain Yogurt (page 36)
1/2 cup (125 ml) water
1/4 teaspoon mustard seeds
1 sprig fresh curry leaves, rinsed and destemmed (about 15 leaves) (optional)

1 Place a medium skillet over medium heat. When the skillet is heated, roast the coconut until it is fragrant and some of it (not necessarily all) starts to turn very light brown, stirring frequently, about 45 seconds. Remove from the skillet and set aside.
2 In the same skillet, pour 1/2 teaspoon of the oil and place over medium heat. When the oil is heated, add the green chili peppers. Roast the peppers until their skins start to bubble, turning frequently, about 1 minute. Place the roasted green chili peppers, roasted coconut, lime juice, salt, yogurt and water in a blender and process until smooth.
3 In the same skillet, pour the remaining 1/2 teaspoon of the oil and place over medium heat. When the oil is heated, add the mustard seeds and let pop, about 10 seconds. Turn off the heat.
4 Add the curry leaves, if using. Stir to combine. Add the contents from the blender. Stir to combine. Enjoy now or refrigerate for later!

1 Wash the mango and pat dry with a kitchen towel. Do not peel it. Using a chef's knife and a lot of force, cut the mango in half lengthwise, cutting through the shell and pit (seed). If the shell is too hard to cut through, use a cleaver and gently tap it with a hammer to break through the shell. Pry the pit out with a knife and discard. (Note: If you do not have a cleaver, you can cut around the shell and discard the shell with the pit inside.)

2 Cut the mango into about 3/4-inch (2-cm) cubes. Pat the pieces dry with a kitchen towel. (*Note:* Do not skip this step. Excess moisture on the mango will cause your pickle to turn moldy.)

3 Place about half of the mustard seeds in a coffee/spice grinder and grind to a fine powder. Place the ground seeds in a small bowl. Repeat with the second half of the mustard seeds.

4 Place the ground mustard seeds, red pepper, salt and oil in a wide-mouth (to make mixing easier) plastic or glass jar. Stir to combine. Add the mango pieces and mix well. Cover and let sit at room temperature for 10 days, mixing the contents once a day with a spoon or by vigorously shaking the jar. The pickled mango will soften and darken in color as it develops in the oil and spices and absorbs the flavors as the days go by.

5 Enjoy a small piece along with each meal, and store the rest in the jar in your pantry or cabinet at room temperature for up to 1 year!

Mango Pickle   Aam ka Aachar

In India, pickling fruits and vegetables, which is the process of preserving foods in salt, oil or vinegar, is done to create a variety of *aachar*, which are pickled condiments. Pickled mango is possibly the most common Indian aachar, yet it has so many different variations in taste and preparation styles. Overall, pickled mango should have a spicy and slightly sour taste to it. A small amount is served along with an Indian meal, and can be bit into between bites. You may also take any Indian bread and sweep a piece of the bread over the pickled mango before scooping up other food with the bread. In India, pickled mango is typically made once a year in the summer when green unripe mangoes are in season, and enough is made to last for the entire year. When you come across the shell in the pickle (the tough layer that surrounds the pit), you simply suck on it and then discard it, but all of the cubed pulp pieces, along with the skin can be eaten.

Pitting and Slicing Mangoes

Cut the mango in half and remove the seed. Cut the mango into about 3/4-inch (2-cm) cubes.

Makes 3 cups (700 g)
Prep time: 15 minutes + 10 days sitting
Refrigerator life: Store up to 1 year in an airtight container at room temperature.
Reheating method: None. Stir before serving.

1 large pickling mango or very green and firm, unripe eating mango (about 1 lb/500 g), unpeeled
1/2 cup (75 g) mustard seeds
1/2 cup (50 g) ground red pepper (cayenne)
4 tablespoons salt
3/4 cup (185 ml) vegetable oil

Crumbled Indian Cheese Paneer

Paneer is the Hindi word for cheese, and this soft Indian cheese is the crumbled form of the Indian Cheese Block (page 43). It is made from boiling milk that is separated into curds and whey by introducing lime juice. The whey is drained, leaving fresh homemade cheese that is used to make the scrumptious Crumbled Indian Cheese and Peas (page 143). It is also used to make delectable desserts such as Sweet Cheese Dessert (page 150) and Sweet Cheese Ball Dessert (page 153). It is best to use whole milk instead of reduced fat milk when making this cheese to get the most yield and a creamier taste and texture.

Makes 1 cup (135 g)
Prep work: 5 minutes   **Cook time:** 5 minutes
Refrigerator life: 1 day   **Reheating method:** None! Simply use to make desired dish.

4 cups (1 liter) whole milk
Juice of 1 lime

1 Pour the milk into a heavy bottomed, medium-sized stockpot. Bring to a rolling boil over high heat, stirring frequently as it comes to a boil. Don't let the milk boil over and out of the pot! Immediately reduce the heat to medium-low.
2 Add the lime juice and gently stir for about 45 seconds, or until the milk separates into curds (solid clumps) and whey (watery liquid). (If the milk does not separate, add more lime juice—2 teaspoons at a time—until it does.) The whey may appear to be light green in color from the lime juice.
3 Fold a large piece of cheesecloth into 4 layers (this will keep the cheese from falling through). Line a colander with the folded cheesecloth and place it in the sink. Gently pour the separated milk into the cheesecloth–lined colander. Let the whey drain through the colander down into the sink.
4 When the whey has stopped draining (about 1 minute), gather up the sides of the cheesecloth to create a bundle. Using the back of a spoon, gently press the bundle against the side of the colander to squeeze out most of the excess whey. It is okay if the cheese is somewhat moist. Be careful, as it will be hot.
5 Remove the cheese from the cheesecloth and place in a small bowl. The *paneer* is now ready to be used in one of the paneer-based recipes in the book or it may be placed in an airtight container and refrigerated up to 1 day before using.

Draining the Whey

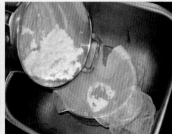

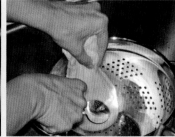

1. Curdled milk.

2. Pouring cheese into cheesecloth (Note that the colander needs to be put over a bowl to collect the whey when making the Indian Cheese Block).

3. Bundle of cheese in cheesecloth to be gently squeezed.

4. Using the back of a spoon to gently press out excess whey.

Unpressed cheese block

Makes 1/4 lb (125 g)
Prep work: 5 minutes
Cook time: 5 minutes + 30 minutes sitting + 1 hour to set in the refrigerator
Refrigerator life: 1 day
Reheating method: None! Simply use to make desired dish.

4 cups (1 liter) whole milk
Juice of 1 lime

1 Pour the milk into a heavy bottomed, medium-sized stockpot. Bring to a rolling boil over high heat, stirring frequently as it comes to a boil. Don't let the milk boil over and out of the pot! Immediately reduce the heat to medium-low.

2 Add the lime juice and gently stir for about 45 seconds, or until the milk separates into curds (solid clumps) and whey (watery liquid). (If the milk does not separate, add more lime juice—2 teaspoons at a time—until it does.) The whey may appear to be light green in color from the lime juice.

3 Fold a large piece of cheesecloth into 4 layers (this will keep the cheese from falling through). Line a colander with the folded cheesecloth and place it over a large bowl to catch the whey. Gently pour the separated milk into the cheesecloth–lined colander. Let the whey drain through the colander down into the bowl.

4 When the whey has stopped draining (about 1 minute), gather up the sides of the cheesecloth to create a bundle. Using the back of a spoon, press the bundle against the side of the colander to squeeze out the excess whey. Be careful, as it will be hot.

5 Place the bundle on a plate. Unfold the cheesecloth and, using your hands (make sure it is not too hot to handle), mold the cheese into a square block about 3/4-inch (2-cm) thick and neatly fold the cheesecloth back over it.

6 Pour the collected whey into the same pot that you boiled the milk in. Place the pot with the whey over the wrapped cheese block for 30 minutes to press any excess whey out of the cheese and to allow it to firm up.

7 Remove the pot and discard the whey. Unfold the cheesecloth and gently place the cheese block on a clean plate. Cover with plastic wrap and refrigerate for a minimum of 1 hour and maximum of 1 day before cutting into cubes and/or pan-frying to make your favorite *paneer*-based dish!

Indian Cheese Block Paneer

Paneer is an easy-to-make Indian homemade cheese that can be used to make many different dishes—from appetizers such as Cheese and Bell Pepper Skewers (page 49) to main dishes such as Creamed Spinach with Cheese Cubes (page 140) and Indian Cheese and Pea Curry (page 142). Once you make paneer, you will be amazed at how easy it is to make cheese at home! To get the optimum yield and creamy taste and texture, it is best to use whole milk instead of reduced fat milk.

Pan-Fried Cheese Cubes

After a block of paneer has been refrigerated for at least an hour, it can be cut into cubes and pan-fried. Traditionally, the cheese cubes are deep-fried before putting them in the main dishes, but I lightly pan-fry the cubes instead just to make the recipes a tad bit easier and healthier!

Makes about 16 cubes
Prep time: 5 minutes
Cook time: 5 minutes
Refrigerator life: 3 days
Freezer life: 1 month
Reheating method: None. Simply drop the refrigerated or frozen pan-fried cheese cubes into the dish you are making.

1 recipe Indian Cheese Block (page 43)
3 tablespoons vegetable oil

1 To cube the cheese block, cut it into 3/4-inch (2-cm)-square pieces. It is okay if the pieces are not perfect cubes. You should get about 16 cubes.
2 To pan-fry the cheese cubes, pour the oil into a medium nonstick skillet and place over medium heat. When the oil is heated, add the cheese cubes. Pan-fry the cheese cubes until all the sides, or at least the top and bottom sides (if not a perfect cube), are lightly golden, gently turning frequently, about 3 minutes.
3 Remove the cubes from the skillet and place on paper towels to drain any excess oil.
4 The fried cheese cubes may be used in a recipe now or they may be placed in an airtight container and refrigerated or frozen for later use.

Garam Masala

This is my mother-in-law's recipe for *garam masala*, a popular roasted spice mix that is used throughout India. Like many Indians, she makes her personal version of garam masala at home, based on the flavors she prefers in her cooking style. I like her personal blend because the flavors are well balanced, and the spices she uses can easily be found at my local grocery store. Garam masala can be used in several dishes in this book, including Chicken Biryani (page 80), Lamb Kebabs (page 113), Easy Shrimp Curry (page 120), Vegetables with Coconut Curry (page 134) and others.

Makes 1/2 cup (40 g)
Cook time: 5 minutes
Refrigerator life: Store up to 3 months in an airtight container at room temperature.

1/2 cup (30 g) coriander seeds
1/2 teaspoon cloves
6 whole green cardamoms
1 tablespoon cumin seeds
1/4 teaspoon black peppercorns
One 1/4-in (6-mm) cinnamon stick

1 Place a small skillet over medium heat. When the skillet is heated, roast the coriander seeds until they are lightly brown and fragrant, stirring frequently, about 2 minutes. Remove from the skillet and set aside.
2 Roast the remaining spices in the same skillet over medium heat until they are fragrant, stirring frequently, about 1 minute. Do not let the cumin seeds burn and turn black. Immediately remove the spices from the skillet and place in a small bowl. Let cool slightly before grinding.
3 Place about half of the roasted seeds and spices in a coffee/spice grinder and grind to a fine powder. Place the ground spices in a small bowl. Repeat with the second half of the roasted seeds and spices.
4 Use now to make a delicious dish, or place in an airtight container at room temperature up to 3 months.

Dosa and Uttapam Batter

This overnight fermented batter is used to make crispy golden Crispy Rice and Lentil Crepes (page 56), Potato Stuffed Crepes (page 56) and Savory Vegetable Pancakes (page 53). Traditionally, it is made with dried and split black lentils (also known as "black gram" or *dhuli urad daal*) and uncooked rice that are soaked and then ground. Since the rice is going to be ground up, usually a cheaper plain white rice is used, instead of more expensive varieties such as Basmati rice. Instead of soaking and grinding the rice, I prefer to use rice flour. It's a great time-saver since the rice is already ground into a flour. Plain white rice flour can be found in the organic section of your grocery store or both the Indian and Asian aisles in the international section of your grocery store and it can be stored in an airtight jar in your pantry up to three months, or up to six months in your freezer. If the batter does not ferment properly, you could still use it, but you might not achieve the classic slightly tart taste and ideal texture that a fully fermented batter provides.

Makes 2 cups (500 ml)
Prep time: 5 hours soaking + overnight sitting (12 hours)
Refrigerator life: 3 days

1/4 cup (45 g) dried, skinned and split black lentils (dhuli urad daal)
1 cup (250 ml) water
3/4 cup (100 g) plain white rice flour (not glutinous, sweetened, Jasmine, brown, etc.)
1/2 teaspoon salt

1 Place the lentils on a plate. Sift through them and remove any grit.
2 Place the lentils in a medium bowl and cover with cold water. Let the lentils soak for 5 hours at room temperature to soften them.
3 Carefully pour the soaking water out of the bowl and discard. Rinse the lentils 3 times by repeatedly filling the bowl with cold water and carefully draining off the water. It is okay if the water is a bit frothy.
4 Process the lentils and 1/4 cup (65 ml) of the water in a blender until smooth and creamy.
5 Mix together the blended lentils, rice flour, salt and the remaining 3/4 cup (185 ml) of water in a medium bowl. Cover the bowl and place in an un-warmed oven to avoid any cool drafts. Let sit undisturbed until the mixture ferments and rises to almost double its size, about 12 hours. Air bubbles will develop along with a slightly sour smell. (If after 12 hours nothing has happened, see the tip below.)
6 Gently stir the batter. The batter will settle down in volume once you stir it, as some of the air bubbles collapse. The fermented mixture should be smooth and creamy, with a texture similar to American pancake batter. If you are not using the batter immediately, you may cover it and refrigerate it for up to 3 days.

> **TIP:** In the summer time, you may simply place the covered bowl in your garage. During any season you could also place the covered bowl by a warm and sunny window, or under a direct light bulb, or any especially warm spot, and it should easily ferment with the heat. In the winter, it may be cooler in your house, so if the batter has not fermented after 12 hours, you can turn on the oven light to provide more heat and keep an eye on it until it doubles in volume. The batter should start to ferment within 6 hours, but you can check back after every hour. Do not let your batter sit more than 20 hours total—by then it will have a rotten smell and not be useable.

Tomato and Cucumber Salad

Instead of a fancy salad that is served before the main course, typically in Indian cuisine, a simple salad of sliced tomatoes, cucumbers and raw onions sprinkled with salt, ground black pepper and lime juice is served along with lunch and dinner to provide a refreshing crunch during the meal. The sliced vegetables are neatly arranged on a plate or serving platter and everyone helps themselves to a few slices on the side of their own plate.

Serves 4
Prep time: 10 minutes
Refrigerator life: Not recommended. Tastes best freshly sliced and served.

1 small fully ripe tomato, such as plum (Roma), sliced crosswise into circles, about 1/4 in (6 mm) thick
1 small cucumber (any variety), peeled and sliced crosswise into circles, about 1/4 in (6 mm) thick
1/2 small onion, sliced into circles, about 1/4 in (6 mm) thick
1/4 teaspoon salt
1/4 teaspoon ground black pepper
Juice of 1 lime

1 Neatly spread out the tomato, cucumber and onion slices on a plate or serving platter. You may arrange them however you think looks best.
2 Evenly sprinkle the salt and black pepper on the tomato, cucumber and onion slices.
3 Sprinkle the lime juice evenly on the slices.
4 Enjoy now along with your meal!

Chapter 1

Appetizers, Snacks and Light Meals

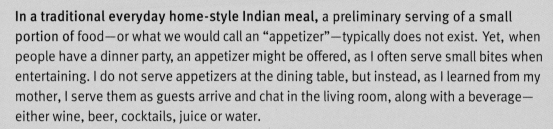

In a traditional everyday home-style Indian meal, a preliminary serving of a small portion of food—or what we would call an "appetizer"—typically does not exist. Yet, when people have a dinner party, an appetizer might be offered, as I often serve small bites when entertaining. I do not serve appetizers at the dining table, but instead, as I learned from my mother, I serve them as guests arrive and chat in the living room, along with a beverage—either wine, beer, cocktails, juice or water.

Pakora, which are Vegetable Fritters (page 61) and *samosa*, which Potato Turnovers (page 50) are typically sold by street vendors and enjoyed as satisfying afternoon snacks in India, but they also make great appetizers. Most snack shops in India also sell these snacks, so it is not too common to make them at home. Even here in the United States, I usually buy *samosa* from the Indian snack shop, but sometimes I do enjoy making them myself, especially with my mom's shortcut technique of using Mexican white flour tortillas!

When entertaining, I particularly enjoy serving Cheese and Bell Pepper Skewers (page 49) and Chicken Kebabs (page 60) as appetizers. Both are easy to prepare and they make a beautiful presentation when skewered on small picks. I also like to serve my mother's Spiced Fruit Cocktail (page 54), which is a medley of different chopped fruits that are spiced and seasoned with ground red pepper (cayenne), salt and ground black pepper and tossed with lime juice.

Pappadums are lentil wafers that are eaten along with the meal to add crunch and flavor. Interestingly, I have noticed that some Indian restaurants in America serve pappadums as appetizers, or place them at the table to munch on before the main course arrives. You can serve them either way.

In the southern states of India, *dosa*, which are Crispy Rice and Lentil Crepes (page 56) and *uttapam*, which are Savory Vegetable Pancakes (page 53) are delicious breakfast and brunch options, and they can also be eaten as a light meal. They are made from the same fermented batter, so when you have the batter ready, you can divide it and make dosa one day and uttapam the next!

Salted Fried Cashews Namkeen Kaju

Fried and salted cashews are an addictive afternoon snack that goes great with a cup of Indian Tea (page 148). They taste great warm right after they are freshly fried, or you can put them in an airtight container to enjoy anytime. These cashews are also excellent to serve as appetizers along with cocktails. When you have a party, fill a beautiful serving dish with these cashews, and watch how quickly they disappear!

Makes 1 lb (500 g)
Cook time: 5 minutes
Refrigerator life: Store up to 1 month in an airtight container at room temperature
Reheating method: None! Simply toss and serve

Vegetable oil, for deep-frying
1 lb (500 g) plain whole cashews
2 teaspoons salt

1 Pour 2 inches (5 cm) of oil into a medium wok or deep stockpot and place over medium-high heat.
2 Test the oil to make sure it is hot by dropping 1 cashew in the wok. If the oil is bubbling around the cashew, the oil is hot and ready. If not, let the oil heat longer. If the cashew turns dark brown immediately, the oil is overheated, so reduce the heat a bit.
3 When the oil is hot, reduce the heat to me-dium so the cashews do not burn while they are cooking. Using a large spoon, carefully slide the cashews in batches into the wok, depending on the size of your wok. Cook until the cashews are light golden, turning frequently, about 30 to 45 seconds.
4 Remove the cashews from the wok with a slotted spoon and place them in a wide bowl lined with paper towels. Immediately sprinkle the salt on the hot cashews and toss well.
5 Allow to cool slightly before serving. Enjoy now or let cool completely and store in a sealed jar at room temperature for later!

> **TIP:** For 1 lb of cashews, I fry them in 5 batches. Keep a very sharp eye on the first batch, as it may take less time since the oil will be very hot.

Cheese and Bell Pepper Skewers

Cheese and Bell Pepper Skewers

Paneer Tikka

These delicious kebabs are a colorful Indian appetizer that is often served at Indian wedding receptions, but you certainly do not have to wait for a wedding to enjoy them! *Tikka* usually refers to bite-size pieces of boneless meat, but small pieces of paneer (Indian cheese) are also called tikka. When entertaining, I like to place the paneer and bell peppers on decorative mini skewers with a pretty ribbon on the end. Just be sure to make plenty of kebabs, as people tend to grab and enjoy them fast!

Serves 4
Prep time: 10 minutes + 1 hour 40 minutes to make Indian Cheese Block
Cook time: 20 minutes + 5 minutes resting
Refrigerator life: Not recommended. (Tastes best when served immediately.)

1 recipe Indian Cheese Block (page 43)
3 tablespoons vegetable oil
1/2 small onion, grated on the largest grating holes on a box grater or in a food processor
1 fully ripe tomato, coarsely chopped
1/4 teaspoon ground red pepper (cayenne)
3/4 teaspoon salt
1/2 teaspoon ground black pepper
1/2 green bell pepper, cut into 3/4-in (2-cm) squares
1/2 red bell pepper, cut into 3/4-in (2-cm) squares
8 to 16 mini bamboo skewers (about 4 to 6 in/10 to 15 cm)

1 Cut the Indian Cheese Block into 3/4-inch (2-cm) cubes. It is okay if the pieces are not perfectly square cubes. You should get about 16 cubes.

2 Pour the oil into a medium nonstick skillet and place over medium heat. When the oil is heated, add the onion. Sauté until the onion is lightly browned, stirring frequently, about 5 minutes.

3 Reduce the heat to medium-low. Add the tomato and cover the skillet. Cook until the tomato becomes completely soft and mashed and is combined with the onion to form a coarse paste, stirring every minute or so and lightly mashing the tomato, about 5 minutes.

4 Add the red pepper, 1/2 teaspoon of the salt and 1/4 teaspoon of the black pepper. Stir to combine. Cook uncovered for 2 minutes, stirring frequently. This is the *masala* (spice base).

5 Increase the heat to medium. Add the cheese cubes. Gently mix to combine. Cook uncovered for 2 minutes, gently stirring frequently and turning the cheese cubes. Push the cheese cubes and masala to one side of the skillet.

6 Add the red and green bell peppers to the other side of the skillet. Sprinkle the remaining 1/4 teaspoon of the salt and black pepper on the bell peppers. Cook uncovered until the bell peppers are just tender with some slight crispness, stirring occasionally, about 5 minutes. While the bell peppers are cooking, gently turn the cheese cubes occasionally so they do not burn.

7 Turn off the heat and cover the skillet. Let rest on the warm stovetop for 5 minutes.

8 On each skewer, thread alternate pieces of the green bell pepper, cheese cube, and red bell pepper, depending on the length of the skewer. Enjoy now!

Potato Turnovers Samosa

A *samosa* is a popular Indian street food that is a turnover stuffed with potatoes and peas and deep-fried. Freshly made samosas are readily available throughout India, so Indians do not typically go through the effort of making them at home. Even in America, samosas are available in Indian restaurants, take-out cafes, and sometimes in the frozen section at a grocery store. However, if you are feeling adventurous, you may make them at home the easy way by using Mexican white flour tortillas instead of making the samosa dough from scratch. And if you are not amazed at how easy and delicious this shortcut way is, I have also provided the method for making samosas the traditional way with homemade dough. Samosas make excellent appetizers and as well as a great afternoon snack along with a cup of Indian Tea (page 148) or Indian Cappuccino (page 149). You may serve samosas with Mint Chutney (page 40), Tamarind Chutney (page 39), ketchup or simply enjoy them as they are!

Makes 10 small samosas

Prep time: 35 minutes to boil the potato (can be done 1 day in advance) + 10 minutes to assemble samosas (*Note*: If you're making homemade Samosa Dough, you will need to add an additional 20 minutes to make and roll out the dough + 30 minutes of resting time)

Cook time: 5 minutes for the filling + 20 seconds per samosa

Refrigerator life: Not recommended. (Tastes best freshly fried and served hot.)

Five 6-in (15-cm) white flour Mexican tortillas or 1 recipe Samosa Dough (recipe on page 52)
Vegetable oil, for deep-frying

Filling

2 tablespoons vegetable oil
1/2 teaspoon cumin seeds
1 medium russet potato (about 1/2 lb/ 250 g), boiled, peeled and diced (see page 24 for tips)
4 tablespoons frozen or fresh parboiled green peas (see page 24)
1/4 teaspoon ground red pepper (cayenne)
1/2 teaspoon salt
1/4 teaspoon ground black pepper

Binding

1 tablespoon all-purpose flour
2 tablespoons water

1 If you're making the samosas with homemade dough, make the Samosa Dough following the recipe on page 52. If you're using tortillas, go to the next step.

2 To make the Filling: Pour the oil into a medium nonstick skillet and place over medium heat. When the oil is heated, add the cumin seeds and let brown, about 10 seconds. Do not let the cumin seeds burn and turn black.

3 Immediately add the diced potato, peas, red pepper, salt and black pepper. Stir to combine. Sauté for 5 minutes, stirring frequently. You may taste the Filling to make sure the seasoning and spices are to your liking, and add more if desired. Remove from the heat.

4 To make the Binding: Place the flour and water in a small bowl. Using a small spoon, mix until thoroughly combined and smooth. (The Binding is the "glue" that holds the samosa together.) If you're making homemade dough, complete Steps 3 through 6 in the recipe for Samosa Dough.

5 When you're ready to assemble the samosas using tortillas, have the Filling and Binding handy on your work surface so you can work quickly to keep the tortillas from drying out. Heat just 1 tortilla in the microwave for 10 seconds to soften it. (This will keep it from breaking when you are folding it, and will help the Binding stick better).

6 Place the tortilla on a flat surface, and using a knife, slice the tortilla down the middle to create two semicircles, in order to create two samosas from each tortilla. (Do this quickly so that the tortilla does not cool down.)

Assembling the Samosas

1 To assemble the samosas, work with one semicircle at a time. Form a cone by folding 1 side of the semicircle to the middle. Dip the tip of your finger in the Binding and wipe it on the folded edge, and on the other side. Fold over the other side and overlap to form a triangle and tightly press to create a seal.

2 Hold the triangle in your hand and open it to form a cone. Pinch the bottom so the Filling will not come out. Place about 1 1/2 tablespoons of the Filling in the cone so it is filled about 1/2 inch (1.25 cm) from the top.

3 Dip the tip of your finger in the glue and line the inside edge of the cone. Tightly pinch the edges together to seal the samosa. (If you're making samosas with homemade dough, place the assembled samosas on a lightly oiled plate so they do not stick to the plate).

4 Repeat this process with the second half of the tortilla or dough circle to assemble another samosa.

5 Continue assembling the rest of the samosas the same way. At this point, you may fry the assembled samosas, or cover and refrigerate them up to 1 day, or cover and freeze up to 1 month.

VARIATION:

Lamb Samosas

Replace the filling for Potato Turnovers with 1/2 recipe Ground Lamb with Peas (page 110).

Samosa with Tamarind Chutney

Assembling the Samosas

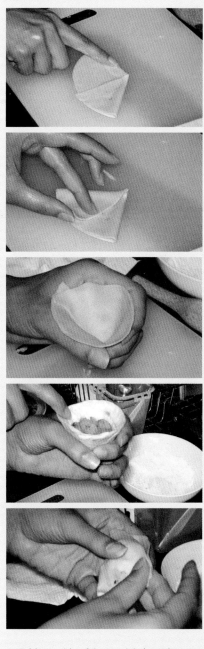

1. Fold one side of the semicircle to the middle and wipe the glue on the edge of the semicircle.
2. Fold over and press tightly to seal.
3. Open the triangle to form a cone. Pinch the bottom to seal it.
4. After filling the cone, wipe the glue on the inside edges of the cone.
5. Pinch the edges together to seal.

TIPS FOR PLANNING AHEAD: You may assemble the samosas and refrigerate, covered, up to 1 day before frying (bring to room temperature before frying). (Spread them out on a plate before refrigerating to avoid them sticking to each other.) You may also assemble the samosas and freeze up to 1 month before frying (defrost and bring to room temperature before frying). (You can freeze them together in a bag, but spread them out and defrost on a plate to avoid them sticking to each other as they thaw.)

Potato Turnovers (continued)

Deep-frying the Samosas

1 To deep-fry the samosas, pour 2 inches (5 cm) of oil into a medium wok or deep stockpot and place over high heat. Before frying the samosas, test the oil to make sure it is hot by pinching a piece of the tortilla (or a pinch of the dough) from a samosa and dropping it into the oil. If the tortilla (or dough) rises quickly to the top, the oil is hot and ready. If not, let the oil heat longer.

2 When the oil is hot, slide the samosas into the wok, about three at a time. Fry the samosas until they are golden, turning frequently, about 20 to 30 seconds. (Samosas made with homemade dough will take a few more seconds.)

3 Remove the samosas from the wok with a slotted spoon and place them on paper towels to allow the excess oil to drain. Fry the remaining samosas the same way. (After you have fried a few samosas, you may notice it is taking longer for them to cook, which means the oil has cooled down. Allow the oil to heat up again before adding more samosas so that they will cook quickly and properly.) Enjoy now while they are crispy and hot!

Samosa Dough

1¼ cups (150 g) all-purpose flour, plus extra flour for dusting
2 tablespoons vegetable oil
4 tablespoons water

1 Place the flour, oil and water in a medium bowl. Using one hand, thoroughly knead the flour mixture for about 5 minutes, using up all the loose flour, to form a firm and smooth dough. Shape the dough into a ball.

2 Wet the inside of a small clean bowl with water and place the dough into the bowl. Cover and let rest at room temperature for 30 minutes, or you may refrigerate up to 2 days. While the dough is resting, make the Filling and Binding.

3 Knead the rested dough for 1 minute. If the dough was refrigerated, let the dough come to room temperature to make it easier to work with, and then knead for 1 minute.

4 Separate the dough into 5 equal pieces. (If the dough is too sticky, dust with a bit of loose flour as needed, but the dough should be firm.) Roll each piece between your hands to form a smooth ball and then slightly flatten it between your palms.

5 Work with 1 flattened dough ball at a time. Dip both sides of the flattened dough ball in loose flour. Place on a flat rolling surface. Using a rolling pin, roll out the dough ball into a circle about 6 inches (15 cm) across. You may flip and turn the circle while rolling to help you get an even thickness and a round shape. The dough will be firm, so it might take a bit of pressure to roll out the circle, and you should not need to dust with too much loose flour. Repeat with the other dough balls.

6 Using a knife, slice each dough circle down the middle to create 2 semicircles, in order to create 2 samosas from each dough circle. You're now ready to assemble and fry the samosas.

Savory Vegetable Pancakes

Savory Vegetable Pancakes Uttapam

An *uttapam* can be described as an Indian pancake, although it is salty, not sweet! I like to add mixed vegetables, fresh chili peppers and coriander for added flavor and a touch of color, but you can also make a plain uttapam with just the batter and salt or with any combination of vegetables you prefer. You may serve this along with a bowl of Split Pea and Vegetable Stew (page 92) and a side of Coconut Chutney (page 40) or Ginger Chutney (page 38) for dipping. Uttapam makes an excellent Indian breakfast or brunch item.

Makes 4 pancakes
Prep time: 5 hours soaking + overnight sitting (12 hours)
Cook time: 5 minutes for each uttapam
Refrigerator life: Not recommended. (Tastes best freshly made and served hot.)

1 recipe Dosa and Uttapam Batter (page 45)
1 small fully ripe tomato, such as plum (Roma), diced
1/2 small onion, diced
1 small carrot, peeled and diced
1 fresh finger-length green chili pepper, diced
1 handful fresh coriander leaves (cilantro) (about 1/4 cup/10 g packed leaves), rinsed and chopped
1/4 teaspoon salt
3 tablespoons vegetable oil

1 Place all the ingredients, except the oil, in a bowl. Mix to combine.

2 Place a large cast-iron skillet (with a low rim to allow easy flipping) over medium heat. When the skillet is heated, pour 1/2 cup (125 ml) of the batter mixture in the center of the skillet. Using the back of a large spoon, quickly spread the batter, moving out from the center, into about a thick 6-inch (15-cm) circle. Small holes may immediately develop on the top of the pancake—a sign of well-fermented batter.

3 Drizzle 1/2 teaspoon of the oil around the outside edge of the pancake. Drizzle 1/2 teaspoon of the oil over the top of the pancake.

4 After about 2 minutes, gently flip the pancake using a spatula. The cooked side will be golden. Sprinkle 1/2 teaspoon of the oil around the outside edge of the pancake. Sprinkle 1/2 teaspoon of the oil on top of the pancake.

5 After about 3 minutes, flip the pancake again. Though cooked, the top side will be whitish in color, and have some golden marks, but it should not be burnt. The pancake will be a bit crisp.

6 After 5 seconds, remove the pancake (uttapam) from the heat, and serve with the whitish side up.

7 Repeat the process until you use up all the batter. Enjoy immediately.

Making Uttapam

1. Pour the batter and spread out with the back of a large spoon (see Tip on page 57).
2. Notice the small holes that come from properly fermented batter.
3. Cooked golden side after first flip.

Spiced Fruit Cocktail Fruit Chaat

In India, fruit is often enjoyed with a sprinkling of salt, ground black pepper, ground red pepper and lime juice. That combination of seasoning is used here to create a quick, easy and beautiful Indian fruit salad that gives a tangy twist to sweet fruits. When in season, guavas are the highlight of this fruit salad, and are an unexpected flavorful treat when people bite into them. I have included my favorite fruits in this recipe, but you may choose any combination of fruits you like. Do remember that bananas are a favorite Indian fruit! The acidity of the lime juice delays the fresh cut fruit from browning, so you can prepare this dish up to an hour in advance before serving. I prefer not to peel any of the fruit (except the banana!), so that we can keep the natural color to make a bright fruit salad.

> **ABOUT GUAVA:** Guava, or *amrood* in Hindi, is a sweet, tropical round fruit that has an amazing fragrance and robust flavor. It has a thin yellowish to light green skin, similar to a pear and ranges in size from a golf ball to a tennis ball. When you cut into them, the fruit varies in color from white to pale yellow to shades of pink. To eat a guava, rinse it first, and then either cut it in cubes, or just bite into it, keeping the skin on. Be careful when eating the seeds, since they can be hard. You could also cut around the middle seeded area. Guavas are in season in the summer months. Look for ones that are slightly tender to the touch, and not too hard. Guava can be stored in the refrigerator up to one week, but you might not want to keep it that long, since the strong aroma permeates the refrigerator, and into the freezer and ice cubes, and your house!

Serves 6 to 8
Prep time: 10 minutes
Refrigerator life: 1 hour (Tastes best freshly tossed & served.)
Reheating method: None! Simply toss and serve

1 guava, chopped into bite-size cubes (peel on)
1 red apple, chopped into bite-size cubes (peel on)
1 pear, chopped into bite-size cubes (peel on)
1 peach, chopped into bite-size cubes (peel on)
1 cup (150 g) green grapes
1 banana
1/4 teaspoon ground red pepper (cayenne)
1/2 teaspoon salt
1/4 teaspoon ground black pepper
Juice of 1 lime
Pomegranate seeds (from 1 small pomegranate), for garnish (optional)

1 Place the guava, apple, pear, peach and grapes in a large serving bowl.
2 Cut the banana into 1/4-inch (6-mm) slices and place in the bowl. Add the red pepper, salt, black pepper and lime juice. Mix well.
3 To extract seeds from a pomegranate, if using, cut off the crown (the small protruding knob) with a knife. Score the pomegranate from the crown end down to the other end, cutting only skin-deep, into four or five sections. Pry the wedges apart with your hands. Working over a bowl, face a wedge downwards and bend it back to allow the seeds to come loose, picking out the seeds with your fingers. Repeat with the other wedges. Sprinkle 2 tablespoons of the seeds over the Spiced Fruit Cocktail. Store leftover seeds in the refrigerator for up to 5 days. Note: Pomegranate juice is very staining so it is a good idea to wear an apron! Enjoy now or refrigerate for later!

Roasted Lentil Wafers Pappadum

Pappadum, also called *pappad*, has a fun name and is enjoyable to eat. They come in different varieties and shapes and sizes, from the round crispy lentil wafers that are heated on an open flame, to colorful square and mini circular ones made from tapioca or rice flour that are deep fried. Here we will make the round pappadums made from lentils. Vendors make raw pappadum wafers from a ground lentil and spice dough that is rolled out into thin circles, and then dried in the sun. People buy the wafers and dry roast them at home, which takes less than a minute. You may serve a pappadum with food, for a crisp bite during the meal. I have also seen pappadum offered at restaurants along with Tamarind Chutney (page 39) for dipping. Look for dried pappadums at the international section at your local grocery store or ethnic grocery store and choose either the plain lentil one, or one that is flavored and spiced. Here I provide two easy methods that offer a more controlled way of cooking them as compared to directly over an open flame: the microwave method, the easiest of all, and the cast-iron skillet method. If you have a gas burner, you can try cooking them directly over the open flame by using tongs to hold a pappadum over the flame and frequently turning it so it cooks evenly.

Serves 4
Cook time: 30 seconds using a cast-iron skillet or 1 minute per pappadum using a microwave

4 dried circular pappadams about 7 in (17.5 cm) across

Microwave Method

1 Place a paper napkin in the center of your microwave. Place a pappadum on the napkin.
2 Run the microwave for about 1 minute. You will see the pappadum start to curl up in places and turn lighter in color as compared to when it is raw. Remove the pappadum while it is still a bit flexible. Within 10 seconds, the pappadum will cool and become crisp.
3 Repeat with the 3 remaining pappadums. Enjoy now!

Cast-iron Skillet Method

1 Place a large cast-iron skillet over high heat. When the skillet is heated, roast a pappadum until it is almost crispy, turning every 5 seconds and pressing it down with a spatula, about 30 seconds. Make sure to evenly press down in the middle and on the sides so it does not curl up and have uncooked spots that did not touch the heat. As the pappadum cooks, it will turn lighter in color as compared to when it is raw and may get some brown spots.
2 Remove from the heat while it is still a bit flexible. Within 10 seconds, the pappadum will cool and become crisp.
3 Repeat with the 3 remaining pappadums. Enjoy now!

Making Plain Crepes

1. Pour batter in the center of the skillet.
2. Using the back of a large spoon, quickly spread the batter outward from the center.
3. Edges will start to curl up when done.
4. Using your finger tips, loosely roll up the dosa.

Crispy Rice and Lentil Crepes Sada Dosa

Dosa is a thin and crispy rice and lentil crepe that makes a delicious breakfast or lunch meal. You may either eat a plain *dosa* (*sada dosa*) or make a *masala* dosa, which is stuffed with potatoes and onions. I have provided both versions, so you can enjoy both types. You may serve dosa with a small bowl of Split Pea and Vegetable Stew (page 92) and with Ginger Chutney (page 38) or Coconut Chutney (page 40). The only thing to keep in mind when making dosas is that spreading out a perfectly thin and circular crepe comes with lots and lots of practice! When I see my mother-in-law making beautiful restaurant-style gigantic dosa so quickly and with such ease, while I still have some difficulty, I have to remind myself that she has been making them for more than thirty years! I keep it easy by making smaller-sized dosas so that not much batter goes to waste if I don't get it quite right!

Makes 4 dosas
Prep time: 5 hours soaking + overnight sitting (12 hours) for the batter
Cook time: 2 minutes for each dosa
Refrigerator life: Not recommended. (Tastes best freshly made and served hot.)

1 recipe Dosa and Uttapam Batter (page 45)
2 tablespoons vegetable oil

1 Place a large cast-iron skillet (with a low rim to allow easy spreading of the batter) over medium-high heat. When the skillet is heated, gently stir the batter and pour 1/2 cup (125 ml) of the batter in the center of the skillet. Using the back of a large spoon, quickly spread the batter outward from the center into about a thin 10-inch (25-cm) circle. Small holes may immediately develop on the top of the crepe—a sign of well-fermented batter.
2 Drizzle 1 teaspoon of the oil around the outside edge of the dosa. Drizzle 1/2 teaspoon of the oil over the top of the dosa.
3 Cook until the bottom of the circle is light golden brown and can easily be lifted with a spatula, about 2 minutes. The edges might start to lift up from the skillet, which is a sign the dosa is cooked. The top side of the dosa will remain white and soft, but the bottom will turn a light golden brown and be slightly crispy.
4 Lift one side of the dosa with the spatula, and then, using your fingertips, loosely roll up the dosa. Remove from the heat and serve folded side down so it does not unroll. You can also simply fold the dosa in half and serve it, rather than loosely rolling it up if that is easier for you. If it breaks while rolling or folding, that means it has become too crisp and is overdone.
5 Repeat the process until you use up all the batter. Enjoy immediately!

VARIATION:

Potato Stuffed Crepes
Masala Dosa

Prepare half the recipe for Sautéed Potatoes with Onions (page 133). After completing Step 3 for Crispy Rice and Lentil Crepes, add 4 heaping table-spoons of the Sautéed Potatoes with Onions down one side of the crepe. Roll up the dosa, following the instructions in Step 4. If you prefer to fold the dosa instead of rolling it, place the Sautéed Potatoes with Onions down the center of the dosa. Repeat the process until you use up all the batter and Sautéed Potatoes with Onions.

Potato Stuffed Crepes

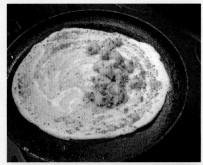

1. Line the potato filling down one side of the crepe.
2. Fold the dosa over the potato filling. Start rolling the dosa.
3. Using your finger tips, loosely roll up the dosa.

DOSA AND UTTAPAM TIP: As when making American breakfast pancakes, the first dosa or *uttapam* you make often doesn't come out great. Just think of the first one as the "test." But I tend to notice that after cooking the first dosa or uttapam, the skillet seems to "adjust" in terms of coming to the proper temperature and having just the right amount of oil on it from the previous dosa or uttapam. You can start off making the first dosa or uttapam smaller, so if it does come out poorly, you have not wasted much batter.

Pepper Shrimp on a Stick Jhinga Kebab

These shrimp is as enticing to the eye as they are to the palate, especially when they are artistically served when threaded on a skewer. In this recipe, I marinate the shrimp in a marinade with roasted and ground cumin seeds, and then quickly cook the shrimp in a hot skillet. I use jumbo shrimp in this recipe, since they can be easily skewered. Prawns, which are popular in India, may also be used for this recipe. The option to skewer the shrimp is up to you, but either way, they will taste delicious!

Serves 4
Prep time: 10 minutes + 15 minutes marinating (you may marinate up to 30 minutes in advance)
Cook time: 5 minutes
Refrigerator life: Not recommended. (Tastes best freshly made.)

12 jumbo shrimp with their tails
2 tablespoons vegetable oil
Juice of 1/2 lime
6 mini bamboo skewers (about 4 to 6 in/ 10 to 15 cm))

Marinade
2 tablespoons minced garlic
Juice of 1 lime
1 tablespoon vegetable oil
3/4 teaspoon roasted and ground cumin seeds (see page 24)
1/2 teaspoon ground coriander
1/2 teaspoon ground red pepper (cayenne)
1/4 teaspoon salt
3/4 teaspoon ground black pepper
2 tablespoons store-bought or Homemade Plain Yogurt (page 36)

1 Remove the shrimp heads, if still on, and peel and devein the shrimp, leaving their tails on. (See "Peeling and deveining shrimp", page 25.) Rinse the shrimp in cold water.
2 Place the ingredients for the Marinade in a medium bowl. Mix well.
3 Add the shrimp and mix well, making sure both sides of the shrimp are coated with the Marinade. Cover and refrigerate for 15 minutes, or up to 30 minutes.
4 Pour the oil into a large cast-iron skillet and place over high heat. When the oil is heated, add the shrimp. Cook until the shrimp are pink and opaque and they curl up, turning frequently, about 5 minutes.
5 Remove from the heat. Sprinkle the juice of the remaining lime evenly on the shrimp.
6 You may evenly thread the shrimp on the skewers before serving. Enjoy now!

Chicken and Bell Pepper Kebabs

Chicken kebabs are both delicious and fun to eat. Here I skewer them with onions and bell peppers to make beautiful kebabs. These kebabs can be cooked in the oven, as described below, but another fun way of cooking them is to use an outdoor grill and have an Indian style barbeque. You can serve these kebabs with a side of Mint Chutney (page 40).

Serves 4
Prep time: 10 minutes + 1 hour marinating, including 30 minutes to soak skewers (you may marinate up to 1 day in advance)
Cook time: 15 minutes
Refrigerator life: 3 days
Freezer life: 1 month
Reheating method: Place the refrigerated or defrosted kebabs in a warmed oven (about 350°F / 175°C) and heat. A less preferred method is to heat the kebabs in a microwave.

1 lb (500 g) boneless, skinless chicken breast
1 tablespoon vegetable oil
8 mini bamboo skewers (about 4 to 6 in/10 to 15 cm), soaked in water for 30 minutes
1 small onion, cut into 8 wedges and layers separated
2 green bell peppers, cut into same size pieces as the onion pieces
Juice of 1 lime

Marinade
1 tablespoon minced garlic
Juice of 1 lime
1/2 teaspoon ground coriander
1/4 teaspoon ground turmeric
1/4 teaspoon ground red pepper (cayenne)
3/4 teaspoon salt
1/2 teaspoon ground black pepper
3 tablespoons store-bought or Homemade Plain Yogurt (page 36)

1 Wash the chicken with cold water and cut into 1-inch (2.5-cm) cubes.
2 Combine all the ingredients for the Marinade in a medium bowl. Add the chicken and mix well. Cover and refrigerate for at least 1 hour, or up to 1 day.
3 Preheat the oven to 450°F (230°C). While the oven is heating up, remove the chicken from the refrigerator to allow it to come to room temperature or at least warm up a bit for faster and even cooking. Spread the oil evenly on a baking sheet.
4 Thread alternate pieces of chicken, onion, and bell pepper on the wooden skewers. Lay the skewers on the oiled baking sheet. Bake the skewers for 8 minutes. Turn the skewers and bake 7 minutes more, or until there are no signs of pink when you insert a knife through the chicken.
5 Remove the skewers from the oven. Sprinkle the lime juice evenly on the skewers. Enjoy now or let cool to room temperature and refrigerate or freeze for later!

Chicken Kebabs   Murgh Tikka

Here is a personal kebab creation I enjoy a lot because they taste great, are easy to make and versatile. These kebabs can be served as an appetizer on short bamboo skewers with a side of Mint Chutney (page 40) or be used to make the ever popular Chicken Tikka Masala (page 105). Traditionally, this dish is cooked in a *tandoor*, which is an open fire pit heated with wood or coal, but you will get similar results simply by using your oven!

Serves 4

Prep time: 15 minutes + a minimum of 1 hour of marinating, including 30 minutes to soak skewers (you may marinate up to 1 day in advance)

Cook time: 15 minutes

Refrigerator life: 3 days

Freezer life: 1 month

Reheating method: Place the refrigerated or defrosted kebabs in a warmed oven (about 350°F /175°C) and heat. A less preferred method is to heat the kebabs in a microwave.

1 lb (500 g) boneless, skinless chicken breast
8 to 12 mini bamboo skewers (about 4 to 6 in/ 10 to 15 cm), soaked in water for 30 minutes

Marinade
4 tablespoons vegetable oil
1 tablespoon minced garlic
Juice of 1 lime
1/4 teaspoon ground nutmeg
1/4 teaspoon ground coriander
3/4 teaspoon paprika
1/4 teaspoon ground red pepper (cayenne)
3/4 teaspoon salt
1/2 teaspoon ground black pepper
2 tablespoons store-bought or Homemade Plain Yogurt (page 36)

1 Wash the chicken with cold water and cut into 3/4-in (2-cm) cubes.

2 To make the Marinade: Mix together 3 tablespoons of the oil and the rest of the ingredients in a medium bowl. Add the chicken cubes and mix well. Cover and refrigerate for 1 hour, or up to 1 day.

3 Preheat the oven to 450°F (230°C). While the oven is heating up, remove the chicken from the refrigerator to allow it to come to room temperature.

4 Spread the remaining 1 tablespoon of oil evenly on a baking sheet. Thread the chicken cubes evenly on the skewers. Lay the skewers on the oiled baking sheet and bake for 8 minutes. Turn and bake for 7 minutes more, or until there are no signs of pink when you insert a knife through the chicken. Enjoy now or let cool to room temperature and refrigerate or freeze for later! You can also now remove the cooked chicken from the skewers and use it make Chicken Tikka Masala (page 105).

Vegetable Fritters   Pakora

Vegetable fritters are made with potatoes, onions, eggplant, cauliflower, fresh fenu-greek, fresh spinach and even big green chili peppers. My personal favorite fritter combination is potatoes, onions and fresh spinach, which is what I make in this recipe. I batter the vegetables in gram flour that is spiced up a bit and then deep-fry them. You may serve these fritters as a snack or appetizer with Mint Chutney (page 40), Tamarind Chutney (page 39), ketchup or eat them as they are! These fritters also go great with a cup of Indian Cappuccino (page 149) or Indian Tea (page 148), although my husband prefers to enjoy them along with an ice-cold beer!

Serves 4
Prep time: 15 minutes + 15 minutes resting
Cook time: about 15 minutes to fry all the fritters, depending on the size of your wok
Refrigerator life: Not recommended. (Tastes best freshly fried and served hot.)

2 cups (200 g) gram flour
3/4 teaspoon ground red pepper (cayenne)
13/4 teaspoons salt
1 teaspoon ground black pepper
1 fresh finger-length green chili pepper, finely chopped
3/4 cup (185 ml) plus 1 tablespoon water
1 small russet potato (about 1/4 lb/125 g)
1 small onion
2 cups (100 g) packed fresh spinach leaves
Vegetable oil, for deep-frying

1 To make the batter: Place the flour, 1/2 teaspoon of the red pepper, 1 1/2 teaspoons of the salt, 1/2 teaspoon of the black pepper, green chili pepper and the water in a medium bowl. Using a spoon, mix to combine, and then beat it vigorously for 2 minutes to smoothen it. Set aside to rest for 15 minutes.

2 Wash and peel the potato. Slice lengthwise into thin ovals, about 1/8-inch (3-mm) thick.

3 Slice the onion into thin rounds, about 1/4-inch (6-mm) thick. Try not to separate the layers.

4 Thoroughly wash the spinach leaves. Finely chop the leaves. Place in a colander and set aside to drain.

5 Spread out the potato and onion rounds on a plate. Evenly sprinkle the remaining 1/4 teaspoon of the red pepper and the salt and 1/2 teaspoon of the black pepper on the slices.

6 Pour 2 inches (5 cm) of oil into a medium wok or deep stockpot and place over medium-high heat. Test the oil to make sure it is hot by dropping a pinch of the batter into the oil. If the batter rises quickly to the top, the oil is hot and ready. If not, let the oil heat longer.

7 When the oil is hot, using your fingers, take a potato slice, dip it in the batter, and gently slide it into the wok. Fry until the fritter has turned golden brown, turning frequently with a slotted spoon, about 2 minutes. To make the fritter crispier, while it is frying, press down on it with a slotted spoon to keep it at the bottom of the wok. Remove the fritter from the oil with a slotted spoon and place it on paper towels to drain any excess oil. Repeat this for the rest of the potato slices in batches, depending on the size of your wok.

8 Repeat the same process with the onion rounds. (After you have fried a few fritters, you may notice it is taking longer for them to cook, which means the oil has cooled down. Allow the oil to heat up again so the fritters will cook quickly and properly.)

9 Squeeze the spinach with your hands to remove any excess water. Add the spinach to the batter. Mix to combine. Place a heaping spoonful of the battered spinach in the wok. Fry until the fritter is crisp and the batter has turned golden brown, turning frequently, about 2 minutes. You may also fry these in batches. Remove the fritters from the oil with a slotted spoon and place on paper towels to drain any excess oil. Place all the fritters on a platter and enjoy!

Chapter 2

Breads and Rice

Bread and rice are the staples of Indian meals. In northern India, where wheat is grown and used to make a variety of tasty Indian breads, a meal would be incomplete without bread. Likewise, in southern India, where rice paddy fields abound, rice is considered an integral part of the meal. In daily home cooking, either rice or breads are served, but at formal dinners and also at Indian restaurant buffets, typically both bread and rice are served with the meal.

Breads are eaten by tearing away pieces of the bread with your hand, and using it to grab the main dish, or scoop up a curry. Many Indian breads are made with *chapati* flour, a whole wheat flour with a bit of all-purpose flour added to lighten the color. Indian breads are both unleavened and leavened. Leavened breads have yeast or yogurt added to the dough which causes fermentation and/or a foaming action, resulting in a soft puffy bread such as *bhatura*, Fried Leavened Breads (page 76), and naan, Oven Baked White Breads (page 66). Although naan might be the bread that first comes to mind when thinking about Indian breads, the most common everyday bread made in Indian homes is chapati, Whole Wheat Flatbreads (page 64), a whole wheat flatbread cooked on a cast-iron skillet. *Paratha* are breads that are cooked on a skillet with a bit of ghee or oil. Naan and *tandoori roti*, Oven Baked Whole Wheat Breads (page 68), are traditionally baked in an Indian clay oven called a *tandoor*, though here I provide a method to bake these breads in a conventional oven so that you can enjoy them at home. Some Indian breads, such as *poori*, Puffed Fried Breads (page 74) and bhatura, Fried Leavened Breads (page 76), are deep-fried and puffed up. All Indian breads are best when served hot and fresh, but if you need to make them in advance, you may refrigerate or freeze them and then reheat them.

Plain white rice is the base of a typical southern Indian meal, as a chapati is the base of a northern Indian meal. Plain rice goes well with the spicy foods of southern India as it balances out the spicy flavor and does not overwhelm the flavor of the main dish. Because the beautiful long-grained and fragrant Basmati rice that is grown in the cooler foothills of the Himalayas in northern India is expensive, it is not typically used in daily cooking, nor ground to make rice flour for *dosa*, Crispy Rice and Lentil Crepes (page 56), but instead a lesser expensive variety of medium- to long-grain white rice is used. However, for certain rice dishes, such as Vegetable Pilaf (page 83) and Chicken Biryani (page 80), Basmati rice is essential for the flavor and texture. For simplicity and added taste, in all my rice recipes, I use Basmati rice, but you may of course use plain white rice if you prefer.

Whole Wheat Flatbreads Chapati

Chapati, also known as *roti*, is whole wheat flatbread. Like most Indians from the northern region of India, I grew up eating hot chapatis with dinner as the basic bread of the meal. A chapati is eaten by tearing away a small piece, and then using that piece to scoop up or grab the vegetable, lentil or meat dish. Making chapatis can get a bit messy. Instead, you can simplify your life and just buy Mexican wheat tortillas and heat them directly on the gas stove burner or on a skillet over medium-high heat to get similar results, which is what I sometimes do! I first attempted to make chapatis when I was eleven years old. For the longest time I struggled with the dough and would roll out the strangest shapes that my mother would refer to as maps of the different continents! Finally, one day I mastered making round chapatis that fluffed up beautifully while cooking, and both my mother and I were pleasantly amazed.

Makes 8 chapati flatbreads

Prep time: 15 minutes + 30 minutes resting (dough can be made up to 2 days in advance)

Cook time: 80 seconds per chapati

Refrigerator life: 2 days, but tastes best freshly made and served hot

Freezer life: 1 month (place a sheet of parchment paper between each chapati before freezing to prevent them from sticking to each other, and then place the stack in an airtight container, plastic bag or tightly wrapped in foil)

Reheating method: Place the refrigerated or defrosted bread in a microwave and heat. Or, place the bread on a skillet over medium-high heat, flipping frequently.

1¹/4 cups (150 g) chapati flour (substitute 1 cup/120 g whole wheat flour plus ¹/4 cup/30 g all-purpose flour), plus extra flour for dusting

¹/2 cup (125 ml) water

2 teaspoons vegetable oil (optional)

> **TIP:** When measuring flour for breads or desserts, use a dry measuring cup and level it off with a knife.

Making and Forming the Dough

1 Place the flour and water in a medium bowl. Using one hand, thoroughly knead the dough for about 5 minutes, using up all the loose flour to form a soft and smooth dough. Shape the dough into a ball.

2 Wet the inside of a clean bowl with water and place the dough ball in the bowl. Cover and let rest at room temperature for 30 minutes, or you may refrigerate up to 2 days.

3 Knead the rested dough for 1 minute. If the dough was refrigerated, let the dough come to room temperature to make it easier to knead. (If the dough is too sticky, dust with a bit of loose flour as needed.)

4 Place a large cast-iron skillet (with a low rim to allow easy flipping) over high heat.

5 While the skillet is heating up, separate the dough into 8 equal pieces. Roll each piece between your hands to form a smooth ball and then slightly flatten it between your palms.

6 Working with 1 flattened dough ball at a time, dip both sides of the flattened dough ball in loose flour. Place on a flat rolling surface. Using a rolling pin, roll out the dough ball into a circle about 5 inches (12.5 cm) across. You may flip and turn the circle while gently rolling to help you get an even thickness and a round shape. Dust with loose flour as needed, but try to use as little extra flour as possible.

Cooking the Chapati

1 When the skillet is hot, carefully slide the rolled-out circle onto your palm and place it on the skillet. Cook for about 30 seconds, and then using a spatula, flip the bread. There should be some brown spots on the flipped side.

2 Cook for about 20 seconds and flip again. There should be brown spots on the flipped side.

3 Cook for 15 seconds, pressing down on the bread with the spatula to encourage the bread to puff up, and flip again.

4 Cook for 15 seconds, pressing down on the bread with the spatula to ensure the bread is well cooked. Remove the puffed bread from the skillet. If desired, lightly spread ¹/4 teaspoon of the oil on it.

5 Continue to roll out and cook the remaining dough balls. Enjoy now or stack them and wrap tightly in foil to keep them warm until ready to serve. You may also refrigerate or freeze for later!

1. Carefully slide the rolled-out circle. onto your palm and place it on the skillet.
2. Press the bread with a spatula to encourage the bread to puff up.
3. Puffed up chapati.
4. Cooked chapati with oil smeared on it.

Slapping the Dough with Grandmother Kesar Devi Bhatia

When rolling out dough to make Indian breads, it is best to use as little loose flour for dusting as possible because the flour will burn and become grainy as the dough cooks. Traditionally, the dough is slapped between the palms before putting it on the skillet or in the *tandoor* to shake off any excess loose flour, but this comes with a lot of practice and creates a bit of a mess! An easier way to decrease the amount of flour on the breads is to wipe any loose flour off your work sur-

face before rolling out the next bread. Also, wipe the skillet with a dry cloth or paper towel after each bread is removed to prevent any loose flour on the skillet from sticking to the next bread as it cooks. Here I am, in a dashing knitted red playsuit, getting a bread "slapping" lesson from my maternal grandmother as we make *tandoori roti* during a visit to India in 1981. My grandmother's clay tandoor, used to bake breads, is shown to my right in the photograph.

Oven Baked White Breads Naan

Naan is the ever popular leavened bread that is served in Indian restaurants. This bread is not typically made in homes, since a *tandoor*, which is an open fire pit heated with wood or coal, is needed, and is not too common in homes, but restaurants have it. You may try to make this bread at home in a conventional oven, and results will be similar but not exactly the same (but still delicious!), since a home oven does not reach the high temperatures of a tandoor. The shape of naan resembles a teardrop shape due to how a chef works with the dough. Typically, a chef slaps the dough between their palms to thin it out, and then pulls it a bit to create a large teardrop shape. I simply roll out an oval, and I keep the overall size smaller so it is easier to handle. With practice, you may soon be serving homemade naan with all of your Indian meals!

Makes 4 small naans
Prep time: 15 minutes + 5 hours resting
Cook time: 3 minutes
Refrigerator life: 2 days, but tastes best freshly made and served hot
Freezer life: 1 month (place a sheet of parchment paper between each naan before freezing to prevent them from sticking to each other, and then place the stack in an airtight container, plastic bag or tightly wrapped in foil)
Reheating method: Place the refrigerated or defrosted bread in a microwave and heat. Or, place the bread on a skillet over medium-high heat, flipping frequently.

1¼ cups (150 g) all-purpose flour, plus extra flour for dusting
¼ teaspoon dry active yeast
¼ heaping teaspoon salt
2 teaspoons store-bought or Homemade Plain Yogurt (page 36)
1 tablespoon plus 2 teaspoons vegetable oil
¼ cup (65 ml) plus 1½ teaspoons warm water (to help the yeast react)

1 Mix the flour, yeast and salt in a medium bowl. Add the yogurt, 1 tablespoon of the oil and the warm water. Using one hand, thoroughly knead the mixture for about 5 minutes, using up all the loose flour to form a soft and smooth dough. Shape the dough into a ball.

2 Wet the inside of a clean bowl with water and place the dough ball in the bowl. Cover and place in an un-warmed oven to avoid any cool drafts. Let sit undisturbed for 5 hours to rise (it will almost double in size).

3 Place a baking sheet in the oven on the highest rack possible (but still allowing about 4 inches/10 cm room for the bread to puff up). Preheat the oven to 500°F (260°C).

4 Separate the dough into 4 equal pieces. (If the dough is too sticky, dust with a bit of loose flour as needed.) Roll each piece between your hands to form a smooth ball and then slightly flatten it between your palms.

5 Working with 1 flattened dough ball at a time, dip both sides of the flattened dough ball in the loose flour. Place on a flat rolling surface. Using a rolling pin, roll out the dough ball into an oval shape, about 7 inches (17.5 cm) long and 5 inches (12.5 cm) wide. You may flip and turn the oval while rolling to help you get an even thickness. The dough will be stretchy, so you might have to use force while rolling. Dust with loose flour as needed, but try to use as little extra flour as possible. Continue to roll out the rest of the dough balls.

6 Remove the heated baking sheet from the oven and place the rolled-out ovals on it. Return the baking sheet to the oven on the high rack. Change the oven setting to broil on high heat. Broil until you see brown spots on the top of the bread, about 3 minutes. The bread might also puff up a bit.

7 Remove from the oven. Spread ½ teaspoon of the remaining oil evenly on each bread and stack them and wrap tightly in foil to keep them warm. It is okay if you flatten them and they crunch a bit, but they will soften after sitting wrapped up.

8 Enjoy now or keep them wrapped until ready to serve. You may also refrigerate or freeze for later!

KNEADING KNOW-HOW *When kneading the breads, it is best to add all the water to the loose flour at one time. If you add the water a little bit at a time, it will be difficult to knead because only parts of the loose flour will absorb the water, instead of the water being evenly distributed at one time. Also, the more you knead the dough, the better it will become. If you think too much water has been added, keep patiently kneading the dough for a few minutes, using up every bit of loose flour in the bowl, and you will see it come together. If you still think too much water was added and the dough is too loose, sprinkle in some loose flour and knead to the correct consistency of the dough. If you think too little water was added, add some water by simply wetting your hands and continuing to knead the dough.*

Oven Baked Whole Wheat Breads

Tandoori Roti

Tandoori roti is a flatbread that is made in a *tandoor*, which is an open fire pit heated with wood or coal. This bread is similar to *chapati*, Whole Wheat Flatbreads (page 64), but it is thicker to withstand the high heat of the oven and has a different flavor and texture since it is oven baked rather than cooked on a stovetop skillet. To make this bread, this dough is stretched out with one's hands and then slapped between the palms to thin it out a bit, resulting in an almost, but not quite perfect circular shape. The dough is then placed on the inside wall of the tandoor, to be cooked by the heat. When it is done, the bread is removed using long tongs. Here is my version of rolling it out and making it in a home oven. Tandoori roti goes well with lentils, legumes, meat, fish and seafood dishes, but you can serve it along with any dish you would serve Chapati or Naan (pages 66 and 68) with.

Makes 4 tandoori roti flatbreads
Prep time: 15 minutes + 30 minutes resting (dough can be made up to 2 days in advance)
Cook time: 4 minutes
Refrigerator life: 2 days, but tastes best freshly made and served hot
Freezer life: 1 month (place a sheet of parchment paper between each tandoori roti before freezing to prevent them from sticking to each other, and then place the stack in an airtight container, plastic bag or tightly wrapped in foil)
Reheating method: Place the refrigerated or defrosted bread in a microwave and heat. Or, place the bread on a skillet over medium-high heat, flipping frequently.

2 cups (240 g) chapati flour (substitute 1 1/2 cups/180 g whole wheat flour plus 1/2 cup/60 g all-purpose flour), plus extra flour for dusting
3/4 cup (185 ml) plus 1 tablespoon water
2 teaspoons vegetable oil (optional)

1 Place the flour and water in a medium bowl. Using one hand, thoroughly knead the flour and water for about 5 minutes, using up all the loose flour to form a soft and smooth dough. Shape the dough into a ball.

2 Wet the inside of a clean bowl with water and place the dough ball in the bowl. Cover and let rest at room temperature for 30 minutes, or you may refrigerate up to 2 days.

3 Knead the rested dough for 1 minute. If the dough was refrigerated, let the dough come to room temperature to make it easier knead. Dust with a bit of loose flour as needed.

4 Place a baking sheet in the oven on the highest rack possible (but still allowing about 4 inches/ 10 cm of room for the bread to puff up). Preheat the oven to 500°F (260°C).

5 Separate the dough into 4 equal pieces. Roll each piece between your hands to form a smooth ball and then slightly flatten it between your palms.

6 Working with 1 flattened dough ball at a time, dip both sides of the flattened dough ball in loose flour. Place on a flat rolling surface. Using a rolling pin, gently roll out the dough into a circular shape about 6 inches (15 cm) across. You may flip and turn the circle while rolling to get an even thickness. Dust with loose flour as needed. Continue to roll out the rest of the dough balls.

7 Carefully remove the heated baking sheet from the oven and place the rolled-out circles on it. Return the baking sheet to the oven on the high rack. Change the oven setting to broil on high heat. Broil until you see brown spots on the top of the bread, about 4 minutes. The bread might also puff up a bit.

8 Remove from the oven. If desired, spread 1/2 teaspoon of oil evenly on each bread. Enjoy now or stack them and wrap tightly in foil to keep them warm until ready to serve. You may also refrigerate or freeze for later!

Gram Flour and Onion Breads   Besan ki Roti

This gram flour (*besan*) bread is square-shaped and is rolled out the same way as Flaky Wheat Breads (page 70). My mom likes to add a touch of oil while cooking this bread so the outside is just a bit crisp and it makes the bread tastier. *Besan ki roti* can be eaten at breakfast, along with homemade Homemade Plain Yogurt (page 36). It can also be eaten plain as an afternoon snack, along with a cup of Indian Tea (page 148). This bread can be kept out at room temperature for one day, which is why my mother tends to pack a dozen of these when going on any trip, so she can snack on and share them when the munchies strike!

Makes 8 besan ki rotis
Prep time: 15 minutes
Cook time: 70 seconds per besan ki roti
Refrigerator life: 2 days refrigerated or 1 day at room temperature
Freezer life: 1 month (place a sheet of parchment paper between each besan ki roti before freezing to prevent them from sticking to each other, and then place the stack in an airtight container, plastic bag or tightly wrapped in foil)
Reheating method: Serve at room temperature, or place the refrigerated or defrosted bread in a microwave and heat. Or, place the bread on a skillet over medium-high heat, flipping frequently.

1¹/2 cups (150 g) gram flour
¹/2 cup (60 g) chapati flour (substitute
  ¹/4 cup/30 g whole wheat flour plus
  ¹/4 cup/30 g all-purpose flour), plus extra
  flour for dusting
¹/2 teaspoon ground red pepper (cayenne)
3/4 teaspoon salt
¹/2 teaspoon ground black pepper
¹/2 small onion, diced
2 tablespoons vegetable oil, plus 4 teaspoons for oiling the bread
1 fresh finger-length green chili pepper,
  finely chopped
¹/4 cup (65 ml) plus 3 tablespoons water

Making the Dough

1 Mix together the flours, red pepper, salt and black pepper in a medium bowl. Add the rest of the ingredients (except the 4 teaspoons extra oil) and, using one hand, thoroughly knead the mixture, using up all the loose flour, until it becomes soft and sticky, about 5 minutes. You might notice the dough is very sticky, so you may dust with loose flour as needed. (*Note*: Do not allow this dough to sit in order to avoid the diced onion from releasing its water.)

2 Place a large cast-iron skillet (with a low rim to allow easy flipping) over medium-high heat.

Forming the Dough

1 While the skillet is heating up, wash your hands so they are clean and it is easier to continue working with the dough. Separate the dough into 8 equal pieces.
2 Roll each piece between your hands to form a smooth ball and then slightly flatten it between your palms. Wash your hands as needed to keep them clean, making it easier to work with the dough.
3 Working with one flattened dough ball at a time, dip both sides of the dough in loose flour. Place on a flat rolling surface. Using a rolling pin, gently roll out the dough into a circle about 4 inches (10 cm) across. You may flip and turn the circle while rolling to get an even thickness and a round shape. Dust with loose flour as needed, but try to use as little extra flour as possible.
4 Fold the top part of the circle halfway down (see the illustrated steps on page 71 for guidance).
5 Fold the bottom part of the circle over the top fold.
6 Fold the left part to the center.
7 Fold the right side over the left fold to form a square.
8 Slightly flatten and smooth out the square by gently pressing down on it with your fingers so it will not break when rolling it out. Dip both sides of the square in loose flour. Place on a flat rolling surface. Use a rolling pin to gently roll out the dough square into about a 4-inch (10-cm) square. You may flip and turn the square while rolling to help get an even thickness. Dust with loose flour as needed, but try to keep it at a minimum.

Cooking the Besan Ki Roti

1 When the skillet is hot, carefully slide the rolled-out square onto your palm and place it on the skillet. Cook for about 30 seconds, and then using a spatula, flip the bread. There should be some brown spots on the bread.
2 Cook for about 30 seconds and flip again. There should be brown spots on the flipped side.
3 Spread ¹/2 teaspoon of oil evenly on the bread and flip it.
4 Cook for 5 seconds, pressing down on the bread with a spatula, and flip again.
5 Cook for 5 seconds, pressing down on the bread with a spatula. Remove the bread from the skillet.
6 Continue to roll out and cook the remaining dough balls. Enjoy now or stack them and wrap tightly in foil to keep them warm until ready to serve. You may also leave them at room temperature for up to one-day, or refrigerate or freeze for later!

Flaky Wheat Breads Sada Paratha

This flaky and buttery wheat flatbread is typically eaten at breakfast or lunch. Sada paratha is usually either square or triangle shaped, but if this is your first time making this bread, any shape will do! *Paratha* refers to breads that are cooked with a bit of oil and are usually made on a skillet. The Hindi word *sada* means "plain," so a sada paratha is a plain paratha, as compared to Aloo ka Paratha (page 72)—a paratha that is stuffed with potatoes. Although I describe these breads as buttery, I make them with vegetable oil instead of the traditional *ghee* (clarified butter) since it is healthier and readily available. Because the bread is hearty, it is usually paired with a simple potato or egg dish, such as Simple Potato Curry (page 127) or Scrambled Breakfast Eggs (page 137), or just Homemade Plain Yogurt (page 36) and Mango Pickle (page 41). Another option is to spread Sweet and Spicy Mango Chutney (page 38) on it, roll it up, and eat it as breakfast on the go on the way out in the morning!

Makes 8 sada parathas

Prep time: 15 minutes + 30 minutes resting (dough can be made up to 2 days in advance)

Cook time: 70 seconds per sada paratha

Refrigerator life: 2 days, but tastes best freshly made and served hot

Freezer life: 1 month (place a sheet of parchment paper between each sada paratha before freezing to prevent them from sticking to each other, and then place the stack in an airtight container, plastic bag or tightly wrapped in foil)

Reheating method: Place the refrigerated or defrosted bread in a microwave and heat. Or, place the bread on a skillet over medium-high heat, flipping frequently.

1¼ cups (150 g) chapati flour (substitute 1 cup/120 g whole wheat flour plus ¼ cup/30 g all-purpose flour), plus extra flour for dusting

½ cup (125 ml) water

8 teaspoons vegetable oil

Making the Dough

1 Place the flour and water in a medium bowl. Using one hand, thoroughly knead the mixture for about 5 minutes, using up all the loose flour to form a soft and smooth dough. Shape the dough into a ball.

2 Wet the inside of a clean bowl with water and place the dough ball in the bowl. Cover and let rest at room temperature for 30 minutes, or you may refrigerate up to 2 days.

3 Knead the rested dough for 1 minute. If the dough was refrigerated, let the dough come to room temperature to make it easier to knead. (If the dough is too sticky, dust with a bit of loose flour as needed.)

4 Place a large cast-iron skillet (with a low rim to allow easy flipping) over high heat.

Forming the Dough

1 While the skillet is heating up, separate the dough into 8 equal pieces.

2 Roll each piece between your hands to form a smooth ball and then slightly flatten it between your palms.

3 Working with one flattened dough ball at a time, dip both sides of the dough in loose flour. Place on a flat rolling surface. Using a rolling pin, gently roll out the dough ball into a circle about 4 inches (10 cm) across. You may flip and turn the circle while rolling to get an even thickness and a round shape). Dust with loose flour as needed, but try to use as little extra flour as possible.

4 Spread 1/2 teaspoon of the oil evenly on the rolled-out circle.

5 Fold the top part of the circle halfway down.

6 Fold the bottom part of the circle over the top fold.

7 Fold the left part to the center.

8 Fold the right side over the left fold to form a square.

9 Slightly flatten the square by gently pressing down on it with your fingers. Dip both sides of the square in loose flour. Place on a flat rolling surface. Using a rolling pin, gently roll out the dough square into about a 4-inch (10-cm) square. You may flip and turn the square while rolling to get an even thickness. Dust with loose flour as needed, but try to keep it at a minimum.

Cooking the Sada Paratha

1 When the skillet is hot, carefully slide the rolled-out square onto your palm and place it on the skillet. Cook for about 30 seconds, and then using a spatula, flip the bread. There should be some brown spots on the flipped side.

2 Cook for about 30 seconds and flip again. There should be brown spots on the flipped side.

3 Spread 1/2 teaspoon of the oil evenly on the bread and flip it.

4 Cook for 5 seconds, pressing down on the bread with a spatula, and flip again. The bread might slightly puff up, which is okay.

5 Cook for 5 seconds, pressing down on the bread with a spatula. Remove the bread from the skillet.

6 Continue to roll out and cook the remaining dough. Enjoy now or stack them and wrap tightly in foil to keep them warm until ready to serve. You may also refrigerate or freeze for later!

Forming the Sada Paratha

1. Spread the oil evenly on the rolled-out circle.
2. Fold the top part halfway down.
3. Fold the bottom part over the top fold.
4. Fold the left half to the center.
5. Fold the right side over the left fold to form a square.
6. Roll out a square and pick it in the palm of your hand to put it in the skillet.

Potato Stuffed Wheat Breads Aloo ka Paratha

Growing up, it was always a treat when my mom made these potato stuffed flat-breads for a weekend breakfast. She served them with a pat of butter on top, and Homemade Plain Yogurt (page 36) and a small piece of Mango Pickle (page 41) on the side. In this recipe, you start by rolling out two dough circles, then place spiced mashed potatoes between them, and then and cook it on a cast-iron skillet. Even today, when we visit my parents for a weekend brunch, I request my mom to make these yummy flatbreads!

Makes 4 potato stuffed parathas
Prep time: 15 minutes + 30 minutes resting (dough can be made up to 2 days in advance) + 35 minutes to boil the potatoes (can be done 1 day in advance)
Cook time: 3 minutes per aloo ka paratha
Refrigerator life: 2 days, but tastes best freshly made and served hot
Freezer life: 1 month (place a sheet of parchment paper between each aloo ka paratha before freezing to prevent them from sticking to each other, and then place the stack in an airtight container, plastic bag or tightly wrapped in foil)
Reheating method: Place the refrigerated or defrosted bread in a microwave and heat. Or, place the bread on a skillet over medium-high heat, flipping frequently.

2 tablespoons vegetable oil
4 thin pats of butter (optional)

Dough
1 1/4 cups (150 g) chapati flour (substitute 1 cup/120 g whole wheat flour plus 1/4 cup/30 g all-purpose flour), plus extra flour for dusting
1/2 cup (125 ml) water

Filling
1 medium russet potato (about 1/2 lb/ 250 g), boiled and peeled (see page 24)
1/2 small onion, diced
1 fresh finger-length green chili pepper, finely chopped
1/2 teaspoon ground red pepper (cayenne)
3/4 teaspoon salt
1/2 teaspoon ground black pepper

1 handful fresh coriander leaves (cilantro) (about 1/4 cup/10 g packed leaves), rinsed and chopped
Juice of 1/2 lime

Making the Dough
1 Place the flour and water in a medium bowl. Using one hand, thoroughly knead the mixture for about 5 minutes, using up all the loose flour to form a soft and smooth Dough. Shape the Dough into a ball.
2 Wet the inside of a clean bowl with water and place the Dough ball in the bowl. Cover and let rest at room temperature for 30 minutes, or you may refrigerate up to 2 days. Just before you're ready to cook the bread, prepare the Filling. (If the Filling is made too far in advance, the onion flavor will become too pronounced.)

Making the Filling
1 In a medium bowl, mash the peeled potato with one hand or a potato masher until there are no lumps. Add the rest of the ingredients for the Filling. Using one hand, mix everything together. Taste a small bit of the potato mixture to make sure the seasoning and spices are to your liking, and add more if desired.
2 Divide the Filling into 4 equal portions. Form each portion into a ball.

Assembling and Cooking the Paratha
1 Knead the rested Dough for 1 minute. If the Dough was refrigerated, let the Dough come to room temperature to make it easier to knead. (If the Dough is too sticky, dust with a bit of loose flour as needed).

2 Place a large cast iron skillet (with a low rim to allow easy flipping) over high heat. Separate the Dough into 8 equal pieces. Roll each piece between your hands to form a smooth ball and then slightly flatten it between your palms. Work with 2 flattened Dough balls at a time to make one paratha. Dip both sides of each flattened Dough ball in the loose flour. Place them on a flat rolling surface. Using a rolling pin, gently roll out both Dough balls into circles about 4 inches (10 cm) across. You may flip and turn the circles while rolling to get an even thickness and a round shape. Dust with loose flour as needed, but try to use as little extra flour as possible.

3 Spread 1/4 teaspoon of the oil evenly on each rolled-out circle. Place 1 portion of the Filling in the center of 1 rolled-out circle. Using your fingers, evenly flatten the Filling to spread it out on the Dough circle, almost to the edges. Place the other Dough circle on top of the one with the Filling, oiled side down. Pinch together the edges of the 2 circles to seal them and keep the Filling from coming out.

4 Using a rolling pin, gently roll out the Dough circle to form a 6½-inch (16.5-cm) circle. You may flip and turn the circle while rolling to get an even thickness and a round shape. Dust with extra flour as needed. (You could also use your fingers and palms to gently pat the dough to flatten it to form a 6½-inch (16.5-cm circle). You may flip and turn the circle while patting it out.)

5 When the skillet is hot, carefully slide the rolled-out circle onto your palm and place it on the skillet. Cook for about 1 minute, and then using a spatula, flip the bread. There should be some brown spots on the flipped side.

6 Cook for about 1 minute and flip again. Now there should be brown spots on both sides. Spread 1 teaspoon of the oil evenly on the bread.

7 Flip it and cook for 30 seconds.

8 Flip once more and cook for an additional 30 seconds. Remove the bread from the skillet.

9 Continue to roll out and cook the remaining Dough balls. Enjoy now or stack them and wrap tightly in foil to keep them warm until ready to serve. If desired, serve with a pat of butter on top of the hot paratha. You may also refrigerate or freeze for later!

How to Stuff the Paratha

1. Spread 1/4 teaspoon oil evenly on each circle.
2. Place 1 portion of the Filling on 1 circle.
3. Flatten the Filling to evenly spread it out.
4. Ready to put the oiled top on.
5. Pinch together the edges to seal.
6. Gently patting the stuffed bread to flatten it.

Puffed Fried Breads Poori

Poori is a fried bread that is similar to *bhatura*, Fried Leavened Breads (page 76), but it does not have yeast in it, and it is smaller and thinner. Pooris are typically served along with Simple Potato Curry (page 127) for breakfast or a light lunch. Served together, this meal is called *aloo poori*, with the word *aloo* meaning "potato." If you prefer a sautéed potato dish instead of a curried potato dish, you may serve poori along with Sautéed Potatoes with Onions (page 133). Whichever potato dish you choose, serve a side of Homemade Plain Yogurt (page 36) to complete the meal. A cup of Indian Tea (page 148) or Indian Cappuccino (page 149) after this simple meal will keep your hunger satisfied for a while!

Makes 8 pooris

Prep time: 10 minutes + 30 minutes resting (dough can be made up to 2 days in advance)
Cook time: 14 seconds per poori
Refrigerator life: 2 days, but tastes best freshly fried and served hot
Freezer life: 1 month (place a sheet of parchment paper between each poori before freezing to prevent them from sticking to each other, and then place the stack in an airtight container, plastic bag or tightly wrapped in foil)
Reheating method: Place the refrigerated or defrosted bread in a microwave and heat. Or, place the bread on a skillet over medium-high heat, flipping frequently.

1 cup (120 g) chapati flour (substitute $3/4$ cup/90 g whole wheat flour plus $1/4$ cup/30 g all-purpose flour), plus extra flour for dusting
2 teaspoons vegetable oil plus extra for deep frying
$1/4$ cup (65 ml) plus 2 tablespoons water

Making and Forming the Dough

1 Place the flour, 2 teaspoons of the oil and water in a medium bowl. Using one hand, thoroughly knead the mixture for about 5 minutes, using up all the loose flour to form a smooth and firm dough. Shape the dough into a ball.
2 Wet the inside of a clean bowl with water and place the dough ball in the bowl. Cover and let rest at room temperature for 30 minutes, or you may refrigerate up to 2 days.
3 Knead the rested dough for 1 minute. If the dough was refrigerated, let the dough come to room temperature to make it easier to knead. (If the dough is too sticky, dust with a bit of the loose flour as needed).
4 Separate the dough into 8 equal pieces, leaving a pinch of dough aside to test the oil.
5 Roll each piece between your hands to form a smooth ball and then slightly flatten it between your palms. If you still feel the dough is too sticky, you may lightly oil your hands, which also helps make a smooth ball.

6 Dip both sides of each flattened dough ball in loose flour. Place the flattened dough balls on a large flat rolling surface. (Because the dough fries very quickly, roll out all the dough balls before frying.) Using a rolling pin, gently roll out each dough ball into a thin circle about $4^{1}/_{2}$ inches (11.5 cm) across. You may flip and turn the circle while rolling to get an even thickness and a round shape. Dust with loose flour as needed, but try to use as little extra flour as possible.

Deep-frying the Poori

1 Pour 2 inches (5 cm) of oil into a medium wok or deep stockpot and place over high heat. Test the oil to make sure it is hot by dropping the pinch of dough in the oil. If it rises quickly to the top, the oil is hot and ready. If not, let the oil heat longer.
2 Slide the dough circles into the wok, one at a time, to deep-fry them. Using a slotted spoon, flip the poori after it puffs up or has started to puff up, no longer than 8 seconds. Fry until the flipped side is golden brown and puffed up (but not fried to a hard crisp), no longer than 6 seconds and, using a slotted spoon, remove the poori from the wok and place on paper towels to allow the excess oil to drain. (While frying, you may press down on the circle with the slotted spoon to encourage the poori to puff up.)
3 Deep-fry the remaining rolled-out dough circles the same way. (After you've fried a few pooris, you may notice it is taking longer for them to cook, which means the oil has cooled down. Allow the oil to heat up again so the breads will cook quickly and properly.)
4 Enjoy now while they are still hot and puffed, or stack the pooris and wrap tightly in foil to keep them warm until ready to serve. You may also refrigerate or freeze for later!

Making Pooris

1. Roll out the dough into a thin circle.
2. Poori will puff up while frying.

Fried Leavened Breads Bhatura

Bhatura is a fried bread that is similar to *poori*, Puffed Fried Breads (page 74), but thicker and leavened since it has yeast in it. This bread goes well with Chickpea Curry (page 94), along with a side of Home-made Plain Yogurt (page 36). Growing up, I used to wake up late on the weekends, and would go down to the kitchen right in time for the bhatura and chickpea curry brunch my mom would have ready. This bread is usually made with all-purpose flour, but I also add a bit of whole wheat flour to make the dough easier to work with and not so stretchy. Typically in India, when this bread is made, it is stretched out by hand into a teardrop-shaped form, and the bread is rather large. To make things easier, I first roll out a circle, and then I stretch it into a small teardrop-shaped form that is easier to manage and deep-fry.

Makes 4 bhathuras
Prep time: 10 minutes + 5 hours resting
Cook time: 20 seconds per bhatura
Refrigerator life: 2 days (Tastes best freshly fried and served hot.)
Freezer life: 1 month (place a sheet of parchment paper between each bhatura before freezing to prevent them from sticking to each other, and then place the stack in an airtight container, plastic bag or tightly wrapped in foil)
Reheating method: Place the refrigerated or defrosted bread in a microwave and heat. Or, place the bread on a skillet over medium-high heat, flipping frequently.

1 cup (120 g) all-purpose flour, plus extra flour for dusting
1/4 cup (30 g) chapati flour or whole wheat flour
1/4 teaspoon dry active yeast
1 tablespoon vegetable oil, plus extra for deep-frying
1/4 cup (65 ml) plus 2 1/2 tablespoons warm water (to help the yeast react)

Making and Forming the Dough

1 In a medium bowl, mix together the flours and yeast. Add the oil and the warm water. Using one hand, thoroughly knead the mixture for about 5 minutes, using up all the loose flour to form a soft and smooth dough. Shape the dough into a ball.

2 Wet the inside of a clean bowl with water and place the dough ball in the bowl. Cover and place in an un-warmed oven to avoid any cool drafts. Let sit undisturbed for at least 5 hours at room temperature so it will ferment and expand to almost double its size, or up to 8 hours.

3 Separate the dough into 4 equal pieces, leaving a pinch of dough aside to test the oil. (If the dough is too sticky, dust with a bit of loose all-purpose flour as needed). Roll each piece between your hands to form a smooth ball and then slightly flatten it between your palms. If you still feel the dough is too sticky, you may lightly oil your hands, which also helps to make a smooth ball.

4 Dip both sides of the flattened dough ball in the loose flour. Place the flattened dough balls on a large flat rolling surface. (Because the dough fries very quickly, roll out all the dough balls before frying.) Using a rolling pin, roll out each dough ball into a thin circle about 5 inches (12.5 cm) across. You may flip and turn the circle while rolling to get an even thickness and a round shape. The dough will be stretchy, so you might have to use force while rolling. Dust with loose flour as needed, but try to use as little extra flour as possible. Using your fingers, slightly pull the dough to form a teardrop shape.

Deep-frying the Bhatura

1 Pour 2 inches (5 cm) of oil into a medium wok or deep stockpot and place over high heat. Test the oil to make sure it is hot by dropping the pinch of dough in the oil. If it rises quickly to the top, the oil is hot and ready. If not, let the oil heat longer.

2 Slide the dough teardrop into the wok, one at a time, to deep-fry them. Using a slotted spoon, flip the bhatura after it puffs up or has started to puff up, no longer than 12 seconds. Fry until the flipped side is golden brown and puffed up, (but not fried to a hard crisp), no longer than 8 seconds and, using a slotted spoon, remove the bhatura from the wok and place on paper towels to allow the excess oil to drain. (While frying, you may press down on the teardrop with the slotted spoon to encourage the bhatura to puff up.)

3 Fry the remaining rolled-out dough teardrops the same way. (After you've fried a few bhaturas, you may notice it is taking longer for them to cook, which means the oil has cooled down. Allow the oil to heat up again so the breads will cook quickly and properly.)

4 Enjoy now while they are still hot and puffed, or stack the bhaturas and wrap tightly in foil to keep them warm until ready to serve. You may also refrigerate or freeze for later! They will soften and deflate as they cool.

Making Bhaturas

1. After rolling out a circle, pull the dough to form a teardrop shape.
2. Press down with a slotted spoon to encourage the bread to puff up.
3. Bread will puff up while being fried.
4. Place on paper towels to drain the excess oil.

Rice with Cumin and Peas   Jeera Matar Chawval

The delicate hint of cumin and beautiful color of green peas in this rice dish make it my favorite everyday rice. It is best to use Basmati rice when making this dish for added taste, beauty, texture and fragrance instead of plain long-grained white rice. This rice dish can be paired with any of the dishes in this book (my favorite pairings are with curries—vegetable or meat), but it is also flavorful enough to be eaten on its own. Or, for a light meal, enjoy this rice with Homemade Plain Yogurt (page 36) on the side or Three Vegetable Raita (page 37) drizzled on top.

Serves 4 as a side dish
Prep time: 5 minutes
Cook time: 15 minutes + 5 minutes to rest
Refrigerator life: 3 days   **Freezer life:** 1 month
Reheating method: Place the refrigerated or defrosted rice in a microwave, sprinkle a few drops of water on it and stir periodically. Or, place the rice in a saucepan, sprinkle a few drops of water on it and warm over medium-low heat, stirring periodically.

1 cup (180 g) uncooked white Basmati rice
3 tablespoons vegetable oil
1 teaspoon cumin seeds
2 cups (500 ml) water
1/2 teaspoon salt
1/2 cup (60 g) frozen or fresh parboiled
  green peas (see page 24)

1 Place the rice in a small bowl. Rinse three or four times by repeatedly filling the bowl with cold water and carefully draining off the water. It is okay if the water is not completely clear, but try to get it as clear as you can. Pour the rice into a sieve to drain.
2 Pour the oil into a medium saucepan and place over medium heat. When the oil is heated, add the cumin seeds and let brown, about 10 seconds. Do not let the cumin seeds burn and turn black. Immediately add the rice and stir thoroughly until all the rice is coated with the oil.
3 Add the water, salt and peas. Stir to combine. Bring to a rolling boil over high heat.
4 Stir and reduce the heat to low. Cover the saucepan. Simmer undisturbed until the water is completely absorbed and you do not see any more water on the bottom of the saucepan if you insert a spoon through the rice, about 7 minutes. You might see dimples formed on the surface of the rice, which is a sign that the water is completely absorbed.
5 Turn off the heat. Let rest, covered, for 5 minutes on the warm stove. Keep covered until ready to serve or let cool to room temperature and refrigerate or freeze for later. Before serving, gently fluff the rice with a fork to mix the cumin seeds and peas.

Plain Boiled Rice   Chawval

Plain rice is simply rice boiled in water. This is the daily rice that is common in the southern part of India. Dishes from that region tend to be rather spicy, and the rice balances out the spices. I use Basmati rice, a fragrant long-grained white rice, to make plain boiled rice, but in India daily rice is usually made with a less expensive variety of white rice. Basmati rice is typically reserved for more elegant rice dishes such as Chicken Biryani (page 63) and Vegetable Pilaf (page 83). If you prefer to buy plain, long-grained white rice for this dish, that will work as well, but you will miss the fragrance you will get from Basmati rice! In this recipe, I soak the rice for 30 minutes to allow every grain of Basmati rice to extend to its fullest length and to reduce cooking time. The short cooking time also prevents the rice grains from overcooking. When choosing a rice to serve as the base of an Indian meal, you can pick this rice or Rice with Cumin and Peas (page 78).

Serves 4 as a side dish
Prep time: 5 minutes + 30 minutes soaking
Cook time: 15 minutes + 5 minutes to rest
Refrigerator life: 3 days   **Freezer life:** 1 month
Reheating method: Place the refrigerated or defrosted rice in a microwave, sprinkle a few drops of water on it and stir periodically. Or, place the rice in a saucepan, sprinkle a few drops of water on it and warm over medium-low heat, stirring periodically.

1 cup (180 g) uncooked white Basmati rice
   (or plain long-grained white rice)
1 1/2 cups (375 ml) water

1 Place the rice in a small bowl and cover with cold water. Let the rice soak for 30 minutes at room temperature.
2 Carefully pour the soaking water out of the bowl. Rinse the rice three or four times by repeatedly filling the bowl with cold water and carefully draining off the water. It is okay if the water is not completely clear, but try to get it as clear as you can. Pour the rice into a sieve to drain.
3 Place the drained rice and water in a medium saucepan. Bring to a rolling boil over high heat. It is okay if the water gets frothy.
4 Stir and reduce the heat to low. Cover the saucepan. Simmer undisturbed until the water is completely absorbed and you do not see any more water on the bottom of the saucepan if you insert a spoon through the rice, about 8

minutes. You might see dimples formed on the surface of the rice, which is a sign that the water is completely absorbed.
5 Turn off the heat. Let rest, covered, for 5 minutes on the warm stove. Keep covered until ready to serve or let cool to room temperature and refrigerate or freeze for later. Before serving, gently fluff the rice with a fork.

VARIATION:
Quick Plain Boiled Rice

If you do not have a spare half-hour to soak the rice, you can make this quick version. Each rice grain might not extend to its fullest potential, which is okay. Because we are not soaking the rice, which allows the rice grains to absorb some water, we need to add twice the amount of water to rice, which is the general rule of thumb when cooking unsoaked rice. To make the rice, place the rice in a small bowl. Rinse the rice, following Step 2 for Plain Boiled Rice (page 79). Follow Step 3 but increase the amount of water to 2 cups (500 ml). Complete the rest of the steps. In Step 4, you may need to increase the time by a few minutes to allow the water to be fully absorbed.

TROUBLESHOOTING TIPS: Making perfect rice can be tricky at first, as common problems are that the rice turns out mushy or it burns and sticks at the bottom of the pan. A good way to avoid burnt rice is to use a heavy bottomed saucepan.

If your rice tends to be mushy: after reducing the heat to low in Step 4, make sure the rice is simmering. If it's just sitting in hot water, it will take a long time to cook, and it will become mushy and sticky. Increase the heat if needed so the rice is simmering. If your rice is still mushy, you may have overcooked it. As soon as you do not see any more water on the bottom of the saucepan if you insert a spoon through the rice, turn off the heat.

If you are new to making rice, for best results for all rice dishes in this chapter, I would first try making the amount in the recipe instead of doubling it. Once you get comfortable with making rice, then you can double the recipe. It is best to gently fluff the rice with a fork after it has cooled a bit so the rice grains do not break apart.

Chicken Biryani

Chicken biryani is a popular Indian dish made with chicken and fragrant Basmati rice that is cooked with an exotic blend of herbs and spices. The chicken is first cooked, and when the rice is partially done, the chicken is added to infuse the rice with the flavors as it finishes cooking. The results are worth the multistep process! This dish is traditionally cooked with bone-in chicken pieces to allow the flavor to be enhanced by the bones, but I actually enjoy biryani with boneless pieces of chicken. I've included the quick steps to make my mother-in-law's simple recipe for *biryani masala*—the blend of ground roasted spices used to flavor this dish. This hearty and flavorful rice dish is served as a main dish with Three Vegetable Raita (page 37) drizzled on top or served in a small bowl on the side.

Serves 4
Prep time: 15 minutes
Cook time: 35 minutes + 5 minutes to rest
Refrigerator life: 3 days
Freezer life: 1 month
Reheating method: Place the refrigerated or defrosted rice in a microwave, sprinkle a few drops of water on it and stir periodically. Or, place the rice in a saucepan, sprinkle a few drops of water on it and warm over medium-low heat, stirring periodically.

Biryani Chicken

2 teaspoons Biryani Masala (recipe follows)
2 tablespoons unsalted butter
1¹/2 teaspoons minced garlic
1¹/2 teaspoons peeled and finely grated fresh ginger
1 small onion, thinly sliced into half moons
2 bay leaves
1 fresh finger-length green chili pepper, cut in half lengthwise
1 lb (500 g) boneless, skinless chicken breast, rinsed and cut into 1-in (2.5-cm) pieces
¹/4 teaspoon ground turmeric
1 teaspoon ground red pepper (cayenne)
1 teaspoon salt
2 tablespoons store-bought or Homemade Plain Yogurt (page 36)
Juice of ¹/2 lime
1 handful fresh coriander leaves (cilantro) (about ¹/2 cup/10 g packed leaves), rinsed and chopped

Biryani Masala (makes 4 teaspoons)

1 teaspoon cloves
10 whole green cardamoms
1 teaspoon fennel seeds
1 teaspoon coriander seeds
One ¹/4-in (6-mm) piece cinnamon stick

Aromatic Rice

1 cup (180 g) uncooked white Basmati rice
3 tablespoons vegetable oil
¹/2 small onion, thinly sliced into half moons
1 handful fresh mint leaves (about ¹/4 cup/ 5 g packed leaves), rinsed and chopped
2 cups (500 ml) water
¹/2 teaspoon salt

1 To make the Biryani Masala: Place a small skillet over medium heat. When the skillet is heated, roast all the spices until they are fragrant, stirring frequently, about 1 minute. Immediately remove the spices from the skillet and place in a small bowl. Let cool a bit before grinding.

2 Grind the roasted spices to a fine powder in a coffee/spice grinder. The yield is enough for two Chicken Biryani dishes. Set 2 teaspoons of the ground spices aside for use now and place the remaining ground spices in an airtight container, where it can be stored at room temperature up to 3 months.

3 To make the Biryani Chicken: Melt the butter in a medium saucepan over medium heat. Add the garlic, ginger, onion, bay leaves and green chili pepper. Sauté until the onion is translucent, stirring frequently, about 3 minutes. Add the chicken, turmeric, red pepper, salt, 2 teaspoons of the Biryani Masala, yogurt, lime juice and coriander leaves. Stir to combine. Cover the saucepan and cook for 10 minutes, stirring occasionally. Remove the cover and cook until the chicken is opaque and the water is cooked off, stirring occasionally, about 5 minutes. Remove from the heat.

4 To make the Aromatic Rice: Place the rice in a small bowl. Rinse three or four times by repeatedly filling the bowl with cold water and carefully draining off the water. It is okay if the water is not completely clear, but try to get it as clear as you can. Pour the rice into a sieve to drain.

5 Pour the oil into a large saucepan and place over medium heat. When the oil is heated, add the onion and mint leaves. Sauté until the onion is translucent, stirring frequently, about 3 minutes. Add the rice and stir thoroughly until all the rice is coated with the oil. Add the water and salt. Stir to combine. Bring to a rolling boil over high heat.

6 Stir and reduce the heat to medium-low. Partially cover the saucepan. Simmer undisturbed until the rice is half-cooked and there is a thin layer of water on top of the rice, about 3 minutes.

7 Add the Biryani Chicken to the rice. Gently stir to combine. Partially cover the saucepan. Simmer undisturbed until the water is completely absorbed, about 5 minutes. Turn off the heat. Let rest, fully covered, for 5 minutes on the warm stove. Keep covered until ready to serve or let cool to room temperature and refrigerate or freeze for later. Before serving, gently fluff the rice with a fork to mix the chicken.

Tamarind Rice Pulihora

This tamarind-flavored rice dish is commonly cooked in homes of the southern states of India such as Andhra Pradesh, Karnatika and Tamil Nadu. Because of the preservative properties of tamarind, this rice dish stays good for two days at room temperature, and is commonly taken on trips since it does not need to be refrigerated. It can be eaten by itself as a snack, or you may serve as a side dish along with Crispy Rice and Lentil Crepes (page 56), Potato Stuffed Crepes (page 56) or Savory Vegetable Pancakes (page 53). If you make this rice in the morning, set aside at room temperature, so by dinner time the flavors have developed, and the rice tastes perfect! Pulihora is an easy dish to serve when entertaining friends, since it can be made ahead of time, and is served at room temperature.

Serves 4 as a side dish
Prep time: 5 minutes + 55 minutes to prepare the rice (or just 25 minutes if you're making Quick Plain Boiled Rice) (you may use rice that has been cooked 1 day in advance)
Cook time: 5 minutes
Refrigerator life: 3 days
Reheating method: Serve at room temperature or just slightly warmed. Allow the refrigerated rice to come to room temperature and fluff with a fork before serving. For faster serving, place the refrigerated rice in a microwave, sprinkle a few drops of water on it and slightly heat, stirring periodically. Or, place the rice in a saucepan, sprinkle a few drops of water on it and slightly warm over medium-low heat, stirring periodically.

1 recipe Plain Boiled Rice (page 79), at room temperature
2 teaspoons plus 3 tablespoons oil
2 teaspoons tamarind concentrate (paste)
1/2 teaspoon ground turmeric
3/4 teaspoon salt
10 whole cashews, split in half lengthwise
4 dried finger-length red chili peppers
2 teaspoons dried, skinned and split brown chickpeas (channa daal)
2 teaspoons dried, skinned and split black lentils (dhuli urad daal)
1/2 teaspoon cumin seeds
1 teaspoon mustard seeds
2 fresh finger-length green chili peppers, cut in half lengthwise
2 sprigs fresh curry leaves, rinsed and destemmed (about 30 leaves) (optional)

1 Place the cooked rice, 2 teaspoons of the oil, tamarind concentrate, turmeric and salt in a serving bowl. Mix to combine, breaking apart any rice lumps.

2 To temper the spices, pour the remaining 3 tablespoons of oil into a small skillet and place over medium heat. When the oil is heated, add the cashews. Cook until the cashews are very lightly browned, stirring frequently, about 30 seconds.

3 Add the dried red chili peppers, chickpeas, lentils, cumin seeds and mustard seeds. Sauté until fragrant and the chickpeas and lentils lightly brown, stirring frequently, about 1 minute. Do not let the cashews burn. Turn off the heat.

4 Immediately add the fresh green chili peppers and curry leaves, if using. Stir until the skin on the green chili peppers starts to bubble, about 20 seconds.

5 Add the tempered spices to the bowl with the cooked rice mixture. Stir to combine. Enjoy now or refrigerate for later, but serve at room temperature.

Vegetable Pilaf Subzee ka Pulao

A pilaf is a rice dish in which the rice is first lightly browned by cooking in oil or butter and with onions to impart a brownish color. Traditionally in India, this dish uses clarified butter (*ghee*), but I use vegetable oil instead since it is healthier and easily available. You could describe this dish as the Indian version of vegetarian fried rice. Since this rice dish is made with aromatic Basmati rice that is infused with fragrant spices and lots of vegetables, it can be eaten as a complete meal along with a side of Homemade Plain Yogurt (page 36) and a small piece of Mango Pickle (page 41).

Serves 4 as a side dish
Prep time: 10 minutes
Cook time: 25 minutes + 5 minutes to rest
Refrigerator life: 3 days
Freezer life: 1 month
Reheating method: Place the refrigerated or defrosted rice in a microwave, sprinkle a few drops of water on it and stir periodically. Or, place the rice in a saucepan, sprinkle a few drops of water on it and warm over medium-low heat, stirring periodically.

1 cup (180 g) uncooked white Basmati rice
4 tablespoons vegetable oil
1 small onion, thinly sliced into half moons
3 cloves
5 black peppercorns
One 1-in (2.5-cm) piece cinnamon stick
1 teaspoon cumin seeds
1 bay leaf
3 whole green cardamom pods
1/2 cup (60 g) frozen or fresh parboiled green peas (see page 24)
1 cup (100 g) fresh or frozen bite-size cauliflower florets (no need to defrost the frozen ones) (see page 25)
1 medium russet potato (about 1/2lb/250 g), peeled and cubed into 1/2-in (1.25-cm) or smaller cubes
1 carrot, peeled and cut into thin matchsticks
2 cups (500 ml) water
1 1/2 teaspoons salt

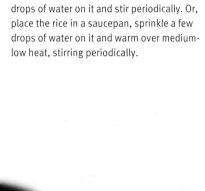

1 Place the rice in a small bowl. Rinse three or four times by repeatedly filling the bowl with cold water and carefully draining off the water. It is okay if the water is not completely clear, but try to get it as clear as you can. Pour the rice into a sieve to drain.

2 Pour the oil into a large saucepan and place over medium heat. When the oil is heated, add the onion, cloves, peppercorns, cinnamon stick, cumin seeds and bay leaf. Open the cardamom pods and add both the seeds and the pods. Sauté until the onion is browned and the edges start to crisp, stirring frequently, about 10 minutes.

3 Add the peas, cauliflower florets, potato and carrot. Cover the saucepan. Cook for 2 minutes, stirring occasionally.

4 Add the rice. Stir thoroughly until all the rice is coated with the oil. Add the water and salt. Stir to combine. Bring to a rolling boil over high heat. Reduce the heat to low and stir.

5 Cover the saucepan and simmer undisturbed until the water is completely absorbed and you do not see any more water on the bottom of the saucepan if you insert a spoon through the rice, about 8 minutes. Turn off the heat. Let rest, covered, for 5 minutes on the warm stove.

6 Keep covered until ready to serve or let cool to room temperature and refrigerate or freeze for later. Before serving, gently fluff the rice with a fork to mix the vegetables. You may leave the whole spices in for presentation.

Lemon Rice Nimmakaya Annam

This lime-flavored rice dish is commonly cooked in homes in the southern Indian state of Andhra Pradesh. Even though this dish is called "lemon rice" it is actually flavored with limes, but in India the terms *lemon* and *lime* are sometimes interchanged, or limes are called lemons! This rice dish is also known as "yellow rice"; it has a bright yellow color from the ground turmeric that is added to the dish. Lemon rice can be served as a side dish along with Crispy Rice and Lentil Crepes (page 56), Potato Stuffed Crepes (page 56) or Savory Vegetable Pancakes (page 53). Although not a typical traditional Indian combination, I actually think this rice dish makes a beautiful and tasty side dish when served along with a fish dish such as Simple Spiced Fish (page 121) or Dad's Baked Salmon (page 116), since typically fish and lemon-lime flavors go well together. This rice can also be eaten on its own as a snack. Since this dish is served at room temperature, it is an easy dish to serve when planning a dinner party because you do not have to worry about warming it up.

Serves 4 as a side dish

Prep time: 5 minutes + 55 minutes to prepare the rice (or just 25 minutes if making Quick Plain Boiled Rice) (you may use rice that has been cooked 1 day in advance)

Cook time: 5 minutes

Refrigerator life: 3 days

Reheating method: Serve at room temperature or just slightly warmed. Allow the refrigerated rice to come to room temperature and fluff with a fork before serving. For faster serving, place the refrigerated rice in a microwave, sprinkle a few drops of water on it and slightly heat, stirring periodically. Or, place the rice in a saucepan, sprinkle a few drops of water on it and slightly warm over medium-low heat, stirring periodically.

1 recipe Plain Boiled Rice (page 79), at room temperature

Juice of 2 limes

1/2 teaspoon ground turmeric

1/2 teaspoon salt

3 tablespoons vegetable oil

10 whole cashews, split in half lengthwise

3 dried finger-length red chili peppers

1 tablespoon dried, skinned and split brown chickpeas (channa daal)

1 tablespoon dried, skinned and split black lentils (dhuli urad daal)

1/2 teaspoon cumin seeds

1/2 teaspoon mustard seeds

2 fresh finger-length green chili peppers, cut in half lengthwise and then cut in half crosswise

1 handful fresh coriander leaves (cilantro) (about 1/4 cup/10 g packed leaves), rinsed and chopped

1 sprig fresh curry leaves, rinsed and destemmed (about 15 leaves) (optional)

1 Place the cooked rice, lime juice, turmeric and salt in a serving bowl. Mix to combine, breaking apart any rice lumps.

2 To temper the spices, pour the oil into a small skillet and place over medium heat. When the oil is heated, add the cashews. Sauté until the cashews are very lightly browned, stirring frequently, about 30 seconds.

3 Tear the red chili peppers in half and add to the skillet. Add the chickpeas, lentils, cumin seeds and mustard seeds. Sauté until fragrant and the chickpeas and lentils lightly brown, stirring frequently, about 1 minute. Do not let the cashews burn. Turn off the heat.

4 Immediately add the fresh green chili peppers, coriander leaves and curry leaves, if using. Stir until the skin on the green chili peppers starts to bubble, about 20 seconds.

5 Add the tempered spices to the bowl with the cooked rice mixture. Stir to combine. Enjoy now or refrigerate for later, but serve at room temperature.

Yogurt Rice Dadhojanam

Yogurt rice is exactly what it sounds! It is rice and Homemade Plain Yogurt (page 36) mixed together with mild spices and vegetables into a porridge-like consistency. This rice and yogurt dish is commonly served at the end of a spicy meal in the homes of the southern Indian states of Andhra Pradesh, Karnatika and Tamil Nadu, since the cuisine from these states tend to be rather spicy. Yogurt calms and soothes the stomach from the acidic spices, and it aids in digestion. This dish is typically served at room temperature, but you may also serve it chilled if you prefer.

Serves 4 as a side dish
Prep time: 5 minutes + 55 minutes to prepare the rice (or just 25 minutes if you're making Quick Plain Boiled Rice) (you may use rice that has been cooked 1 day in advance)
Cook time: 5 minutes
Refrigerator life: 3 days

Reheating method: None! Stir the refrigerated rice and serve either chilled or at room temperature. If you see that this dish has dried up a bit after refrigerating it, you can add more plain yogurt to it until the desired consistency is achieved.

1 recipe Plain Boiled Rice (page 79), at room temperature or chilled
3 cups (750 g) store-bought or Homemade Plain Yogurt (page 36)
1 teaspoon salt
3 tablespoons vegetable oil
1 dried finger-length red chili pepper
1 teaspoon dried, skinned and split brown chickpeas (channa daal)
1 teaspoon dried, skinned and split black lentils (dhuli urad daal)
1/2 teaspoon cumin seeds
1/2 teaspoon mustard seeds
2 fresh finger-length green chili peppers, cut in half lengthwise and then cut in half crosswise
1 handful fresh coriander leaves (cilantro) (about 1/4 cup/10 g packed leaves), rinsed and chopped
1 sprig fresh curry leaves, rinsed and destemmed (about 15 leaves) (optional)

1 Place the cooked rice, yogurt and salt in a serving bowl. Mix to combine, breaking apart any rice lumps.
2 To temper the spices, pour the oil into a small skillet and place over medium heat. When the oil is heated, tear the red chili pepper in half and add to the skillet. Add the chickpeas, lentils, cumin seeds and mustard seeds. Sauté until fragrant and the chickpeas and lentils lightly brown, stirring frequently, about 1 minute. Turn off the heat.
3 Immediately add the fresh green chili peppers, chopped coriander leaves and curry leaves, if using. Stir until the skin on the green chili peppers starts to bubble, about 20 seconds. Add the tempered spices to the bowl with the cooked rice mixture. Stir to combine. Enjoy now or refrigerate for later!

VARIATION:
Mother-in-law Yogurt Rice

My mother-in-law likes to add onions and carrots to this dish to add some crunch, more flavor and a bit of color. To make Mother-in-Law Yogurt Rice, dice half a small onion and peel and dice 1 carrot. Add the onion and carrot in Step 3 in the recipe for Yogurt Rice.

Rice and Lentil Porridge Kichidi

Kichidi is a rice and lentil dish best known as a comforting cure-all for those feeling under the weather. To this day, if I complain of a tummy ache, my mom will suggest a light and nutritious meal of kichidi and a side of Homemade Plain Yogurt (page 36). In India, this dish is also a common choice for older people and babies, both of whom need light meals that don't require chewing, go down easily and are gentle on the stomach. Depending on the amount of water added, kichidi can be cooked in different consistencies, from thin to porridge-like as I do here, to a thicker, dryer form. For a bit of kick to a kichidi and yogurt meal, you may add a small chunk of Mango Pickle (page 41) on the side. But remember, you don't have to be sick, a baby or an elderly person to enjoy kichidi and yogurt—you can have this light meal anytime! Kichidi is usually made with a less expensive variety of plain white rice, as my grandmother would have used, because this dish is a simple porridge—not worthy of the beautiful long grains of Basmati rice or its special flavor, but you may use it if you wish!

Serves 4
Prep time: 5 minutes
Cook time: 25 minutes + 5 minutes to rest
Refrigerator life: 2 days
Freezer life: 1 month
Reheating method: Place the refrigerated or defrosted kichidi in a microwave, sprinkle a few drops of water on it and stir periodically. Or, place the kichidi in a saucepan, sprinkle a few drops of water on it and warm over medium-low heat, stirring periodically.

1/2 cup (100 g) dried, skinned and split green lentils (dhuli moong daal)
1/2 cup (90 g) uncooked white Basmati rice (or plain white rice)
3 tablespoons vegetable oil
1 teaspoon cumin seeds
4 cups (1 liter) water
1 teaspoon salt

1 Place the lentils on a plate. Sift through them and remove any grit. Place the lentils and rice in a small bowl. Rinse three or four times by repeatedly filling the bowl with cold water and carefully draining off the water. It's okay if the water is not completely clear. Pour the lentils and rice into a sieve to drain.

2 Pour the oil into a medium saucepan and place over medium heat. When the oil is heated, add the cumin seeds and let brown, about 10 seconds. Do not let the cumin seeds burn and turn black. Immediately add the lentils and rice. Stir thoroughly until all the lentils and rice are coated with the oil. Add the water and salt. Stir to combine. Bring to a rolling boil over high heat. It is okay if the water gets frothy.

3 Stir and reduce the heat to medium. Cook for 5 minutes, stirring occasionally. Stir and reduce the heat to low. Cover the saucepan. Simmer until the lentils are soft, stirring occasionally, about 15 minutes. The dish should have a mushy porridge-like consistency.

4 Turn off the heat. Stir and cover. Let rest for 5 minutes on the warm stove. Keep covered until ready to serve or let cool to room temperature and refrigerate or freeze for later!

Chapter 3
Lentils, Legumes and Soups

This is a great chapter for vegetarians, since lentils, called *daal* in Hindi, are a delicious and excellent source of protein. These easy-to-cook pulses (dried seeds from the legume family) are served year-round at most Indian meals. The soupy consistency of the lentil dishes makes them a perfect accompaniment to dry, sautéed vegetables, such as Sautéed Okra with Onions (page 135) or Stuffed Bell Peppers (page 130). Lentils come in a variety of shapes and colors, and when split and shelled, they reveal different colors and flavors. In this chapter, I use two different types of lentils, *moong daal* (green lentils) and *masoor daal* (red lentils), and I will show you how to cook them whole and when they are split and shelled. I will also show you how to sprout whole green lentils to toss with turnips, tomatoes, cucumbers, onions and red bell peppers to create a colorful and nutritious lentil salad!

In addition to lentils, other legumes such as chickpeas, kidney beans and black-eyed peas make hearty curries that are also a good source of protein. Sambar (page 92) is a delicious stew made from yet another legume, the split pigeon pea, called *toor daal* in Hindi. Sambar tastes excellent by itself, but it is usually served along with a *dosa*, which are Crispy Rice and Lentil Crepes (page 56) or with *uttapam*, Savory Vegetable Pancakes (page 53).

A separate soup course is not part of a traditional Indian meal—thus the relatively small number of soups in this chapter. There are some "Indian-inspired" soups, such as the popular Creamy Mulligatawny Soup (page 91) which is made from split and shelled green lentils that are puréed, to which heavy cream is added to give it a creamy base. I add potatoes and peas to make it heartier for a satisfying light meal. I've also included a recipe for Spiced Tomato Soup (page 90), known more commonly as *rasam*, that is eaten with Plain Boiled Rice (page 79).

Feel free to enjoy these varieties of lentils, legumes and soups as an appetizer or soup course, or serve them along with the meal the traditional Indian way!

Spiced Tomato Soup Rasam

Rasam is a hot and spicy thin tomato soup from the southern region of India. With each sip, you will initially get a hint of lime and tomato flavors, and then you will feel the warmth of the roasted red chili peppers as it goes down. This dish can be spooned over Plain Boiled Rice (page 79), or you can serve it in individual bowls as a soup or appetizer. Rasam gets its flavor from *rasam masala* (also called rasam powder), which is a spicy blend of ground roasted spices that I also show you how to make. My sinuses get cleared after I have a bowl of rasam since the dried red chili peppers in the rasam masala do the job, but you can use less chili peppers if you prefer.

Serves 4 to 6
Prep time: 10 minutes
Cook time: 20 minutes
Refrigerator life: 3 days
Freezer life: 1 month

Reheating method: Place the refrigerated or defrosted rasam in a microwave, cover and stir periodically. Or, place it in a saucepan over medium-low heat and stir periodically.

2¹/2 teaspoons Rasam Masala (recipe follows)
3 fully ripe tomatoes, each cut into 4 pieces
4 cups (1 liter) water
¹/4 teaspoon ground turmeric
1¹/2 teaspoons salt
Juice of ¹/2 lime
1 handful fresh coriander leaves (cilantro) (about
    ¹/4 cup/10 g packed leaves), rinsed and chopped
1 tablespoon vegetable oil
¹/2 teaspoon cumin seeds
³/4 teaspoon mustard seeds
1 sprig fresh curry leaves, rinsed and destemmed
    (about 15 leaves) (optional)

Rasam Masala (makes 4 tablespoons)
5 dried finger-length red chili peppers
1¹/2 teaspoons coriander seeds
1 tablespoon cumin seeds
1 teaspoon mustard seeds
1¹/2 teaspoons black peppercorns

1 To make the Rasam Masala: Heat a small skillet over medium heat. Roast all the ingredients until they are fragrant, stirring frequently, about 2 minutes. The red chili peppers will slightly puff up, and you will hear the mustard seeds pop. Immediately remove the spices from the skillet and place in a small bowl. Let cool a bit before grinding to a fine powder in a coffee/spice grinder. Set 2¹/2 teaspoons of the mix for use now and place the remaining mix in an airtight container, where it can be stored at room temperature up to 3 months.

2 Place the tomatoes and water in a large saucepan. Bring to a rolling boil over high heat. Cook, uncovered, for 5 minutes to soften the tomatoes. Turn off the heat and transfer the contents to a blender. Purée until smooth (it may also get frothy, which is ok). Pour the blended tomatoes back into the saucepan. (Or, use an immersion blender and purée right in the saucepan.) Add the turmeric, salt, 2¹/2 teaspoons of the Rasam Masala, lime juice and coriander leaves. Stir to combine. Bring to a rolling boil over high heat. Turn off the heat.

3 To temper the spices, pour the oil into a small skillet and place over medium heat. When the oil is heated, add the cumin seeds and mustard seeds. Cook until the cumin seeds turn brown and you hear the mustard seeds pop, about 10 seconds. Do not let the cumin seeds burn and turn black. Turn off the heat. Add the curry leaves, if using, and stir to combine.

4 Add the tempered spices to the tomato mixture. Stir to combine. Enjoy now or let cool to room temperature and refrigerate or freeze for later!

1/2 cup (100 g) dried, skinned and split green
   lentils (dhuli moong daal)
3 1/4 cups (815 ml) water
1 small fully ripe tomato, such as plum (Roma),
   cut in half
1/2 cup (60 g) frozen or fresh parboiled green
   peas (see page 24)
1 small russet potato (about 1/4 lb/125 g),
   peeled and cut into 1/2-in (1.25-cm) cubes
1/4 teaspoon ground turmeric
1/4 teaspoon ground red pepper (cayenne)
3/4 teaspoon salt
1/2 teaspoon ground black pepper
1/4 cup (65 ml) heavy cream
8 to 12 fresh mint leaves, rinsed (for garnish)
   (optional)

1 Place the lentils on a plate. Sift through them and
remove any grit. Transfer the lentils to a small bowl.
Rinse the lentils three times by repeatedly filling the
bowl with cold water and carefully draining off the
water. It is okay if the water is a bit frothy.

2 Place the lentils, water and tomato in a medium
saucepan. Bring to a rolling boil over high heat. It is
okay if the water gets frothy. Stir and reduce the heat
to medium. Cook for 10 minutes, stirring occasionally
and lightly mashing the tomato. Reduce the heat to
low and cover the saucepan. Simmer until the lentils
are completely soft, stirring occasionally and continuing to mash the tomato, about 7 minutes. Turn off the
heat and transfer the contents to a blender.

3 Purée until smooth. Pour the blended lentil mixture back into the saucepan. (Or, use an immersion
blender and purée right in the saucepan.) Add the
peas, potato, turmeric, red pepper, salt and black
pepper. Stir to combine. Bring to a rolling boil over
high heat.

4 Stir and reduce the heat to medium-low. Cover the
saucepan and cook for 5 minutes, stirring every minute or so to keep the soup from burning at the bottom
of the pan.

5 Add the heavy cream. Stir to combine. Cover the
saucepan. Cook, stirring every minute, until you can
easily insert a knife through the potato cubes, about
5 minutes. Enjoy now or let cool to room temperature
and refrigerate or freeze for later! Garnish each portion with 2 or 3 mint leaves before serving.

Creamy Mulligatawny Soup

Mulligatawny soup is not a true Indian dish, but a recipe that was created from a
blend of British and Indian tastes. The word *mulligatawny* originally comes from
the Indian dialect, Tamil, and translates to "pepper water." I was actually first
introduced to this dish while watching the Seinfeld television show, in which the
"soup Nazi" character selectively served his mulligatawny soup to customers he
thought were worthy of the taste. This soup is made with skinned and split green
lentils (called *dhuli moong daal* in Hindi), and I like to add peas and potatoes to it.
This soup gets its rich consistency from heavy cream, which also makes this soup
heartier! You may serve this soup as an appetizer, or along with the main course, or
you can even serve it by itself for a light meal!

Serves 4
Prep time: 5 minutes
Cook time: 30 minutes
Refrigerator life: 3 days
Freezer life: 1 month

Reheating method: Place the refrigerated or
defrosted soup in a microwave, cover and stir
periodically. Or, place it in a saucepan over
medium-low heat and stir periodically.

Split Pea and Vegetable Stew Sambar

Sambar is a stew made with split pigeon peas (called *toor daal* in Hindi) and vegetables, and is typically eaten in the southern Indian states of Andhra Pradesh, Karnatika, Tamil Nadu and Kerala. This dish is made with whole grayish-tan pigeon peas that are skinned and split, revealing a yellow pea. The unique flavor of sambar comes from a blend of ground roasted spices, known as *sambar masala*, or sambar powder, which I have included the recipe for. Sambar can be served in individual bowls along with Crispy Rice and Lentil Crepes (page 56), Potato Stuffed Crepes (page 56) and Savory Vegetable Pancakes (page 53). Sambar also goes well with Plain Boiled Rice (page 79).

Serves 4
Prep time: 10 minutes
Cook time: 55 minutes
Refrigerator life: 3 days
Freezer life: 1 month
Reheating method: Place the refrigerated or defrosted sambar in a microwave, cover and stir periodically. Or, place it in a saucepan over medium-low heat and stir periodically. If the reheated sambar seems too thick, you may add a bit of water to it.

2 teaspoons Sambar Masala (recipe follows)
1/2 cup (100 g) dried, skinned and split pigeon peas (toor daal) (not oily)
4 1/2 cups (1.1 liters) water
1 small fully ripe tomato, such as plum (Roma), cut in half
1/2 small onion, diced
1 small carrot, peeled and sliced into 1/2-in (1.25-cm)-thick circles
1 fresh finger-length green chili pepper, cut in half lengthwise

1 teaspoon tamarind concentrate (paste)
1 teaspoon salt
2 tablespoons vegetable oil
2 dried finger-length red chili peppers
1/2 teaspoon cumin seeds
1/2 teaspoon mustard seeds
1 handful fresh coriander leaves (cilantro) (about 1/4 cup/10 g packed leaves), rinsed and chopped
1 sprig fresh curry leaves, rinsed and destemmed (about 15 leaves) (optional)

Sambar Masala (Makes 5 tablespoons)
4 dried finger-length red chili peppers
2 teaspoons dried, skinned and split black chickpeas (channa daal)
1 teaspoon dried, skinned and split black lentils (dhuli urad daal)
1 teaspoon cumin seeds
2 tablespoons coriander seeds
1/2 teaspoon black peppercorns
1 pinch ground turmeric

1 To make the Sambar Masala: Place a small skillet over medium heat. When the skillet is heated, roast all the ingredients except the turmeric until they are fragrant, stirring frequently, about 2 minutes. The red chili peppers will slightly puff up. Do not let the cumin seeds burn and turn black. Immediately remove the spices from the skillet and place in a small bowl. Let cool a bit before grinding.

2 Grind the roasted spices in a coffee/spice grinder, to a fine powder. Place the ground spices in a small bowl. Add the turmeric and mix to combine. Set 2 teaspoons of the mix aside for use now and place the remaining mix in an airtight container, where it can be stored at room temperature up to 3 months.

3 Place the split pigeon peas on a plate . Sift through them and remove any grit.

4 Transfer the pigeon peas to a small bowl. Rinse the peas three times by repeatedly filling the bowl with cold water and carefully draining off the water. It is okay if the water is a bit frothy.

5 Place the pigeon peas, water and tomato in a large saucepan. Bring to a rolling boil over high heat. It is okay if the water gets frothy. Stir and reduce the heat to medium.

6 Partially cover the saucepan and cook until the pigeon peas are completely soft, about 30 minutes, stirring occasionally. Make sure the water does not boil over and out of the saucepan. Turn off the heat and transfer the contents to a blender.

7 Purée until smooth. Pour the blended mixture back into the saucepan. (Or, use an immersion blender and purée right in the saucepan.)

8 Add the onion, carrot, green chili pepper, tamarind, salt and 2 teaspoons of the Sambar Masala. Stir to combine. Bring to a rolling boil over high heat.

9 Reduce the heat to medium. Partially cover the saucepan. Simmer until the onion is translucent and the carrot is tender, stirring occasionally, about 15 minutes. Turn off the heat. The consistency of the sambar should be smooth—not too thin, and not too thick. If the sambar seems too thick, add a little water,

about 1/4 cup (65 ml) at a time, to create desired consistency.

10 To temper the spices, pour the oil into a small skillet and place over medium heat. When the oil is heated, tear the red chili peppers in half and add to the skillet. Add the cumin seeds and mustard seeds. Cook until the cumin seeds turn brown and you hear the mustard seeds pop, about 10 seconds. Do not let the cumin seeds burn and turn black. Turn off the heat. Add the coriander leaves and curry leaves, if using. Stir to combine.

11 Add the tempered spices to the pigeon peas. Stir to combine. Enjoy now or let cool to room temperature and refrigerate or freeze for later!

VARIATION:

Vegetable Medley Sambar

To make a heartier sambar, follow Steps 1 through 7 for Split Pea and Vegetable Stew (page 92). In Step 8 add 1/2 cup (50 g) fresh or frozen bite-size cauliflower florets (there's no need to defrost frozen cauliflower); 1/2 unpeeled Japanese or Chinese eggplant or 1 unpeeled Indian eggplant, cut into 1/2-inch (1.25-cm) cubes; and 1/2 green bell pepper, chopped. Continue with the rest of the directions. If the sambar becomes too thick after adding the vegetables, add a little water, about 1/4 cup (65 ml) at a time, to create desired consistency. Check for seasoning and add some salt if needed.

Chickpea Curry Channa Masala

Cream-colored chickpeas (also called garbanzo beans), or *kabuli channa* in Hindi, make a delicious curry dish. The quickest way to make this dish is to use canned chickpeas since they are already precooked. All we have to do then is make the spice base (*masala)*, and add the canned chickpeas. If you use dried chickpeas, you will first need to soak them overnight and then boil them. This dish is typically eaten with Fried Leavened Breads (page 76) or Puffed Fried Breads (page 74). You may even eat this dish with Plain Boiled Rice (page 79) or Rice with Cumin and Peas (page 78). It is common to serve this dish with lime wedges and a small bowl of tossed tomatoes, onions and green chili peppers on the side, allowing each person the opportunity to garnish as he or she likes.

Serves 4 to 6
Prep time: 5 minutes + overnight soaking (12 hours) if using dried chickpeas
Cook time: 30 minutes + an additional 50 minutes if using dried chickpeas
Refrigerator life: 3 days   **Freezer life:** 1 month
Reheating method: Place the refrigerated or defrosted curry in a microwave, cover and stir periodically. Or, place it in a saucepan over medium-low heat and stir periodically.

3 tablespoons vegetable oil
1¹/2 teaspoons minced garlic
1 tablespoon peeled and finely grated fresh ginger
¹/2 small onion, grated on the largest grating holes on a box grater or shredded in a food processor
1 fully ripe tomato, cut into 4 pieces
³/4 teaspoon cumin seeds, roasted and ground (see page 24)
¹/4 teaspoon ground turmeric
¹/2 teaspoon ground red pepper (cayenne)
³/4 teaspoon salt
¹/2 teaspoon ground black pepper.
1 fresh finger-length green chili pepper, diced
Two 15-oz (425-g) cans precooked chickpeas with liquid from cans or 1 cup (180 g) dried chickpeas, soaked overnight and cooked, with cooking liquid
¹/4 cup (65 ml) water if using canned chickpeas (see Note)

Side Accompaniments
¹/2 small onion, diced

1 small fully ripe tomato, such as plum (Roma), diced
1 fresh finger-length green chili pepper, sliced into thin rings
1 lime, cut into 4 to 6 wedges

1 Pour the oil into a medium saucepan and place over medium heat. When the oil is heated, add the garlic, ginger and onion. Sauté until the onion is golden brown, stirring frequently, about 5 minutes.
2 Reduce the heat to medium-low. Add the tomato and cover the saucepan. Cook until the tomato becomes completely soft and mashed and is combined with the onion to form a coarse paste, stirring every minute or so and lightly mashing the tomato, about 5 minutes.
3 Add the cumin, turmeric, red pepper, salt, black pepper and green chili pepper. Cook uncovered for 6 minutes, stirring frequently. This is the *masala* (spice base).
4 Add the canned chickpeas with their liquid and the additional ¹/4 cup (65 ml) water and bring to a rolling boil over high heat. (Or add the boiled chickpeas with 2 cups (500 ml) of their cooking liquid and bring to a rolling boil over high heat.)
5 Reduce the heat to medium-low. Simmer uncovered for 15 minutes to thicken the curry and let the flavors infuse, stirring occasionally. Enjoy now or let cool to room temperature and refrigerate or freeze for later! Before serving, prepare the Side Accompaniments, if using. Place the onion, tomatoes and green chili peppers in a small bowl and toss. Place the lime wedges on a small plate.

> **NOTE:** When buying canned chickpeas, it is okay if you do not exactly find 15-oz (425-g) cans, as long as they are about that size. The amount of liquid in the can varies slightly depending on the brand, so you may add a bit more or less water than the suggested ¹/4 cup (65 ml) to achieve the desired consistency. I like to use the liquid in the can since it has flavor to it, just as the broth does when boiling dried chickpeas. The liquid in the can also lends to a desirable consistency of the curry in the dish.

Preparing Dried Chickpeas

1 Place the dried chickpeas on a plate, sift through them and remove any grit, or any blemished chickpeas.

2 Transfer the chickpeas to a large bowl and cover with cold water. Cover the bowl and let soak overnight at room temperature to allow the chickpeas to expand and become tender.

3 The next morning, place a colander in the sink. Pour the soaked chickpeas into the colander and rinse thoroughly.

4 Place the drained chickpeas, 4 cups (1 liter) of water and 3/4 teaspoon salt in a large saucepan. Bring to a rolling boil over high heat. It is okay if the water gets frothy.

5 Reduce the heat to medium-low. Cover the saucepan. Simmer until the chickpeas are very soft, stirring occasionally, about 45 minutes.

6 Keep 2 cups (500 ml) of the cooking liquid (broth) and discard the rest. If for some reason you do not have at least 2 cups (500 ml) of cooking liquid, add some water.

Fresh Lentil Sprout Salad

You can make a colorful and nutritious lentil salad by sprouting whole green lentils, called *sabut moong daal* in Hindi. This beautiful dish makes a healthy snack, or it can be served along with Dad's Baked Salmon (page 116) and a side of Rice with Cumin and Peas (page 78) or even Lemon Rice (page 85) for a complete meal. For fun, put a few sprouted lentils in the ground and water them daily, and watch your own lentil plant grow!

Serves 4 to 6
Prep time: 15 minutes + overnight soaking (12 hours) + 1 day sitting (24 hours)
Refrigerator life: 1 hour (Tastes best freshly tossed and served.)

1/2 cup (100 g) dried whole green lentils (sabut moong daal)
1 small fully ripe tomato, such as plum (Roma), diced
1 small turnip, peeled and diced
1/2 small onion, diced
1/2 red bell pepper, diced
4 tablespoons peeled and diced cucumber (any variety) (see page 37)
1 handful fresh coriander leaves (cilantro) (about 1/4 cup/10 g packed leaves), rinsed and chopped
1/4 teaspoon ground red pepper (cayenne)
1/2 teaspoon salt
1/2 teaspoon ground black pepper
Juice of 2 limes

1 Place the lentils on a plate. Sift through them and remove any grit. Transfer the lentils to a small bowl. Rinse the lentils three times by repeatedly filling the bowl with cold water and carefully draining off the water. Add cold water to cover the lentils. Cover the bowl and let soak overnight at room temperature.

2 By the next morning, the lentils should be tender. Drain the water from the bowl. Cover the bowl and place aside at room temperature until the following morning. Before going to bed, you can peek at the lentils to find small sprouts. The next morning, you will see longer sprouts. At this point, if you're not ready to make the salad, you may cover and refrigerate the sprouted lentils up to 1 day.

3 Place the sprouted lentils and the rest of the ingredients in a serving bowl. Mix to combine. Enjoy now or refrigerate up to 1 hour!

Kidney Bean Curry Rajma

Known as *rajma*, this popular kidney bean curry is from the northern Indian state of Punjab. This dish is traditionally eaten with Plain Boiled Rice (page 79), and when served together, this meal is called *rajma chawval*, which means "kidney bean curry and rice." When my parents lived in college dorms in India, once a week the cafeteria would serve rajma chawval, and that was the day everyone looked forward to and would go back in line for seconds and sometimes even thirds! Even today, my dad always looks forward to this meal when my mom makes it. If you prefer, you may also eat this dish with Whole Wheat Flatbreads (page 64), Oven Baked White Breads (page 66) or Oven Baked Whole Wheat Breads (page 68). The quickest way to make this recipe is to use precooked canned kidney beans instead of dried beans, which have to be soaked overnight and then boiled, but I do provide both cooking methods.

Serves 4 to 6

Prep time: 5 minutes + overnight soaking (12 hours) if using dried kidney beans

Cook time: 30 minutes + an additional 1 hour 20 minutes if using dried kidney beans

Refrigerator life: 3 days

Freezer life: 1 month

Reheating method: Place the refrigerated or defrosted curry in a microwave, cover and stir periodically. Or, place it in a saucepan over medium-low heat and stir periodically.

3 tablespoons vegetable oil
1¹/2 teaspoons minced garlic
1 tablespoon peeled and finely grated fresh ginger
¹/2 small onion, grated on the largest grating holes on a box grater or shredded in a food processor
1 fully ripe tomato, cut into 4 pieces
3/4 teaspoon Garam Masala (page 44)
¹/2 teaspoon ground red pepper (cayenne)
3/4 teaspoon salt
3/4 teaspoon ground black pepper
Two 15-oz (425-g) cans precooked dark red kidneys beans with liquid from cans or 1 cup (180 g) dried dark red kidney beans, soaked overnight and cooked, with cooking liquid
¹/2 cup (125 ml) water if using canned kidney beans (see Note on page 97)

1 Pour the oil into a medium saucepan and place over medium heat. Add the garlic, ginger and onion. Sauté until the onion is golden brown, stirring frequently, about 5 minutes.

2 Reduce the heat to medium-low. Add the tomato and cover the saucepan. Cook until the tomato becomes completely soft and mashed and is combined with the onion to form a coarse paste, stirring every minute or so and lightly mashing the tomato, about 5 minutes.

3 Add the Garam Masala, red pepper, salt and black pepper. Cook uncovered for 6 minutes, stirring frequently. This is the *masala* (spice base).

4 Add the canned kidney beans with their liquid and the additional ¹/2 cup (125 ml) water and bring to a rolling boil over high heat. (Or add the boiled kidney beans with 2 cups (500 ml) of their broth and bring to a rolling boil over high heat.)

5 Reduce the heat to medium-low. Simmer, uncovered, for 15 minutes to thicken the curry and let the flavors infuse, stirring occasionally. Enjoy now or let cool to room temperature and refrigerate or freeze for later!

> **NOTE:** When buying canned kidney beans, it is okay if you do not exactly find 15-oz (425-g) cans, as long as they are about that size. The amount of liquid in the can varies slightly depending on the brand, so you may add a bit more or less water than the suggested 1/2 cup (125 ml) to achieve the desired consistency. I prefer to use the liquid in the can since it has flavor to it, just as the broth does when boiling dried kidney beans. The liquid in the can also lends to a desirable consistency of the curry in the dish. Most canned kidney beans also have sugar or corn syrup, which may bring a slight sweet hint to the finished dish. Try to look for canned beans without the sugar or corn syrup, but if you can't find them, you may simply squeeze in a little lime juice to balance the taste if you prefer.

Preparing Dried Kidney Beans

1 Place the dried kidney beans on a plate, sift through them and remove any grit, or any blemished kidney beans.

2 Transfer the beans to a large bowl and cover with cold water. Cover the bowl and let soak overnight at room temperature to allow the kidney beans to expand and become tender.

3 The next morning, place a colander in the sink. Pour the soaked kidney beans into the colander and rinse thoroughly.

4 Place the drained kidney beans, 5 cups (1.25 liters) of water and 3/4 teaspoon salt in a large saucepan. Bring to a rolling boil over high heat. It is okay if the water gets frothy.

5 Reduce the heat to medium-low. Cover the saucepan. Simmer until the kidney beans are very soft, stirring occasionally, about 1 hour 15 minutes.

6 Keep 2 cups (500 ml) of the cooking liquid (broth) and discard the rest. If for some reason you do not have at least 2 cups (500 ml) of the cooking liquid, you may add some water to make up the balance.

Stewed Whole Red Lentils

Sabut Masoor Daal

Whole red lentils, called *sabut masoor daal* in Hindi, are an easy lentil dish that takes just a bit longer to cook than Punjabi Split Red Lentil Stew (page 100) since here the dried lentil is in its whole form with the reddish/light brownish skin on, which gives it a different flavor and appearance. This dish can be served in individual bowls, along with an Indian bread such as Whole Wheat Flatbreads (page 64), Oven Baked White Breads (page 66) or Oven Baked Whole Wheat Breads (page 68), and be paired with Sautéed Green Beans and Potatoes (page 132). This lentil dish also goes well spooned over Plain Boiled Rice (page 79).

Serves 4
Prep time: 5 minutes
Cook time: 45 minutes
Refrigerator life: 2 days
Freezer life: 1 month
Reheating method: Place the refrigerated or defrosted daal in a microwave, cover and stir periodically. Or, place it in a saucepan over medium-low heat and stir periodically. If the reheated daal seems too thick, you may add a bit of water to it.

1/2 cup (100 g) dried whole red lentils (sabut masoor daal)
2 1/2 cups (625 ml) water
1 small fully ripe tomato, such as plum (Roma), cut in half
1/4 teaspoon ground turmeric
1/4 teaspoon ground red pepper (cayenne)
1/2 teaspoon salt
2 tablespoons vegetable oil
1/4 teaspoon cumin seeds
1/2 small onion, diced
1 fresh finger-length green chili pepper, finely chopped

1 Place the lentils on a plate. Sift through them and remove any grit.

2 Transfer the lentils to a small bowl. Rinse the lentils three times by repeatedly filling the bowl with cold water and carefully draining off the water.

3 Place the lentils, 2 1/2 cups (625 ml) water, tomato, turmeric, red pepper and salt in a medium saucepan. Stir to combine. Bring to a rolling boil over high heat.

4 Stir and reduce the heat to medium-low and cover the saucepan. Simmer until the lentils are completely soft, stirring occasionally and lightly mashing the tomato, about 35 minutes. It should not look like the lentils are floating individually in the water and you can pick them out; instead they should come together with the water when fully cooked should be similar to a thick soup with an even consistency. Turn off the heat.

5 To temper the spices, pour the oil into a small skillet and place over medium heat. When the oil is heated, add the cumin seeds and let brown, about 10 seconds. Do not let the cumin seeds burn and turn black.

6 Immediately add the onion. Sauté the onion until it is browned, stirring frequently, about 6 minutes. Add the green chili pepper and stir.

7 Add the tempered spices to the lentils. Stir to combine. Enjoy now or let cool to room temperature and refrigerate or freeze for later!

Prep time: 5 minutes + overnight soaking (12 hours) if using dried black-eyed peas
Cook time: 30 minutes + an additional 1 hour 20 minutes if using dried black-eyed peas
Refrigerator life: 3 days
Freezer life: 1 month
Reheating method: Place the refrigerated or defrosted curry in a microwave, cover and stir periodically. Or, place it in a saucepan over medium-low heat and stir periodically.

3 tablespoons vegetable oil
1½ teaspoons minced garlic
1 tablespoon peeled and finely grated fresh ginger
1 small onion, grated on the largest grating holes on a box grater or shredded in a food processor
1 fully ripe tomato, cut into 4 pieces
¼ teaspoon ground turmeric
½ teaspoon ground red pepper (cayenne)
¾ teaspoon salt
½ teaspoon ground black pepper
Two 15-oz (425-g) cans precooked black-eyed peas with liquid from cans or 1 cup (180 g) dried black-eyed peas, soaked overnight and cooked, with cooking liquid
½ cup (125 ml) water if using canned black-eyed peas (see Note on page 99)

1 Pour the oil into a medium saucepan and place over medium heat. When the oil is heated, add the garlic, ginger and onion. Sauté until the onion is golden brown, stirring frequently, about 6 minutes.
2 Reduce the heat to medium-low. Add the tomato and cover the saucepan. Cook until the tomato becomes completely soft and mashed and is combined with the onion to form a coarse paste, stirring every minute or so and lightly mashing the tomato, about 5 minutes.
3 Add the turmeric, red pepper, salt and black pepper. Cook uncovered for 6 minutes, stirring frequently. This is the *masala* (spice base).
4 Add the canned black-eyed peas with their liquid and the additional ½ cup (125 ml) of the water and bring to a rolling boil over high heat. (Or add the boiled black-eyed peas with 1½ cups (375 ml) of their broth

Black-Eyed Pea Curry Lobhia

This black-eyed pea curry, or *rongi*, as my mom calls it in Punjabi, is one of my favorite Indian dishes. This legume gets its name from the tiny black marking in the center of it which actually looks like the eye of the pea! You won't believe how easy it is to make a flavorful black-eyed pea curry using precooked and canned black-eyed peas until you try it yourself! For those strict traditionalists, instructions are provided for using dried peas. If you do use dried black-eyed peas, you will have to soak them overnight and then boil them to make them soft. This dish has a saucy consistency and can be eaten with Plain Boiled Rice (page 79) or with Indian breads such as Whole Wheat Flatbreads (page 64), Oven Baked White Breads (page 66) or Oven Baked Whole Wheat Breads (page 68).

and bring to a rolling boil over high heat.)

5 Reduce the heat to medium-low. Simmer uncovered for 10 minutes to thicken the curry and let the flavors infuse, stirring occasionally. Enjoy now or let cool to room temperature and refrigerate or freeze for later!

> NOTE: When buying canned black-eyed peas, it is okay if you do not exactly find 15-oz (425 g) cans, as long as they are about that size. The amount of liquid in the can varies slightly depending on the brand, so you may add a bit more or less water than the suggested 1/2 cup (125 ml) to achieve the desired consistency. I prefer to use the liquid in the can since it has flavor to it, just as the broth does when boiling dried black-eyed peas. The liquid in the can can also lends to a desirable consistency of the curry in the dish.

Preparing Dried Black-eyed Peas

1 Place the dried black-eyed peas on a plate and sift through them and remove any grit, or any blemished black-eyes peas.

2 Transfer the beans to a large bowl and cover with cold water. Cover the bowl and let soak overnight at room temperature to allow the black-eyed peas to expand and become tender.

3 The next morning, place a colander in the sink. Pour the soaked black-eyed peas into the colander and rinse thoroughly.

4 Place the drained black-eyed peas, 4 cups (1 liter) of water and 3/4 teaspoon salt in a large saucepan. Bring to a rolling boil over high heat. It is okay if the water gets frothy.

5 Reduce the heat to medium-low. Cover the saucepan. Simmer until the black-eyed peas are very soft, stirring occasionally, about 1 hour.

6 Keep 1 1/2 cups (375 ml) of the boiled water (broth) and discard the rest. If for some reason you do not have at least 1 1/2 cups (375 ml) of the broth left over, you may add some water to make up for the balance.

Whole Green Lentil Stew

Sabut Moong Daal

Whole green lentils, called *sabut moong daal* in Hindi, is an easy lentil dish that takes just a bit longer to cook than Stewed Split Green Lentils (page 101) since here the dried lentil is in its whole form with the green skin on, which gives it a different flavor and appearance. This dish can be served in individual bowls, along with an Indian bread such as Whole Wheat Flatbreads (page 64), Oven Baked White Breads (page 66) or Oven Baked Whole Wheat Breads (page 68) and be paired with Spiced Cauliflower and Potatoes (page 131). This lentil dish also goes well spooned over Plain Boiled Rice (page 79).

Serves 4
Prep time: 5 minutes
Cook time: 50 minutes
Refrigerator life: 2 days
Freezer life: 1 month
Reheating method: Place the refrigerated or defrosted daal in a microwave, cover and stir periodically. Or, place it in a saucepan over medium-low heat and stir periodically. If the reheated daal seems too thick, you may add a bit of water to it.

1/2 cup (100 g) dried whole green lentils (sabut moong daal)
3 1/2 cups (875 ml) water
1 small fully ripe tomato, such as plum (Roma), cut in half
3 garlic cloves, slits cut into them to help release the flavor
1/4 teaspoon ground turmeric
1/2 teaspoon ground red pepper (cayenne)
3/4 teaspoon salt
2 tablespoons vegetable oil
1/4 teaspoon cumin seeds
1/2 small onion, diced
1 teaspoon peeled and finely grated fresh ginger

1 Place the lentils on a plate. Sift through them and remove any grit.

2 Transfer the lentils to a small bowl. Rinse the lentils three times by repeatedly filling the bowl with cold water and carefully draining off the water.

3 Place the lentils, 3 1/2 cups (875 ml) water, tomato, 1 garlic clove, turmeric, red pepper and salt in a medium saucepan. Stir to combine. Bring to a rolling boil over high heat.

4 Stir and reduce the heat to medium-low. Cover the saucepan. Simmer until the lentils are completely soft, stirring occasionally and lightly mashing the tomato, about 40 minutes. It should not look like the lentils are floating individually in the water and you can pick them out; instead they should come together with the water when fully cooked when fully cooked should be similar to a thick soup with an even consistency. Turn off the heat.

5 To temper the spices, pour the oil into a small skillet and place over medium heat. When the oil is heated, add the cumin seeds and let brown, about 10 seconds. Do not let the cumin seeds burn and turn black.

6 Immediately add the onion, ginger and the 2 remaining garlic cloves. Sauté the onion until it is browned, stirring frequently, about 6 minutes.

7 Add the tempered spices to the lentils. Stir to combine. Enjoy now or let cool to room temperature and refrigerate or freeze for later! Before serving, remove the garlic cloves and discard.

Punjabi Split Red Lentil Stew

Dhuli Masoor Daal

Split red lentils make a rich and savory lentil dish (*daal*). In the northern Indian state of Punjab, it is common to add butter to lentil dishes, and in this recipe I indulge in this tradition! This dish is made with whole red lentils that are skinned and split, revealing an orange lentil, which surprisingly turns a darker shade of yellow when cooked (partially due to the turmeric)! Split red lentils, called *dhuli masoor daal* in Hindi, can be served in individual bowls with an Indian bread, such as Whole Wheat Flatbreads (page 64), Oven Baked White Breads (page 66) or Oven Baked Whole Wheat Breads (page 68), and Stuffed Bell Peppers (page 130). This lentil dish also goes well spooned over Plain Boiled Rice (page 79).

Serves 4
Prep time: 5 minutes
Cook time: 25 minutes
Refrigerator life: 2 days
Freezer life: 1 month
Reheating method: Place the refrigerated or defrosted daal in a microwave, cover and stir periodically. Or, place it in a covered saucepan over medium-low heat and stir periodically. If the reheated daal seems too thick, you may add a bit of water to it.

1/2 cup (80 g) dried, skinned and split red lentils (dhuli masoor daal)
2 1/4 cups (565 ml) water
1 small fully ripe tomato, such as plum (Roma), cut in half
1/4 teaspoon ground turmeric
1/4 teaspoon ground red pepper (cayenne)
1/2 teaspoon salt
1 tablespoon vegetable oil
1/4 teaspoon cumin seeds
1/2 small onion, diced
1 tablespoon unsalted butter
1 handful fresh coriander leaves (cilantro) (about 1/4 cup/10 g packed leaves), rinsed and chopped

1 Place the lentils on a plate. Sift through them and remove any grit.

2 Transfer the lentils to a small bowl. Rinse the lentils three times by repeatedly filling the bowl with cold water and carefully draining off the water. It is okay if the water is a bit frothy.

3 Place the lentils, water, tomato, turmeric, red pepper and salt in a medium saucepan. Stir to combine. Bring to a rolling boil over high heat. It is okay if the water gets frothy.

4 Stir and reduce the heat to medium. Cook for 10 minutes, stirring occasionally and lightly mashing the tomato.

5 Reduce the heat to low and cover the saucepan. Simmer until the lentils are completely soft, stirring occasionally and continuing to mash the tomato, about 5 minutes. It should not look like the lentils are floating individually in the water and you can pick them out; instead they should come together with the water when fully cooked and should be similar to a thick soup with an even consistency. Turn off the heat.

6 To temper the spices, pour the oil into a small skillet and place over medium heat. When the oil is heated, add the cumin seeds and let brown, about 10 seconds. Do not let the cumin seeds burn and turn black.

7 Immediately add the onion. Sauté the onion until it is browned, stirring frequently, about 6 minutes.

8 Add the tempered spices and butter to the lentils. Stir to combine until the butter is melted. Enjoy now or let cool to room temperature and refrigerate or freeze for later! Just before serving, sprinkle the chopped coriander leaves on top.

Punjabi Split Red Lentil Stew

Stewed Split Green Lentils Dhuli Moong Daal

This is my favorite Indian lentil dish. A similar version of this dish is also commonly served as an appetizer at Middle Eastern restaurants. This dish is made with whole green lentils that are skinned and split, revealing a yellow lentil that is called *dhuli moong daal* in Hindi. These lentils can be served in individual bowls along with an Indian bread, such as Whole Wheat Flatbreads (page 64), Oven Baked White Breads (page 66) or Oven Baked Whole Wheat Breads (page 68), and be paired with Sautéed Okra with Onions (page 135). Or, it may simply be spooned over Plain Boiled Rice (page 79).

Serves 4
Prep time: 5 minutes
Cook time: 20 minutes
Refrigerator life: 2 days
Freezer life: 1 month
Reheating method: Place the refrigerated or defrosted daal in a microwave, cover and stir periodically. Or, place it in a covered saucepan over medium-low heat and stir periodically. If the reheated daal seems too thick, you may add a bit of water to it.

1/2 cup (100 g) dried, skinned and split green lentils (dhuli moong daal)
2 1/4 cups (565 ml) water
1 small fully ripe tomato, such as plum (Roma), cut in half
1/4 teaspoon ground turmeric
1/4 teaspoon ground red pepper (cayenne)
1/2 teaspoon salt
1 tablespoon vegetable oil
1/4 teaspoon cumin seeds
1 handful fresh coriander leaves (cilantro) (about 1/4 cup/10 g packed leaves), rinsed and chopped
1 lime, cut into 4 wedges

1 Place the lentils on a plate. Sift through them and remove any grit.

2 Transfer the lentils to a small bowl. Rinse the lentils three times by repeatedly filling the bowl with cold water and carefully draining off the water. It is okay if the water is a bit frothy.

3 Place the lentils, water, tomato, turmeric, red pepper and salt in a medium saucepan. Stir to combine. Bring to a rolling boil over high heat. It is okay if the water gets frothy.

4 Stir and reduce the heat to medium. Cook for 10 minutes, stirring occasionally and lightly mashing the tomato.

5 Reduce the heat to low and cover the saucepan. Simmer until the lentils are completely soft, stirring occasionally and continuing to mash the tomato, about 7 minutes. It should not look like the lentils are floating individually in the water and you can pick them out; instead they should come together with the water when fully cooked and should be similar to a thick soup with an even consistency. Turn off the heat.

6 To temper the spices, pour the oil into a small skillet and place over medium heat. When the oil is heated, add the cumin seeds and let brown, about 10 seconds. Do not let the cumin seeds burn and turn black.

7 Add the tempered spices to the lentils. Stir to combine. Enjoy now or let cool to room temperature and refrigerate or freeze for later! Just before serving, sprinkle the chopped coriander leaves on top, and serve with a wedge of lime to be squeezed onto the lentils.

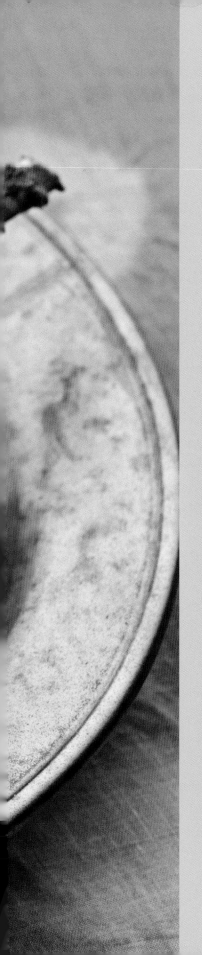

Chapter 4
Chicken and Lamb

By far, my favorite dish in this chapter is Chicken Tikka Masala (page 105). And I know I am not alone! Its creamy curry base is simply heaven. It's normally found only in restaurants, but after experimenting a lot in my kitchen, I finally came up with a recipe that I personally think is comparable to the restaurant version! Now I can enjoy this dish as often as I want, and I hope you enjoy my recipe just as much as I do!

Though I might be obsessed with Chicken Tikka Masala, I know many of you may want to learn to make some other Indian meat or chicken dishes at home. And Indian cuisine offers a great variety of recipes—from spicy Lamb Vindaloo Curry (page 108) to elegant Lamb Chops with Indian Spice Rub (page 112) and Oven Baked Tandoori Chicken (page 107), that can even be prepared on your outdoor grill.

For economic, cultural and religious reasons, poultry and meat are not eaten daily or ever eaten in many households throughout India. Some communities, such as the Muslim community in the state of Andhra Pradesh, enjoy a greater variety of flavorful meat dishes. Some of their dishes, such as Chicken Biryani (page 80) and Ground Lamb with Peas (page 110), have become popular throughout the world. And many Hindu homes will make chicken or other meat dishes when having a party or celebrating an event. For example, every time I visit India, my family is sure to get a live chicken from the market and cook it fresh for us.

The cow is a respected animal in India: it is used to plow the land, provides milk to the population and is prevalent in Hindu mythology. For these cultural and religious reasons, beef dishes are not common in India. Instead, goat is the mainstream red meat. In the United States, goat meat is neither popular nor readily available. Instead tender, young lamb meat, which comes from a sheep less than one-year-old, is preferred. So I've used a variety of cuts of lamb in this chapter—from ground, rib chops, leg and loin chops. Goat meat is tougher than lamb meat, but you can still use goat meat if you prefer, although you might have to cook it a bit longer for the desired tenderness.

Prep time: 10 minutes
Cook time: 30 minutes
Refrigerator life: 3 days
Freezer life: 1 month
Reheating method: Place the refrigerated or defrosted chicken in a skillet over medium-low heat and stir periodically. A less preferred method is to place the chicken in a microwave and stir periodically.

1¹⁄₄ **lbs (600 g) boneless, skinless chicken breast**
4 **tablespoons vegetable oil**
1 **tablespoon minced garlic**
2¹⁄₂ **teaspoons peeled and finely grated fresh**
   ginger
1 **onion, grated on the largest grating holes on a**
   box grater or shredded in a food processor
³⁄₄ **teaspoon cumin seeds**
4 **whole green cardamom pods**
1 **large fully ripe tomato, cut into 4 pieces**
¹⁄₄ **heaping teaspoon ground turmeric**
³⁄₄ **teaspoon ground red pepper (cayenne)**
³⁄₄ **teaspoon salt**
³⁄₄ **teaspoon ground black pepper**

1 Wash the chicken with cold water and cut into ³⁄₄-inch (2-cm) pieces.

2 Pour the oil into a large skillet and place over medium heat. When the oil is heated, add the garlic, ginger and onion. Sauté until the onion is golden brown, stirring frequently, about 7 minutes.

3 Add the cumin seeds. Open the cardamoms and add the seeds and the pods. Stir to combine. Reduce the heat to medium-low. Add the tomato and cover the skillet. Cook until the tomato becomes completely soft and mashed and is combined with the onion to form a coarse paste, stirring every minute or so and lightly mashing the tomato, about 5 minutes.

4 Add the turmeric, red pepper, salt and black pepper. Stir to combine. Cook uncovered for 7 minutes, stirring frequently. This is the *masala* (spice base).

5 Add the chicken. Stir to combine and increase the heat to medium. Cook uncovered until there are no signs of pink when you insert a knife though the chicken, stirring occasionally, about 10 minutes. Remove the cardamom pods and discard. Enjoy now or let cool to room temperature and refrigerate or freeze for later!

Cardamom Chicken Masala Murgh

My mother makes this quick-and-easy chicken dish by first making her fancy version of *masala* (tomato and onion spice base), to which she adds some cardamom. Once the *masala* picks up the subtle cardamom flavor, she then adds the chicken (*murgh*) and sautés it until it is done. Masala murgh can be eaten with Indian breads such as Whole Wheat Flatbreads (page 64), Oven Baked White Breads (page 66) or Oven Baked Whole Wheat Breads (page 68). It can even be served with Plain Boiled Rice (page 79) or Rice with Cumin and Peas (page 78). Add your favorite curried vegetable dish and a side of Three Vegetable Raita (page 37), and you have a complete and balanced Indian meal.

Chicken Tikka Masala

Chicken *tikka masala* most likely does not need an introduction! Of all the popular chicken dishes served at Indian restaurants, this is my favorite, and so I tried to recreate it at home and have come up with this recipe. This is a two-part recipe: first you need to make the chicken *tikka* (small pieces of chicken) following the recipe for Chicken Kebabs (page 60); then you make the *masala*—a spiced tomato and onion base that is mixed with heavy cream to give an indulgent taste. You can save preparation and cooking time by cooking the kebabs a day in advance. Chicken tikka masala tastes great with Oven Baked White Breads (page 99), Whole Wheat Flatbreads (page 64) or Oven Baked Whole Wheat Breads (page 68). I personally enjoy this dish served on a bed of Rice with Cumin and Peas (page 78), but you may also serve it with Plain Boiled Rice (page 79). Because of the heavy cream, try to resist making this dish too frequently for your own good!

Serves 3 to 4
Prep time: 10 minutes + 1 1/2 hours to make the chicken kebabs (can be done 1 day in advance)
Cook time: 20 minutes
Refrigerator life: 3 days
Freezer life: 1 month

Reheating method: Place the refrigerated or defrosted chicken tikka masala in a saucepan over medium-low heat and stir periodically. A less preferred method is to place the chicken tikka masala in a microwave, cover and stir periodically.

1/2 recipe Chicken Kebabs (page 60)
3 tablespoons vegetable oil
2 teaspoons minced garlic
2 teaspoons peeled and finely grated fresh ginger
1 onion, diced
1 fully ripe tomato, chopped
1/2 teaspoon cumin seeds
1/2 teaspoon ground coriander
1 teaspoon paprika
1/2 teaspoon ground red pepper (cayenne)
3/4 teaspoon salt
1/2 teaspoon ground black pepper
1 1/2 teaspoons sugar
One 1-in (2.5-cm) cinnamon stick
2 tablespoons butter
Juice of 1/2 lime
1/4 cup (65 ml) heavy cream
3 tablespoons water

1 Prepare the Chicken Kebabs, if you have not already done so.

2 Pour the oil into a medium saucepan and place over medium heat. When the oil is heated, add the garlic, ginger and onion. Sauté until the onion is golden brown, stirring frequently, about 6 minutes.

3 Reduce the heat to medium-low. Add the tomato. Cover the saucepan. Cook until the tomato becomes completely soft and mashed and is combined with the onion to form a coarse paste, stirring every minute or so and lightly mashing the tomato, about 5 minutes.

4 Add the cumin seeds, coriander, paprika, red pepper, salt, black pepper and sugar. Stir to combine. Cook uncovered for 5 minutes, stirring frequently. This is the *masala* (spice base). Transfer the masala (be careful, since it is hot) to a blender and blend until a smooth paste is formed.

5 Return the smooth paste to the saucepan. Add the cinnamon stick, butter, lime juice, heavy cream and water. Bring to a rolling boil over high heat. Reduce the heat to medium-low. Add the chicken. Simmer for 5 minutes, stirring occasionally. Enjoy now or let cool to room temperature and refrigerate or freeze for later!

Fragrant Chicken Curry

Chicken curry is perhaps one of the most common dishes in Indian cuisine, yet there are so many different versions of it. One thing that remains constant is that chicken curry is typically made with bone-in pieces of chicken for added flavor. This dish goes great with Plain Boiled Rice (page 79) or Rice with Cumin and Peas (page 78). You may also serve this dish with Indian breads such as Whole Wheat Flatbreads (page 64), Oven Baked White Breads (page 66) or Oven Baked Whole Wheat Breads (page 68). Pick your favorite sautéed vegetable dish, add a side of Three Vegetable Raita (page 37) and enjoy a great Indian meal!

Serves 4
Prep time: 15 minutes
Cook time: 30 minutes
Refrigerator life: 3 days
Freezer life: 1 month
Reheating method: Place the refrigerated or defrosted chicken curry in a saucepan over medium-low heat and stir periodically. A less preferred method is to place the chicken curry in a microwave, cover and stir periodically.

2½ lbs (1.25 kg) bone-in chicken pieces of your choice (see "Shopping Tip," below)
3 tablespoons vegetable oil
¼ teaspoon cumin seeds
¼ teaspoon mustard seeds
1 tablespoon minced garlic
1 tablespoon peeled and finely grated fresh ginger
1 small onion, diced
¼ teaspoon ground turmeric
¾ teaspoon ground red pepper (cayenne)
1¼ teaspoon salt
2½ teaspoons Garam Masala (page 44)
1 handful fresh mint leaves (about ¼ cup/5 g packed leaves), rinsed and chopped
1 handful fresh coriander leaves (cilantro) (about ¼ cup/10 g packed leaves), rinsed and chopped
Juice of ½ lime
1 cup (250 ml) water

1 If your butcher has cut the chicken pieces into sections, remove the skin and wash the cut chicken with cold water. If the chicken is not yet cut, remove the skin and cut the chicken into 2-inch (5-cm) sections with a chef's knife or cleaver. (Legs may be left whole if desired.) Wash the cut pieces of chicken with water.

2 Pour the oil into a large saucepan and place over medium heat. When the oil is heated, add the cumin seeds and mustard seeds. Sauté until the cumin seeds turn brown and you hear the mustard seeds pop, stirring frequently, about 10 seconds. Do not let the cumin seeds burn and turn black.

3 Add the garlic, ginger and onion. Stir to combine. Sauté until the onion is translucent, stirring frequently, about 3 minutes.

4 Add the chicken, turmeric, red pepper, salt, Garam Masala, mint leaves, coriander leaves, lime juice and water. Stir to combine. Bring to a rolling boil over high heat.

5 Reduce the heat to medium. Partially cover the saucepan. Simmer until the chicken is tender and cooked so that it separates easily with a fork when done, stirring occasionally, about 25 minutes. Enjoy now or let cool to room temperature and refrigerate or freeze for later!

> **SHOPPING TIP:** The chicken pieces will need to be broken down into 2-inch (5-cm) sections. If you have a helpful butcher, ask him or her to cut them into sections. It will make things easier for you because the bones are tough to cut.

Oven Baked Tandoori Chicken

Oven Baked Tandoori Chicken

This is my version of *tandoori* chicken—the red-hued oven-baked chicken served at almost every Indian restaurant. The bright red hue usually comes from artificial food coloring, but I like to get a hint of natural color by using paprika. As the name suggests, tandoori chicken is traditionally cooked in a *tandoor*, which is an open fire pit heated with coal or wood, but you can get similar results in an oven, or you may even use an outdoor grill. I like to make this dish when having a dinner party, since it is so easy to make. I marinate the chicken the day before, and then an hour before the guests arrive, I will ask my husband to cook the chicken. Then I will place the cooked chicken in a serving platter, cover it with foil, and keep it in the warm oven until dinner is served. This way it does not dry out, stays warm, and make cooking dinner a breeze! Tandoori chicken goes well with the Indian breads like Oven Baked Whole Wheat Breads (page 68) or Oven Baked White Breads (page 66) and a side of Mint Chutney (page 50), along with a curried vegetable dish of your choice. You may even serve this with Plain Boiled Rice (page 79) or Rice with Cumin and Peas (page 78) instead of bread.

Serves 3 to 4
Prep time: 15 minutes + 1 hour marinating (you may marinate up to 1 day in advance)
Cook time: 30 minutes
Refrigerator life: 3 days
Freezer life: 1 month
Reheating method: Place the refrigerated or defrosted chicken in a warmed oven (about 350°F/175°C) and heat. A less preferred method is to heat the chicken in a microwave.

Approximately 2 lbs (1 kg) bone-in chicken pieces (thighs and drumsticks)
2 tablespoons vegetable oil
Juice of 1 lime
1 small onion, sliced into thin circles

Marinade

1 tablespoon minced garlic
Juice of 1 lime
3 tablespoons vegetable oil
3/4 teaspoon cumin seeds, roasted and ground (see page 24)
1/2 teaspoon ground coriander
1 teaspoon paprika
1/2 teaspoon ground red pepper (cayenne)
3/4 teaspoon salt
1/2 teaspoon ground black pepper
1 1/2 teaspoons store-bought or Home-made Plain Yogurt (page 36)

1 Remove the skin from the chicken pieces. Wash the pieces with cold water and cut deep diagonal slashes in the pieces.
2 Place all the ingredients for the Marinade in a large bowl. Mix well. Add the chicken to the bowl with the Marinade and mix well, making sure all sides of the chicken and the inside of the slashes are coated with the Marinade. Cover and place in the refrigerator to marinate for at least 1 hour, or up to 1 day.
3 Preheat the oven to 500°F (260°C). While the oven is heating up, remove the chicken from the refrigerator to allow it to come to room temperature or at least warm up a bit for faster and even cooking.
4 Spread 1 tablespoon of the oil evenly on a baking sheet. Place the chicken pieces on the oiled baking sheet and pour any excess Marinade over them. Bake for 15 minutes.
5 Using tongs, turn the chicken. Brush on the remaining 1 tablespoon of oil. Bake for 15 minutes more, or until there are no signs of pink when you insert a knife though the chicken.
6 Remove the chicken from the oven. Sprinkle the lime juice evenly on the chicken. Enjoy now or let cool to room temperature and refrigerate or freeze for later! Serve with the onion slices.

Lamb Vindaloo Curry

Vindaloo is a spicy dish that is common in homes in the western Indian state of Goa. The origins of this dish and its name come from Portugal. In the sixteenth century, when the Portugese came to Goa, they brought pork preserved in vinegar and garlic (*vin* meaning vinegar, and *aloo*, from the Portugese word *alho* for garlic) for their long journey. They also brought chili peppers, and Indians embraced them so well, that they spiced up the original Portuguese dish, and used chilies in some form or another in almost every other Indian dish! Today, this dish is made with meats such as pork, lamb, chicken and shrimp, but lamb seems to be a common favorite. This is the spiciest dish in this book, but if you feel you may not be able to handle the fiery intensity, you may reduce the number of red chili peppers to your tolerance level. This dish can be eaten with Indian breads such as Whole Wheat Flatbreads (page 64), Oven Baked White Breads (page 66) or Oven Baked Whole Wheat Breads (page 68), or with Plain Boiled Rice (page 79). It would also be a good idea to serve with a side of Homemade Plain Yogurt (page 36) to calm and sooth your stomach from the fiery peppers!

Serves 3 to 4

Prep time: 10 minutes + 35 minutes to boil the potato (can be done 1 day in advance) + 2 1/2 hours to make the lamb kebabs (can be done 1 day in advance)

Cook time: 20 minutes

Refrigerator life: 3 days

Freezer life: 1 month

Reheating method: Place the refrigerated or defrosted vindaloo in a saucepan over medium-low heat and stir periodically. A less preferred method is to place the vindaloo in a microwave, cover and stir periodically. If the reheated vindaloo seems too thick, you may add a bit of water to it.

1/2 recipe Lamb Kebabs (page 113)
1 medium russet potato (about 1/2 lb/250 g), boiled and cooled (see page 24)
5 dried finger-length red chili peppers, stems removed
1/2 teaspoon cumin seeds
1/2 teaspoon black peppercorns
One 1/4-in (6-mm) cinnamon stick
4 cloves
3 tablespoons vegetable oil
1 small onion, finely diced
1 fully ripe tomato, coarsely chopped
3 large garlic cloves
1 1/2 teaspoons peeled and coarsely chopped fresh ginger
1 tablespoon vinegar
1 tablespoon light brown sugar
1 teaspoon paprika
1/4 teaspoon ground turmeric
1/2 teaspoon salt
1 cup (250 ml) water

1 Prepare the Lamb Kebabs, if you have not already done so.

2 Peel the potato and cut into 1-inch (2.5-cm) cubes.

3 Grind the red chili peppers, cumin seeds, peppercorns, cinnamon stick and cloves to a fine powder in a coffee/spice grinder. Set aside.

4 Pour the oil into a medium saucepan and place over medium heat. When the oil is heated, add the onion. Sauté until the onion is very brown (but not black and burnt!), stirring frequently, about 10 minutes.

5 Process the tomato, garlic, ginger, vinegar and browned onion in a blender until smooth. Add the blended ingredients to the saucepan. Add the ground spices, brown sugar, paprika, turmeric and salt. Stir to combine. Cook for 3 minutes over medium heat, stirring frequently. The mixture will turn darker in color as it cooks.

6 Add the cubed potato, Lamb Kebabs and water. Stir to combine. Cook for 4 minutes, stirring occasionally. The dish will have a saucy consistency. Enjoy now or let cool to room temperature and refrigerate or freeze for later! Make sure everyone has a tall glass of water on the table before serving!

Chicken Vindaloo Curry

In this version the chicken is cooked right in the sauce, rather than precooking it first, because chicken does not take as much time as it does to cook lamb. To make Chicken Vindaloo, wash 1/2 lb (250 g) of boneless, skinless chicken breast with cold water and cut it into 1-inch (2.5-cm) cubes. Follow Steps 2 to 5 for Lamb Vinda-loo Curry. Add the chicken, stirring to com-bine, and cook for 2 minutes over medium heat, stirring frequently. Add the water and bring to a rolling boil over high heat.

Reduce the heat to medium and cover the saucepan. Simmer for 5 minutes, stirring occasionally. Add the cubed potato and cook uncovered until there are no signs of pink when you insert a knife though the chicken, stirring occasionally, about 4 minutes. The sauce will thicken a bit as it cooks. Enjoy now or let cool to room temperature and refrigerate or freeze for later! Don't forget to have lots of water at the table!

1 lb (500 g) ground lamb
2 tablespoons vegetable oil
1 dried finger-length red chili pepper
$^1/_2$ teaspoon cumin seeds
$^1/_2$ teaspoon mustard seeds
2 fresh finger-length green chili peppers, cut in half lengthwise
1 tablespoon minced garlic
1 tablespoon peeled and finely grated fresh ginger
$^1/_2$ onion, diced
$^1/_2$ cup (60 g) frozen or fresh parboiled green peas (see page 24)
$^1/_4$ teaspoon ground turmeric
$^1/_2$ teaspoon ground red pepper (cayenne)
$1^1/_4$ teaspoons salt
4 teaspoons Garam Masala (page 44)
6 large fresh mint leaves, rinsed, and chopped

1 Wash the ground lamb with cold water in a colander.
2 Cook the ground lamb in a medium skillet over medium heat, covered, stirring every minute or so with a spatula to break it apart, about 6 minutes. The lamb is fully cooked when it turns from pink to light brown. A lot of fatty liquid will be released as the lamb cooks. There should be no signs of pink left.
3 Drain the fatty liquid by carefully tilting the skillet into a bowl and holding back the meat with the cover. Discard the fat, but do not pour the fat down the sink or else you will clog it. Put the drained and cooked lamb aside in another bowl.
4 Pour the oil into the same skillet and place over medium heat. When the oil is heated, tear the red chili pepper in half and add to the skillet. Add the cumin seeds and mustard seeds. Sauté until the cumin seeds turn brown and you hear the mustard seeds pop, stirring frequently, about 10 seconds. Do not let the cumin seeds burn and turn black.
5 Add the green chili peppers, garlic, ginger, onion and peas. Stir to combine. Cook until the onions turn translucent, stirring frequently, about 5 minutes.
6 Add the cooked ground lamb, turmeric, red pepper, salt, Garam Masala and mint leaves. Stir to combine. Cover and cook, stirring every minute or so to allow the flavors to come together, about 3 minutes. Enjoy now, use to make Lamb Samosas (page 50), or let cool to room temperature and refrigerate or freeze for later!

Ground Lamb with Peas Keema Matar

In this dish, ground lamb and peas are sautéed and spiced with my mother-in-law's spice blend for Garam Masala (page 44). Keema matar goes best with Whole Wheat Flatbreads (page 64), Oven Baked White Breads (page 66) or Oven Baked Whole Wheat Breads (page 68), a curried vegetable dish of your choice, and a side of Three Vegetable Raita (page 37). You may even put this lamb and pea dish in a pita bread pocket, and drizzle some raita on top! This dish can also be used to do a meat variation on the traditional Potato Turnovers (page 50).

Serves 3 to 4
Prep time: 10 minutes
Cook time: 15 minutes
Refrigerator life: 3 days
Freezer life: 1 month

Reheating method: Place the refrigerated or defrosted keema matar in a skillet over medium-low heat and stir periodically. A less preferred method is to place the keema matar in a microwave and stir periodically.

Easy Lamb Curry

Lamb curry is an easy and flavorful curry that I make with bone-in loin chops, which are a tender cut of meat from the upper buttocks area of the lamb. If you prefer another cut of lamb meat, you may use that as well; just make sure it is a bone-in cut as the bones give extra flavor to the curry. This dish goes great with Plain Boiled Rice (page 79) or Rice with Cumin and Peas (page 78). You may also serve this dish with Indian breads such as Whole Wheat Flatbreads (page 64), Oven Baked White Breads (page 66) or Oven Baked Whole Wheat Breads (page 68).

Serves 3 to 4
Prep time: 10 minutes
Cook time: 40 minutes
Refrigerator life: 3 days
Freezer life: 1 month
Reheating method: Place the refrigerated or defrosted lamb curry in a saucepan over medium-low heat and stir periodically. A less preferred method is to place the lamb curry in a microwave, cover and stir periodically.

4 bone-in lamb loin chops, about 1 lb (500 g) total (see "Shopping Tip" below)
3 tablespoons vegetable oil
1/4 teaspoon cumin seeds
1/4 teaspoon mustard seeds
1 tablespoon minced garlic
1 tablespoon peeled and finely grated fresh ginger
1 small onion, diced
1/4 teaspoon ground turmeric
3/4 teaspoon ground red pepper (cayenne)
3/4 teaspoon salt
2 teaspoons Garam Masala (page 44)
1 handful fresh mint leaves (about 1/4 cup/5 g packed leaves), rinsed and chopped
1 1/2 cups (375 ml) water

1 If your butcher has cut the chops for you, trim any excess fat and discard and then wash the lamb pieces with cold water. If the loin chops are not yet cut, trim any excess fat and discard. If you have a sturdy cleaver, cut the chops into 1-inch (2.5-cm) or larger pieces. Or, simply cut the meat away from the bone and then cut it into 1-inch (2.5-cm) pieces. Leave some meat on the bones so there will be boneless and bone-in pieces to enjoy. Wash the cut loin chops with water.
2 Pour the oil into a medium saucepan and place over medium heat. When the oil is heated, add the cumin seeds and mustard seeds. Sauté until the cumin seeds turn brown and you hear the mustard seeds pop, stirring frequently, about 10 seconds. Do not let the cumin seeds burn and turn black.
3 Add the garlic, ginger and onion. Stir to combine. Sauté until the onion is translucent, stirring frequently, about 3 minutes.
4 Add the loin chop pieces, turmeric, red pepper, salt, Garam Masala, mint leaves and water. Stir to combine. Bring to a rolling boil over high heat.
5 Reduce the heat to medium-low. Cover the saucepan. Simmer until the meat is tender and cooked so that you can easily cut through it with a knife when done, stirring occasionally, about 35 minutes. Enjoy now or let cool to room temperature and refrigerate or freeze for later!

SHOPPING TIP: The lamb chops need to be broken down into 1-inch (2.5-cm) or larger pieces. If you have a helpful butcher, ask him or her break the chops or other bone-in cut of lamb down into pieces. It will make things easier for you because the bones are tough to cut! Of course, if you forget to ask your butcher to do this, there is an easier back-up method (described in Step 1).

Lamb Chops with Indian Spice Rub

This recipe for lamb chops is a quick-and-easy way to make a fancy restaurant-style dish. First, I marinate the lamb chops and then sear them in a hot skillet, which causes the outside to cook and seal in the juices, keeping the inside tender. If you prefer lamb cooked to medium-well doneness, you have the option of finishing them off in the oven. This dish is made with tender lamb rib chops, which are small cuts of bone-in meat taken from the rib section. I prefer to get Frenched chops, in which the bone end of the chop is trimmed of fat and exposed, which adds a bit of elegance to the presentation. These lamb chops go well with Oven Baked White Breads (page 66) or Oven Baked Whole Wheat Breads (page 68), along with a side of Mint Chutney (page 40).

Serves 4
Prep time: 5 minutes + 2 hours marinating (you may marinate up to 1 day in the refrigerator)
Cook time: 12 to 22 minutes
Refrigerator life: 3 days
Freezer life: 1 month
Reheating method: Place the refrigerated or defrosted lamb chops in a warmed oven (about 350°F /175°C) and heat. A less preferred method is to heat the lamb chops in a microwave.

8 lamb rib chops
3 to 4 tablespoons vegetable oil

Indian Spice Rub

2 tablespoons minced garlic
Juice of 1 lime
1/2 teaspoon cumin seeds, roasted and ground (see page 24)
1/2 teaspoon ground nutmeg
1/2 teaspoon ground red pepper (cayenne)
3/4 teaspoon salt
1/2 teaspoon ground black pepper
1 handful fresh mint leaves (about 1/4 cup/ 5 g packed leaves), rinsed and finely chopped

1 Wash the rib chops with cold water.
2 To make the Indian Spice Rub: Place all the ingredients in a small bowl. Mix well.
3 Rub all sides of the chops with the Indian Spice Rub. Place the chops on a plate. Cover and refrigerate for 2 hours, or up to 1 day. About 15 minutes before you plan to cook the lamb, remove it from the refrigerator to allow it to come to room temperature.
4 If you prefer lamb medium-well to well-done, preheat the oven to 400°F (200°C). (The chops will be finished off in the oven after first pan-searing them.)
5 Pour 2 tablespoons of the oil into a large cast-iron skillet and place over medium-high heat. When the oil is heated, add 4 of the chops. Cook until the bottoms are seared, about 3 minutes. They will be brown and slightly crusted when properly seared.
6 Using tongs, turn all the lamb chops. Cook until the underside is seared, about 3 minutes. The inside will be pink and tender, and the outside will be nicely seared. Remove from the skillet.
7 Add 1 tablespoon of the oil and the remaining 4 lamb chops to the skillet and cook the same way. If you prefer lamb cooked medium-rare, you may enjoy the lamb chops now. If you prefer lamb medium-well to well-done, go on to the next step.
8 Spread the remaining 1 tablespoon of oil evenly on a baking sheet. Lay the seared lamb chops on the oiled baking sheet. Bake the chops for 5 minutes. Using tongs, turn the chops and bake to desired doneness, about 5 minutes more for almost well-done. The lamb will have just a hint of dark pink when you insert a knife through it when it is well-done. Enjoy now or let cool to room temperature and refrigerate or freeze for later!

Lamb Kebabs

For these kebabs, small chunks of lamb are skewered on bamboo sticks and baked in an oven. When the weather is pleasant, you can cook these lamb kebabs on an outdoor grill. You may serve these kebabs on a bed of Rice with Cumin and Peas (page 78) or you may eat them with Oven Baked Whole Wheat Breads (page 68) or Oven Baked White Breads (page 66). Whichever way you serve them, you can add a side of Mint Chutney (page 40). You may also use these kebabs to make the fiery hot Lamb Vindaloo Curry (page 108). In this recipe, I use boneless leg of lamb, but if you prefer goat meat, which is more common in India, you may use that instead. (*Note*: If you use goat meat for this recipe, marinate the goat meat for a minimum of three hours since goat meat is tougher than lamb.)

Serves 3 to 4

Prep time: 10 minutes + 2 hours marinating, including 30 minutes to soak skewers (you may marinate up to 1 day in advance)

Cook time: 15 to 20 minutes

Refrigerator life: 3 days

Freezer life: 1 month

Reheating method: Place the refrigerated or defrosted kebabs in a warmed oven (about 350°F /175°C) and heat. A less preferred method is to heat the kebabs in a microwave.

1 lb (500 g) boneless leg of lamb
1 tablespoon vegetable oil
Four 12-in (30.5-cm) wooden skewers, soaked in water for 30 minutes

Marinade

2 tablespoons minced garlic
1 tablespoon peeled and finely grated fresh ginger
1/4 teaspoon ground turmeric
1/4 teaspoon ground red pepper (cayenne)
3/4 teaspoon salt
1/4 teaspoon ground black pepper
2 teaspoons Garam Masala (page 44)
3 tablespoons store-bought or Homemade Plain Yogurt (page 36)
1 handful fresh mint leaves (about 1/4 cup/5 g packed leaves), rinsed and finely chopped
1 tablespoon vegetable oil

1 Wash the lamb with cold water and cut into 1-inch (2.5cm) cubes.

2 Place the ingredients for the Marinade in a large bowl. Mix well. Add the lamb and mix well. Cover and refrigerate for at least 2 hours, or up to 1 day.

3 Preheat the oven to 450°F (230°C). While the oven is heating up, remove the lamb from the refrigerator to allow it to come to room temperature or at least warm up a bit for faster and even cooking. Spread the 1 tablespoon of the oil evenly on a baking sheet.

4 Thread the pieces of lamb evenly on the wooden skewers. Lay the skewers on the oiled baking sheet. Bake the skewers for 10 minutes.

5 Turn the skewers and bake to desired doneness—about 5 minutes more for medium-well or 10 minutes more for well-done. The lamb will be slightly pink when you insert a knife through it when it is medium-well, and will have just a hint of dark pink in the inside when it is well-done. Enjoy now or let cool to room temperature and refrigerate or freeze for later, or use these kebabs to make Lamb Vindaloo Curry (page 108)!

Chapter 5
Fish and Seafood

Seafood is very popular throughout India's vast coastal regions (it is surrounded by water on all sides except the north). And where meat, or certain types of meat, is not eaten regularly by all Indians, whether for economic or religious reasons, seafood is generally enjoyed by many Indians living in the coastal regions. Fishermen go out early in the morning in their small boats and with fishing nets to catch as many fish as they can, and return to the bustling markets and docks to sell their fresh catch to individuals, restaurant chefs or anyone who gets there first for the best deal and the freshest choices. Some fish are exported to international markets.

Fish and seafood is cooked in a variety of ways, from curries, to fried fish, to baked fish in the Indian *tandoor* oven, and more. I have chosen recipes with simple cooking techniques so that you can easily make and enjoy fish and seafood Indian style! I have even created a recipe using scallops, which are not common in Indian cuisine, but are quite popular in America. I use my mother's style of making a spiced tomato and onion base called a *masala*, and then cook the scallops in the masala for a few minutes to create Masala Scallops with Tomatoes and Onions (page 118). My dad enjoys fish and seafood, and he sometimes bakes salmon in an oven with Indian spices, and I share his recipe for Dad's Baked Salmon (page 116) with you as well.

Prawns are very popular in India, although I substitute shrimp because they are easily available in different sizes. Fish such as pomfret, king fish and mackerel are commonly found in the waters around India, but you may use any fish you prefer and is easy to find, even though it is not what I use in the recipe. If you would like to use a different fish than what I indicate in the recipe, try to use one that is similar in texture and flavor (such as flaky or firm, and mild or full flavored fish). Ask your fish monger to suggest a fish substitute . . . I find they are very knowledgeable and helpful since they work with fish all day!

Serves 4

Prep time: 5 minutes + 30 minutes marinating (you may marinate up to 1 hour in the refrigerator)

Cook time: 10 minutes

Refrigerator life: 1 day (best if served immediately)

Reheating method: Cover the refrigerated fish in foil so it does not dry out while reheating. Place in a warmed oven (about 350°F/175°C) and heat.

4 boneless salmon fillets with skin on (about 4 to 6 oz/125 to 175 g each)

1 tablespoon vegetable oil

Dad's Spice Rub

1½ tablespoons minced garlic

Juice of 2 limes

1 teaspoon carom seed (ajwain) or dried thyme leaves

½ teaspoon ground coriander

½ teaspoon ground red pepper (cayenne)

¾ teaspoon salt

½ teaspoon ground black pepper

1 Wash the fish with cold water. Combine all the ingredients for the Dad's Spice Rub in a small bowl. Gently rub all sides of the fish fillets with Dad's Spice Rub. Place the fillets on a plate, skin side down. Cover and refrigerate for 30 minutes, or up to 1 hour.

2 Preheat the oven to 450°F (230°C). While the oven is heating up, remove the fish from the refrigerator to allow it to come to room temperature or at least warm up a bit for faster and even cooking.

3 Spread the oil evenly on a baking sheet. Gently place the fillets on the oiled baking sheet, skin side down, and bake until the fish is opaque and flakes easily with a fork, about 10 minutes. Enjoy now or let cool to room temperature and refrigerate for later!

Dad's Baked Salmon

My dad does not cook frequently, but ever since he created this quick and easy recipe for baked salmon, I often hear him raving about it and he insisted I try it out! Well I did try it, and it is indeed quite simple. I actually do not prefer a full-flavored fish like salmon, but I have to say this dish is delicious. My dad especially likes the flavor of salmon, which is not readily available in India. So he then decided to make salmon "Indian style" and that is how he came up with this recipe. I like to cook salmon with the skin on because it helps to hold the delicate and flaky salmon flesh together when cooking and serving it. You can eat the skin, or leave it on your plate, whichever you prefer. For a light and healthy protein packed meal, you may pair this salmon dish along with my Fresh Lentil Sprout Salad (page 95) and a side of Rice with Cumin and Peas (page 78) or Lemon Rice (page 85).

Fish Curry

Traditionally in India, fish curry has pieces of fish with the bone-in and skin-on to add more flavor, but you can use boneless, skinless pieces if you prefer, as I do in this recipe. Here I use red snapper, although king fish, seerfish (a member of the mackerel family) or pomfret is more commonly used in India, but you may use any fish. I first marinate this fish in a simple spiced marinade, and then add it to a *masala* (cooked and spiced tomatoes and onions), and finish it off with water to create the curry consistency. This dish can be eaten with Whole Wheat Flatbreads (page 64), Oven Baked White Breads (page 66) or Oven Baked Whole Wheat Breads (page 68), or with Plain Boiled Rice (page 79) or Rice with Cumin and Peas (page 78). This dish tastes even better after being refrigerated for one day, simply because the flavors in the curry have more time to develop.

Serves 3 to 4
Prep time: 10 minutes + 30 minutes marinating (you may marinate up to 1 hour in advance)
Cook time: 30 minutes
Refrigerator life: 2 days

Reheating method: Place the refrigerated fish curry in a saucepan over medium-low heat and stir periodically. Or, place the fish curry in a microwave, cover and stir periodically.

1 lb (500 g) boneless, skinless red snapper fillets
3 tablespoons vegetable oil
2 teaspoons minced garlic
1 teaspoon peeled and finely grated fresh ginger
1/2 small onion, grated on the largest grating holes on a box grater or in a food processor
1 fully ripe tomato, cut into 4 pieces
1/4 teaspoon ground turmeric
1/4 teaspoon ground red pepper (cayenne)
1/2 teaspoon salt
1/2 teaspoon ground black pepper
1 cup (250 ml) water

Marinade
2 teaspoons minced garlic
1 teaspoon peeled and finely grated fresh ginger
Juice of 2 limes
1/4 teaspoon ground turmeric
1/4 teaspoon ground red pepper (cayenne)
1/4 teaspoon salt
1/4 teaspoon ground black pepper

1 Wash the fish with cold water and cut into 2-inch (5-cm) pieces. Spread out the cut pieces in a wide dish.
2 Combine all the ingredients for the Marinade in a small bowl. Pour half of the Marinade evenly over the fish pieces. Turn over the fish pieces and pour the rest of the marinade over them. Cover and refrigerate for 30 minutes, or up to 1 hour.
3 Pour the oil into a wide saucepan and place over medium heat. When the oil is heated, add the garlic, ginger and onion. Sauté until the onion is golden brown, stirring frequently, about 6 minutes.
4 Reduce the heat to medium-low. Add the tomato and cover the saucepan. Cook until the tomato becomes completely soft and mashed and is combined with the onion to form a coarse paste, stirring every minute or so and lightly mashing the tomato, about 5 minutes.
5 Add the turmeric, red pepper, salt and black pepper. Stir to combine. Cook uncovered for 6 minutes, stirring frequently. This is the *masala* (spice base).
6 Add the fish and any excess Marinade to the saucepan. Stir to combine. Cook for 5 minutes, gently stirring occasionally. Add the water and stir to combine.
7 Bring to a rolling boil over high heat. Reduce the heat to medium. Cook until the fish is opaque and flakes easily with a fork, about 6 minutes. Enjoy now or let cool to room temperature and refrigerate for later!

Masala Scallops with Tomatoes and Onions

Scallops are shellfish that grow inside a beautiful hinged shell. There are different types of scallops such as the smaller bay scallops and the larger sea scallops. Scallops are not commonly found in India, but I know how popular scallops are among my American friends, which inspired me to make them in a delectable Indian style. In this dish, the scallops are seared in a *masala* (spiced tomato and onion base) that has a unique peppery punch from carom seeds. This dish can be eaten with Indian breads such as Whole Wheat Flatbreads (page 64), Oven Baked White Breads (page 66) or Oven Baked Whole Wheat Breads (page 68). It can even be served with Plain Boiled Rice (page 79) or Rice with Cumin and Peas (page 78).

Serves 4
Prep time: 10 minutes
Cook time: 25 minutes
Refrigerator life: 2 days
Reheating method: Place the refrigerated scallops in a skillet over medium-low heat and turn periodically. Or, place the scallops in a microwave and turn periodically.

12 to 14 sea scallops (about 1 lb/500 g)
4 tablespoons vegetable oil
2 tablespoons minced garlic
1 small onion, grated on the largest grating holes on a box grater or in a food processor
1 fully ripe tomato, cut into 4 pieces
1/2 teaspoon cumin seeds
1 teaspoon carom seeds (ajwain) or dried thyme leaves
1/4 teaspoon ground turmeric
1/2 teaspoon ground red pepper (cayenne)
3/4 teaspoon salt
3/4 teaspoon ground black pepper

1 Remove the muscle from the scallop by feeling around the scallop to locate the tough and rubbery opaque muscle. If you do not find it, it may have already been removed. Using your fingers, grab the muscle and pull it off and discard. Wash the scallops with cold water.

2 Pour the oil into a large skillet and place over medium heat. When the oil is heated, add the garlic and onion. Sauté until the onion is golden brown, stirring frequently, about 6 minutes.

3 Reduce the heat to medium-low. Add the tomato. Cover the skillet. Cook until the tomato becomes completely soft and mashed and is combined with the onion to form a coarse paste, stirring every minute or so and lightly mashing the tomato, about 5 minutes.

4 Add the cumin seeds, carom seeds, turmeric, red pepper, salt and black pepper. Stir to combine. Cook uncovered for 5 minutes, stirring frequently. This is the *masala* (spice base).

5 Add the scallops, making sure they do not overlap. Stir to combine. Increase the heat to medium. Cook for about 6 minutes, turning the scallops once after 3 minutes. Spoon some of the masala on top of the scallops as they cook so the flavors will be absorbed. When cooked, the scallops will be opaque throughout. Enjoy now or let cool to room temperature and refrigerate for later!

> **TIP:** Scallops are typically sold shucked (removed from the shell) and fresh, or shucked and frozen. If you bought frozen scallaps, thaw them in the refrigerator the same day you plan to cook them.

Easy Shrimp Curry Masala Jhinga

In this dish, shrimp are cooked in a *masala* (spiced tomato and onion base) in which I combined the cooking styles and flavor of northern and southern India. The masala base is a northern Indian style used by my mother, but I have added mustard seeds as a spice, which are common in southern Indian cooking and are used by my mother-in-law. I then add a little bit of water to give a saucy currylike consistency to the final dish. Since this shrimp dish has a saucy consistency, it goes well with Plain Boiled Rice (page 79) or Rice with Cumin and Peas (page 78), or even with Indian breads such as Whole Wheat Flatbreads (page 64), Oven Baked White Breads (page 66) or Oven Baked Whole Wheat Breads (page 68).

Serves 3 to 4
Prep time: 10 minutes
Cook time: 25 minutes
Refrigerator life: 2 days

Reheating method: Place the refrigerated shrimp curry in a saucepan over medium-low heat and stir periodically. Or, place the shrimp curry in a microwave and stir periodically.

1 lb (500 g) shrimp (in the 40 to 50 per lb range)
3 tablespoons vegetable oil
2 dried finger-length red chili peppers
3/4 teaspoon cumin seeds
3/4 teaspoon mustard seeds
1 small onion, grated on the largest grating holes on a box grater or in a food processor
1 fully ripe tomato, cut into 4 pieces
1/4 teaspoon ground turmeric
1/2 teaspoon ground red pepper (cayenne)
1/2 teaspoon salt
3/4 teaspoon ground black pepper
1 1/2 teaspoons Garam Masala (page 44)
1/4 cup (65 ml) water

1 If you're using shrimp with their peels and heads on, remove their heads, peel the shrimp, remove their tails and devein them. (See "Peeling and deveining shrimp", page 25.) Rinse the peeled shrimp in cold water.

2 Pour the oil into a medium nonstick skillet and place over medium heat. When the oil is heated, tear open and add the red chili peppers, cumin seeds and mustard seeds. Sauté until the cumin seeds turn brown and you hear the mustard seeds pop, stirring frequently, about 10 seconds. Do not let the cumin seeds burn and turn black. Immediately add the onion. Sauté until the onion is golden brown, stirring frequently, about 6 minutes.

3 Reduce the heat to medium-low. Add the tomato and cover the saucepan. Cook until the tomato becomes completely soft and mashed and is combined with the onion to form a coarse paste, stirring every minute or so and lightly mashing the tomato, about 5 minutes.

4 Add the turmeric, red pepper, salt, black pepper and Garam Masala. Stir to combine. Cook uncovered for 6 minutes, stirring frequently. This is the *masala* (spice base).

5 Add the shrimp. Stir to combine. Add the water and increase the heat to medium. Cook until the shrimp are opaque and they curl up, stirring frequently, about 5 minutes. Enjoy now or let cool to room temperature and refrigerate for later!

1 lb (500 g) boneless, skinless tilapia fillets
3 tablespoons vegetable oil
2 teaspoons minced garlic
1 teaspoon peeled and finely grated fresh ginger
1 small onion, grated on the largest grating holes on a
  box grater or shredded in a food processor
1 fully ripe tomato, cut into 4 pieces
1/2 teaspoon carom seeds (ajwain) or dried thyme
  leaves
1/4 teaspoon ground turmeric
1/4 teaspoon ground red pepper (cayenne)
3/4 teaspoon salt
1/2 teaspoon ground black pepper

Marinade
2 teaspoons minced garlic
1 teaspoon peeled and finely grated fresh ginger
Juice of 2 limes
2 teaspoons carom seeds (ajwain) or dried thyme
  leaves
1/4 teaspoon ground red pepper (cayenne)
1/4 teaspoon salt
1/4 teaspoon ground black pepper

1 Wash the fish with cold water and cut into 2-inch (5-cm) pieces. Spread out the cut pieces in a wide dish.
2 Place the ingredients for the Marinade in a small bowl. Mix well. Pour half of the Marinade evenly over the fish pieces. Turn over the fish pieces and pour the rest of the Marinade over them. Cover and refrigerate for 30 minutes, or up to 1 hour.
3 Pour the oil into a large nonstick skillet and place over medium heat. When the oil is heated, add the garlic, ginger and onion. Sauté until the onion is golden brown, stirring frequently, about 6 minutes.
4 Reduce the heat to medium-low. Add the tomato and cover the saucepan. Cook until the tomato becomes completely soft and mashed and is combined with the onion to form a coarse paste, stirring every minute or so and lightly mashing the tomato, about 5 minutes.
5 Add the carom seeds, turmeric, red pepper, salt and black pepper. Cook uncovered for 6 minutes, stirring frequently. This is the *masala* (spice base).
6 Add the fish and any excess Marinade to the skillet. Try not to overlap the fish pieces. Gently stir. Cook for 4 minutes. Gently turn all the pieces of fish. Cook until the fish is opaque and flakes easily with a fork, about 3 minutes. Enjoy now or let cool to room temperature and refrigerate for later!

Simple Spiced Fish   Masala Machlee

In this fish dish, I first marinate the fish in a lime juice marinade with carom seeds ("bishops weed" or *ajwain* in Hindi), and then I sauté the marinated fish in a *masala* (cooked tomatoes and onions) spiced with more carom seeds for a peppery punch. When making this dish, I use Tilapia since I prefer mild flavor fish, but you can use any boneless, skinless fish fillets of your choice. This dish goes best with Whole Wheat Flatbreads (page 64), Oven Baked White Breads (page 66) or Oven Baked Whole Wheat Breads (page 68), but you may also serve it along with Plain Boiled Rice (page 79) or Rice with Cumin and Peas (page 78).

Serves 3 to 4
Prep time: 10 minutes + 30 minutes marinating (you may marinate up to 1 hour in advance)
Cook time: 25 minutes

Refrigerator life: 2 days
Reheating method: Place the refrigerated fish in a skillet over medium-low heat and turn periodically. Or, place the fish in a microwave and turn periodically.

Serves 3 to 4
Prep time: 10 minutes   **Cook time:** 25 minutes + 30 minutes resting
Refrigerator life: 2 days   **Reheating method:** Place the refrigerated fish curry in a saucepan over medium-low heat and stir periodically. Or, place the fish curry in a microwave, cover and stir periodically.

2 to 3 whole catfish (heads removed) (2¹/₂ lbs/1.25 kg total), (see "Shopping Tip" below)
3 tablespoons vegetable oil
2 dried finger-length red chili peppers
¹/₂ teaspoon cumin seeds
¹/₂ teaspoon mustard seeds
1 onion, diced
1 tablespoon minced garlic
1 tablespoon peeled and finely grated fresh ginger
2 fresh finger-length green chili peppers, cut in half lengthwise
1 teaspoon tamarind concentrate (paste)
2 cups (500 ml) water
¹/₄ teaspoon ground turmeric
¹/₄ teaspoon ground red pepper (cayenne)
1 teaspoon salt
2 teaspoons Garam Masala (page 44)
Juice of 1 lime
1 handful fresh coriander leaves (cilantro) (about ¹/₄ cup/10 g packed leaves), rinsed and chopped

Tamarind Fish Curry Chepala Pulusu

This catfish dish is a *pulusu*, which is a tamarind-based curry dish from the southern Indian state of Andhra Pradesh. This dish is typically made with whole bone-in catfish that is cut into two or three pieces. The bones add flavor to the curry, and hold together the delicate pieces of catfish. Fish pulusu is typically served with Plain Boiled Rice (page 79), but you may also serve it with Whole Wheat Flatbreads (page 64), Oven Baked White Breads (page 66) or Oven Baked Whole Wheat Breads (page 68). This dish tastes best when it's allowed to sit for thirty minutes after it has finished cooking so the fish can absorb even more flavor.

1 Remove the tail, fins and skin of each catfish. Wash the catfish with cold water and cut each fish crosswise into 2 or 3 pieces (steaks), about 3-inch (7.5-cm) each.

2 Pour the oil into a wide stockpot and place over medium heat. When the oil is heated, tear open and add the red chili peppers, cumin seeds and mustard seeds. Sauté until the cumin seeds turn brown and you hear the mustard seeds pop, stirring frequently, about 10 seconds. Immediately add the onion, garlic, ginger and green chili peppers. Cook for 2 minutes, stirring frequently.

3 Add the tamarind, water, turmeric, red pepper, salt and Garam Masala. Bring to a rolling boil over high heat. Reduce the heat to medium. Cover and simmer until the onion is translucent, stirring occasionally, about 8 minutes.

4 Add the lime juice and coriander leaves. Stir to combine. Add the fish pieces, making sure not to overlap them. Bring to a rolling boil over high heat. Reduce the heat to medium. Cook, covered, for 5 minutes.

5 Gently turn the fish. Cook, covered, until the fish is opaque and flakes easily with a fork, about 4 minutes. Turn off the heat and let rest covered for 30 minutes. Enjoy now or refrigerate for later!

SHOPPING TIP: Whole catfish are typically sold with the head already removed. To make things easier, ask your fish monger to remove the tail, fins and skin of each whole fish. If your fish monger is in a very helpful mood, also ask him or her to cut each fish crosswise into 2 or 3 pieces (steaks), about 3 inches (7.5 cm) each. Then all you need to do is wash the steaks with cold water when you get home and proceed to Step 2.

Fish with Coconut Curry

I had once dined at a Spanish tapas (small plates) restaurant and my friend had ordered monkfish in coconut curry. At first I was a bit hesitant to try the dish, since I had seen an actual monkfish before, and it was not a beautiful sight! But the spices, color, and aroma of the coconut curry enticed me, so I went ahead and tried the dish, and I was pleasantly surprised at the delicious, delicately sweet taste. Coconut curry based fish and seafood dishes are common in the southern region of Indian, but monkfish is not commonly found in India, so I decided to make an Indian flavored coconut curry dish with monkfish. This dish may be served with Plain Boiled Rice (page 79) or Rice with Cumin and Peas (page 78), or with Indian breads such as Whole Wheat Flatbreads (page 64) or Oven Baked White Breads (page 66).

Serves 3 to 4
Prep time: 10 minutes   **Cook time:** 25 minutes
Refrigerator life: 2 days
Reheating method: Place the refrigerated fish curry in a saucepan over medium-low heat and stir periodically. Or, place the fish curry in a microwave, cover and stir periodically.

1 lb (500 g) boneless, skinless monkfish fillets
3 tablespoons vegetable oil
2 teaspoons minced garlic
1 teaspoon peeled and finely grated fresh ginger
1/2 small onion, grated on the largest grating holes on a box grater or in a food processor
1 fully ripe tomato, cut into 4 pieces
1/4 teaspoon ground turmeric
1/2 teaspoon ground red pepper (cayenne)
1/2 teaspoon salt
1 teaspoon Garam Masala (page 44)
2 fresh finger-length green chili peppers, cut in half lengthwise
1 cup (250 ml) coconut milk
1/4 cup (65 ml) water

1 Wash the fish with cold water and cut into 3-inch (7.5-cm) pieces.
2 Pour the oil into a medium saucepan and place over medium heat. When the oil is heated, add the garlic, ginger and onion. Sauté until the onion is golden brown, stirring frequently, about 6 minutes.
3 Reduce the heat to medium-low. Add the tomato and cover the saucepan. Cook until the tomato becomes completely soft and mashed and is combined with the onion to form a coarse paste, stirring every minute or so and lightly mashing the tomato, about 5 minutes.
4 Add the turmeric, red pepper, salt and Garam Masala. Stir to combine. Cook uncovered for 2 minutes, stirring frequently. This is the *masala* (spice base).
5 Add the fish. Cook for 2 minutes, stirring gently. Add the green chili peppers, coconut milk and water. Stir to combine. Bring to a rolling boil over high heat.
6 Reduce the heat to medium-low and cover the saucepan. Simmer until the fish is opaque, stirring occasionally, about 5 minutes. Enjoy now or let cool to room temperature and refrigerate for later!

chapter 6
Vegetarian Dishes

This is the go-to chapter for vegetarians, or for meat eaters who love a diverse table with a contrast of flavors and textures (and, of course, a balanced diet). Vegetables are a major part of Indian cuisine since they are relatively easy and economical to grow and cook, and many Indians are vegetarian due to economic, cultural and religious reasons.

In Hindi, vegetables and vegetable dishes are called *subzee*. During my childhood summer vacations in India, when I would be lounging in my grandmother's home, I would sometimes hear the vegetable vendor melodiously yell out the names of all the vegetables on his big flat wooden cart as he pushed it through the neighborhood streets. I would run out and stop him while my grandmother caught up, and then I would watch her pick though the colorful vegetables to choose the best ones. If my mother and I were out shopping or sightseeing and we missed the vegetable cart in the day or we wanted to take home some extra vegetables, we would stop by the neighborhood vegetable store and choose some vegetables to make for dinner. The shop owner sat in the middle of his elevated shop with his scale, surrounded with fresh vegetables all around him. He would put the chosen vegetables on one end of the scale, and measured weights on the other end to price it for us. Then he would wrap the vegetables in newspapers, and we would place them in our tote and walk home, in anticipation of the subzee Grandmother would prepare!

Cooking vegetables Indian style is simply amazing! The flavors, textures and colors that can be achieved by cooking vegetables with Indian spices are so complex, that I hope after making these recipes, you'll see vegetables in a different light and you will never think of eating plain steamed or bland vegetables again! You can take any vegetable and easily turn it into a unique and flavorful Indian dish.

Along with vegetables, this chapter includes dishes made with *paneer*, the famous Indian cheese that is easy to make at home. I love dishes made from homemade paneer and can never get enough of them, especially my all-time favorite Creamed Spinach with Cheese Cubes (page 140), which is commonly known as *saag paneer*. Eggs, too, are delicious when cooked Indian style, and they can be served at any meal, not just breakfast or brunch. My mother's Scrambled Breakfast Eggs (page 137) is one of my husband's favorite dishes!

If you are not a vegetarian yet, this chapter just might make one out of you! These vegetarian dishes are easy to make, taste wonderful and are great for your health!

Potato and Pea Curry Aloo Matar

This recipe starts off looking like a thin curry, but as the water is cooked off, a nice thick sauce is created, and if cooked further, until all the water cooks off, it becomes a dry dish. My grandmother used to cook off all the water and pack this dish for my mom's school lunch since it packed well as a dry lunch (not runny liquid) along with a soft and buttery Flaky Wheat Breads (page 70) and a small piece of Mango Pickle (page 41). But when guests would come over, to make it go further, she would add a bit more water and cook it just until a thick curry was left. This dish can be eaten with Indian breads, such as Whole Wheat Flatbreads (page 64), Oven Baked White Breads (page 66) or Oven Baked Whole Wheat Breads (page 68), or with Plain Boiled Rice (page 79) or Rice with Cumin and Peas (page 78).

Serves 4
Prep time: 10 minutes
Cook time: 35 minutes
Refrigerator life: 3 days
Freezer life: 1 month
Reheating method: Place the refrigerated or defrosted curry in a microwave, cover and stir periodically. Or, place it in a saucepan over medium-low heat and stir periodically.

3 tablespoons vegetable oil
1 teaspoon peeled and finely grated fresh ginger
1/2 small onion, grated on the largest grating holes on a box grater or shredded in a food processor
1 small fully ripe tomato, such as plum (Roma), cut into 4 pieces
1/4 teaspoon ground turmeric
1/4 teaspoon ground red pepper (cayenne)
1/2 teaspoon salt
1/2 teaspoon ground black pepper
1 medium russet potato (about 1/2 lb/ 250 g), peeled and cut into 1 in (2.5 cm) cubes
1 cup (120 g) frozen or fresh parboiled green peas (see page 24)
1 cup (250 ml) water

1 Pour the oil into a medium saucepan and place over medium heat. When the oil is heated, add the ginger and onion. Sauté until the onion is golden brown, stirring frequently, about 5 minutes.
2 Reduce the heat to medium-low. Add the tomato. Cover the saucepan. Cook until the tomato becomes completely soft and mashed, and is combined with the onion to form a coarse paste, stirring every minute or so and lightly mashing the tomato, about 5 minutes.
3 Add the turmeric, red pepper, salt and black pepper. Stir to combine. Cook uncovered for 6 minutes, stirring frequently. This is the *masala* (spice base). Add the potato, peas and water. Stir to combine. Bring to a rolling boil over high heat.
4 Stir and reduce the heat to medium. Simmer uncovered for 10 minutes, stirring occasionally. Cover the saucepan. Cook, stirring every minute, until you can easily insert a knife through the potato cubes, about 5 minutes. The water should be almost all cooked off, leaving a saucy consistency, or you can cook it until all the water is gone to create a dry "sauté"-style dish. Enjoy now or let cool to room temperature and refrigerate or freeze for later!

Potato and Pea Curry

Simple Potato Curry Tharee Aloo

Potato curry is a simple and hearty dish for breakfast or lunch, but you can enjoy it any time in the day. Here, I use boiled potatoes, which easily release their starches in the curry, creating a thicker consistency than when raw potatoes are used. This dish goes best with Flaky Wheat Breads (page 70) or Puffed Fried Breads (page 74), and served with a side of Homemade Plain Yogurt (page 36). You can also serve this with Plain Boiled Rice (page 79) or Rice with Cumin and Peas (page 78).

Serves 4
Prep time: 5 minutes + 35 minutes to boil the potatoes (can be done 1 day in advance)
Cook time: 25 minutes
Refrigerator life: 3 days
Freezer life: 1 month
Reheating method: Place the refrigerated or defrosted curry in a microwave, cover and stir periodically. Or, place it in a saucepan over medium-low heat and stir periodically.

2 medium russet potatoes (total 1 lb/ 500 g), boiled (see page 24)
3 tablespoons vegetable oil
1 fully ripe tomato, cut into 4 pieces
1/2 teaspoon cumin seeds
1/4 teaspoon ground turmeric
1/4 teaspoon ground red pepper (cayenne)
1 teaspoon salt
1/2 teaspoon ground black pepper
1 1/2 cups (375 ml) water

1 Peel the potatoes and cut into 3/4-inch (2-cm) cubes.
2 Pour the oil into a medium saucepan and place over medium heat. When the oil is heated, add the tomato. Cover the saucepan and cook until the tomato becomes completely soft and mashed, stirring every minute or so and lightly mashing the tomato, about 5 minutes.
3 Add the cumin seeds, turmeric, red pepper, salt and black pepper. Stir to combine. Cook uncovered for 3 minutes, stirring frequently. This is the *masala* (spice base).
4 Add the potatoes and water. Bring to a rolling boil over high heat.
5 Reduce the heat to medium. Simmer uncovered for 10 minutes, stirring occasionally. The curry will thicken a bit as it cooks. Enjoy now or let cool to room temperature and refrigerate or freeze for later! You will notice that the curry thickens a bit more as the dish cools.

Roasted Eggplant Baingan Bharta

Smoked eggplant is one of my favorite Indian dishes, and is fun to make, although it might make a small mess on your stove! The eggplant is roasted directly over the open flame on a gas stovetop. If you don't have a gas stove, you could roast the eggplant under an oven broiler—it is not as messy, but you will not get the smoky taste that comes from cooking directly over an open flame. This dish can be served with Whole Wheat Flatbreads (page 64), Oven Baked White Breads (page 66) or Oven Baked Whole Wheat Breads (page 68). When serving this dish, one lucky person will get the stem of the eggplant which they can enjoy by sucking on it to get all the cooked eggplant flesh out from it.

Serves 4
Prep time: 5 minutes
Cook time: 25 minutes if using gas stove
Refrigerator life: 3 days
Freezer life: 1 month
Reheating method: Place the refrigerated or defrosted eggplant in a microwave and stir periodically. Or, place it in a saucepan over medium-low heat and stir periodically.

1 large eggplant, globe variety (about
   1 lb/500 g)
3 tablespoons vegetable oil (plus 1 extra
   teaspoon oil if using an oven)
1 small onion, diced
1 fully ripe tomato, coarsely chopped
1/4 teaspoon ground red pepper (cayenne)
1/2 teaspoon salt

1 If you're using a gas stove to roast the eggplant, place aluminum foil under a large burner to make clean-up easier. Wash and dry the eggplant. Place the eggplant directly on the gas burner on high heat. Using tongs, frequently turn the eggplant to make sure all sides are evenly cooked, about 8 minutes. When done, the eggplant will become very soft and mushy. The skin will be charred, and it will have collapsed in on itself. Also, some liquid will be coming out of it during the cooking process, which will be caught by the foil. Remove from the heat and let cool. Discard the foil.
2 If you're using your oven to roast the eggplant, preheat the broiler to high. Wash and dry

the eggplant. Rub 1 teaspoon of the oil on the eggplant so it will not dry out while cooking. Place the eggplant on a baking sheet on the highest rack possible near the broiler and turn frequently until the eggplant is evenly charred and the flesh is soft and mushy, about 25 minutes. Remove from the heat and let cool.
3 Using your fingers, peel the skin off the eggplant and discard. After you have removed the skin, hold the eggplant over your sink by the stem with one hand. Wet your other hand and very gently grab the eggplant and run your wet hand down it to help take off any small remaining bits of skin.
4 Place the eggplant in a shallow dish. Holding the eggplant by the stem, use a potato masher to mash the eggplant flesh and break it apart. (The stem will become separated from the eggplant flesh. Do not discard the stem.)
5 Pour the oil into a medium saucepan and place over medium heat. When the oil is heated, add the onion. Sauté until the onion is lightly browned, stirring frequently, about 4 minutes.
6 Add the tomato. Cook until the tomato pieces become soft, stirring frequently, about 5 minutes. Add the mashed eggplant (including the stem and the juices), red pepper and salt. Stir to combine. Cook for 5 minutes, stirring occasionally.
7 Serve the eggplant on a platter, along with the stem, or let cool to room temperature and refrigerate or freeze for later!

EGGPLANT TIP: Eggplants, also known as "brinjal" in India and "aubergine" in Europe, come in many different shapes, varieties and colors from white to green to a range of light to dark purples—each having slight variances in taste and textures. In America, the most common one is the big, globe eggplant (also called an "American eggplant"), which I use to make Roasted Eggplant (recipe on this page). This eggplant has a thicker skin than other varieties, and is sometimes peeled before being cooked, depending on what dish it is being used in. When making the Vegetable Medley Sambar (page 93), I use Indian, Chinese or Japanese eggplants, depending on which is easier to find. Chinese and Japanese eggplants are narrow instead of plump and have a more delicate, somewhat sweet flavor than the globe variety. Chinese eggplants are light purple and a bit longer than the darker purple Japanese eggplants. Indian eggplants look like round mini versions of the globe eggplant and are slightly smaller than a tennis ball. They are usually found only at ethnic grocery stores. The Indian, Chinese and Japanese eggplants have a smooth, glossy skin that is thin, so it's not necessary to peel them before cooking. When buying an eggplant, pick out ones that are not too firm, and not too soft, but tender to the touch, since they will have less seeds. Also look for ones that do not have brown spots or discoloration on the skin. Eggplants can be refrigerated up to one week until ready to use.

Stuffed Bell Peppers Aloo Bharee Shimla Mirch

This dish reminds me of the Mexican dish, *chili relllenos*, which translates to "stuffed peppers." The Mexican version commonly uses poblano peppers, and also sometimes bell peppers, which are typically stuffed with cheese and sometimes meat. In this Indian dish, we stuff the bell peppers with boiled potatoes that are mashed and spiced. This beautiful dish looks fanciful, but is surprisingly easy to make. This dish can be served with Whole Wheat Flatbreads (page 64), Oven Baked White Breads (page 66) or Oven Baked Whole Wheat Breads (page 68). It might seem as if we are adding a bit too many spices to the potatoes, but some of these spices will be absorbed in the bell peppers as they cook, so it will be okay!

Serves 4
Prep time: 10 minutes + 35 minutes to boil potatoes (can be done 1 day in advance)
Cook time: 35 minutes
Refrigerator life: 3 days
Freezer life: 1 month
Reheating method: Place the refrigerated or defrosted bell peppers in a microwave and turn periodically. Or, place them in a skillet over medium-low heat and turn periodically.

2 medium russet potatoes (total 1 lb/
   500 g), boiled and peeled (see page 24)
Juice of 1 lime
1/2 teaspoon turmeric
1 teaspoon ground red pepper
   (cayenne)
2 teaspoons salt
1/2 teaspoon ground black pepper
1 handful fresh coriander leaves (cilantro)
   (about 1/4 cup/10 g packed leaves), rinsed
   and chopped
4 small green bell peppers
4 tablespoons vegetable oil

1 Place the potatoes in a medium bowl. Using one hand or a potato masher, mash the potatoes until there are no lumps.
2 Add the lime juice, turmeric, red pepper, salt, black pepper and coriander leaves. Using one hand, mix everything together.
3 To stuff each bell pepper: core the pepper with a paring knife. Remove the stem and set aside. Remove as many of the seeds and as much of the membrane as possible. Rinse each pepper. With a small spoon, evenly stuff the peppers with the spiced mashed potato filling. Place the stems back on the peppers.
4 Pour the oil into a medium nonstick skillet and place over medium heat. When the oil is heated, add the stuffed bell peppers and lay on their sides. Cook until all sides are dark brown and seared, about 35 minutes, turning every few minutes or so. The bell peppers will be soft and tender when done. Enjoy now or let cool to room temperature and refrigerate or freeze for later!

Spiced Cauliflower and Potatoes

Aloo Gobi

India is one of the top producers of cauliflower, so it's no wonder that this dish is very popular in Indian cuisine. *Aloo gobi* can be eaten with Indian breads such as Whole Wheat Flatbreads (page 64), Oven Baked White Breads (page 66) or Oven Baked Whole Wheat Breads (page 68), and even though it does not have a curry consistency that makes it easy to mix with rice, you can still eat it with Plain Boiled Rice (page 79) or Rice with Cumin and Peas (page 78). When selecting fresh cauliflower heads, look for ones that are firm and creamy white, without any brown markings. You can keep them up to one week in your refrigerator before cooking them. My mom sometimes makes "Indian burritos" for my dad's lunch by rolling some of this dish in a Whole Wheat Flatbreads (page 64) or Flaky Wheat Breads (page 70). It tastes great at room temperature without needing to reheat in the office microwave and filling the office with the aroma of Indian spices!

Serves 4
Prep time: 5 minutes (15 minutes if using fresh head of cauliflower)
Cook time: 30 minutes
Refrigerator life: 3 days
Freezer life: 1 month
Reheating method: Place the refrigerated or defrosted cauliflower in a microwave and stir periodically. Or, place it in a skillet over medium-low heat and stir periodically.

1 large head fresh cauliflower (about 2 lbs/1 kg) or
    1 lb (500 g) frozen bite-size cauliflower florets
3 tablespoons vegetable oil
1 fully ripe tomato, cut into 4 pieces
1 medium russet potato (about 1/2 lb/250 g), peeled and
    cut into 3/4-in (2-cm) cubes
2 teaspoons peeled and finely grated fresh ginger
1 teaspoon cumin seeds
1/2 teaspoon ground turmeric
1/4 teaspoon ground red pepper (cayenne)
1 1/4 teaspoons salt
1/4 teaspoon ground black pepper
1 handful fresh coriander leaves (cilantro) (about
    1/4 cup/10 g packed leaves), rinsed and chopped

1 If you're using frozen cauliflower, do not defrost. If you're using fresh cauliflower, cut the florets off the cauliflower head into large bite-size pieces and wash with cold water (see page 25 on how to cut cauliflower).

2 Pour the oil into a large nonstick skillet and place over medium heat. When the oil is heated, add the tomato. Cover the skillet. Cook until the tomato becomes soft and mashed, stirring every minute or so and lightly mashing the tomato, about 5 minutes.

3 Add the cauliflower, potato, ginger, cumin seeds, turmeric, red pepper, salt and black pepper. Stir to combine until everything is stained yellow from the turmeric. Increase the heat to medium-high. Cook covered for 7 minutes, stirring every minute or so.

4 Reduce the heat to medium. Remove the cover to avoid letting the cauliflower become mushy. Cook until the cauliflower is tender and you can easily insert a knife through the potato cubes, stirring occasionally, about 10 minutes. You may sprinkle some water in the skillet if you feel the cauliflower is drying up while the potatoes are cooking.

5 Turn off the heat. Let rest covered for 5 minutes on the warm stove. Enjoy now or let cool to room temperature and refrigerate or freeze for later! Just before serving, sprinkle the chopped coriander leaves on top.

Sautéed Green Beans and Potatoes

Aloo France Beans

This easy to make green bean and potato sautéed dish goes best with Indian breads such as Whole Wheat Flatbreads (page 64), Oven Baked White Breads (page 66) or Oven Baked Whole Wheat Breads (page 68). You may also eat it with Plain Boiled Rice (page 79) or Rice with Cumin and Peas (page 78), although it might be hard to mix together with rice because this dish does not have a liquid curry base. When shopping for fresh green beans, look for the bright green and crisp, firm ones rather than the softer, flimsy ones. The best ones will make a snapping noise when broken in half. Green beans are also called snap beans and string beans.

Serves 4
Prep time: 5 minutes (15 minutes if using fresh green beans)
Cook time: 30 minutes
Refrigerator life: 3 days
Freezer life: 1 month
Reheating method: Place the refrigerated or defrosted beans in a microwave and stir periodically. Or, place them in a skillet over medium-low heat and stir periodically.

1 lb (500 g) fresh green beans or frozen, chopped or French cut green beans
3 tablespoons vegetable oil
1 teaspoon cumin seeds
1 medium russet potato (about 1/2 lb/ 250 g), peeled and cut into 1/2-in (1.25-cm) cubes
1/2 teaspoon ground turmeric
1/2 teaspoon ground red pepper (cayenne)
1 teaspoon salt
1/2 teaspoon ground black pepper

1 If you're using frozen green beans, do not defrost them. If you're using fresh green beans, wash them. Trim the tip and head and discard. Chop the green beans into 1/4-inch (6-mm) pieces.
2 Pour the oil into a large nonstick skillet and place over medium heat. When the oil is heated, add the cumin seeds and let brown, about 10 seconds. Do not let the cumin seeds burn and turn black. Immediately add the green beans, potato, turmeric, red pepper, salt and black pepper. Stir thoroughly. Cover the skillet and cook for 5 minutes, stirring occasionally.
3 Remove the cover. Cook, stirring frequently, until the beans are tender and you can easily insert a knife through the potato cubes, about 20 minutes. Turn off the heat. Let rest covered for 5 minutes on the warm stove. Enjoy now or let cool to room temperature and refrigerate or freeze for later!

Sautéed Potatoes with Onion Sukha Aloo

This potato and onion dish is most commonly folded inside Potato Stuffed Crepes (page 56). You may also serve this dish with breads such as Puffed Fried Breads (page 74) or Flaky Wheat Breads (page 70) along with a side of Homemade Plain Yogurt (page 36) and a small piece of Mango Pickle (page 41) for a breakfast or lunch meal. I like to make a toaster sandwich by putting these potatoes and onions between two slices of white bread in a sandwich press. This toasted potato sandwich makes an interesting lunch to look forward to when at the office! You do not have to warm it up, since it tastes great and stays well at room temperature.

Serves 4
Prep time: 10 minutes
Cook time: 15 minutes
Refrigerator life: 3 days
Freezer life: 1 month
Reheating method: Place the refrigerated or defrosted potatoes in a microwave and stir periodically. Or, place them in a skillet over medium-low heat and stir periodically.

2 tablespoons vegetable oil
2 dried finger-length red chili peppers
1 teaspoon cumin seeds
1 teaspoon mustard seeds
1 fresh finger-length green chili pepper, cut in half lengthwise and then cut in half crosswise
2 medium russet potatoes (total 1 lb/ 500 g), diced
1 onion, thinly sliced into half moons
1 handful fresh coriander leaves (cilantro) (about 1/4 cup/10 g packed leaves), rinsed and chopped
1/4 teaspoon ground turmeric
1 teaspoon salt

1 Pour the oil into a large nonstick skillet and place over medium heat. When the oil is heated, tear each red chili pepper into 3 pieces and add to the saucepan.
2 Add the cumin seeds and mustard seeds. Sauté until the cumin seeds turn brown and you hear the mustard seeds pop, about 10 seconds. Do not let the cumin seeds burn and turn black. Immediately add the rest of the ingredients. Stir to combine.
3 Reduce the heat to medium-low and cover the skillet. Cook, stirring every few minutes or so, until you can easily insert a knife through the potatoes, about 15 minutes. Enjoy now or let cool to room temperature and refrigerate or freeze for later, or use to make Potato Stuffed Crepes (page 56)!

Serves 4
Prep time: 15 minutes
Cook time: 25 minutes
Refrigerator life: 3 days
Freezer life: 1 month
Reheating method: Place the refrigerated or defrosted curry in a microwave, cover and stir periodically. Or, place it in a saucepan over medium-low heat and stir periodically.

2 tablespoons vegetable oil
2 teaspoons minced garlic
1 teaspoon peeled and finely grated fresh ginger
1 fully ripe tomato, cut into 4 pieces
1/2 teaspoon ground turmeric
1/4 teaspoon ground red pepper (cayenne)
1/2 teaspoon salt
1 teaspoon Garam Masala (page 44)
1/2 small onion, thinly sliced into half moons
1 cup (120 g) frozen or fresh parboiled green peas (see page 24)
1 medium russet potato (about 1/2 lb/250 g), peeled and cut into 1-in (2.5-cm) cubes
1 carrot, peeled and cut into matchsticks
1 cup (250 ml) coconut milk
1/4 cup (65 ml) water

1 Pour the oil into a medium saucepan and place over medium heat. When the oil is heated, add the garlic and ginger. Sauté until the garlic is lightly browned, stirring frequently, about 30 seconds.

2 Reduce the heat to medium-low and add the tomato. Cover the saucepan and cook until the tomato becomes completely soft and mashed, stirring every minute or so and lightly mashing the tomato, about 5 minutes.

3 Add the turmeric, red pepper, salt and Garam Masala. Stir to combine. Cook uncovered for 2 minutes, stirring frequently. This is the *masala* (spice base).

4 Add the onion, peas, potato, carrot, coconut milk and water. Stir to combine. Bring to a rolling boil over high heat.

5 Reduce the heat to medium-low and cover the saucepan. Simmer until the onion is translucent and the potato and carrot are tender, stirring occasionally, about 15 minutes. Enjoy now or let cool to room temperature and refrigerate or freeze for later!

Vegetables with Coconut Curry

Coconut-curried dishes are some of my personal favorite foods, and I usually enjoy them at Thai restaurants. In the tropical southern states of India, where many people have coconut trees in their backyards, coconut-based dishes are very common. This coconut curry dish is my own creation, using influences from Thai restaurants and my mother-in-law's recipe for Garam Masala (page 44). This dish may be served with Plain Boiled Rice (page 79) or Rice with Cumin and Peas (page 78), or with Indian breads such as Whole Wheat Flatbreads (page 64), Oven Baked White Breads (page 66) or Oven Baked Whole Wheat Breads (page 68).

Sautéed Okra with Onions Bhindi Pyaz

Okra, known as "lady's fingers" in India, has a beautiful fresh, bright green color and looks wonderful on the table. When buying fresh okra, avoid the flimsy, flexible ones. Look for crisp ones in which the tail end can be snapped off. Avoid the very hard okra that are over-ripe with brown seeds instead of the ideal white seeds. I also never cover okra when cooking because doing so will darken its color. Okra can be eaten with Indian breads, such as Whole Wheat Flatbreads (page 64), Oven Baked White Breads (page 66) or Oven Baked Whole Wheat Breads (page 68), or with Plain Boiled Rice (page 79) or Rice with Cumin and Peas (page 78), but it might be tricky to mix with rice since it does not have a curry consistency. Okra also goes very well with lentil dishes.

Serves 4
Prep time: 5 minutes (15 minutes if using fresh whole okra)
Cook time: 35 minutes
Refrigerator life: 3 days
Freezer life: 1 month
Reheating method: Place the refrigerated or defrosted okra in a microwave and stir periodically. Or, place it in a skillet over medium-low heat and stir periodically.

1 lb (500 g) fresh okra or frozen, precut okra
3 tablespoons vegetable oil
Juice of 1/2 lime
1 small onion, thickly sliced into half moons
1/2 teaspoon ground turmeric
1/2 teaspoon ground red pepper (cayenne)
1 teaspoon salt
1/2 teaspoon ground black pepper

1 If you're using frozen okra, do not defrost. If you're using fresh okra, wash the okra and pat dry with a kitchen towel. Trim the tip and head and discard. Slice each okra into 1/4-inch (6-mm) pieces.
2 Pour the oil into a large nonstick skillet and place over medium heat. (Place over high heat if using frozen okra.) When the oil is heated, add the okra and lime juice. Sauté for 5 minutes, stirring frequently.
3 Reduce the heat to medium-low. Add the onion, turmeric, red pepper, salt, and black pepper. Stir to combine. Sauté until the okra is tender and the onion becomes translucent, stirring frequently, about 30 minutes.
4 Enjoy now or let cool to room temperature and refrigerate or freeze for later!

> **OKRA TIP:** Okra has a peculiar slimy substance that is released when the okra is cut and washed. The first time I cooked okra, I washed it after I chopped it and had slime everywhere! That is why it is important to wash it and pat dry before chopping to reduce the release of the sticky material. If you're using frozen okra, it is best not to defrost it first, since it will become flimsy and release a lot of slimy substance. When okra is cooked with lime juice, the slime disappears as the okra cooks.

8 oz (250 g) fresh whole or pre-sliced mushrooms
3 tablespoons vegetable oil
1/2 small onion, grated on the largest grating
holes on a box grater or shredded in a food
processor
1 fully ripe tomato, cut into 4 pieces
1/4 teaspoon ground turmeric
1/4 teaspoon ground red pepper (cayenne)
1/2 teaspoon salt
1/2 teaspoon ground black pepper
1/2 cup (60 g) frozen or fresh parboiled green
peas (see page 24)
2 tablespoons store-bought or Homemade
Plain Yogurt (page 36), stirred vigorously
with a spoon until smooth
1/2 cup (125 ml) water (see tip)

1 If you're using whole mushrooms, clean them by
placing them in a colander and running cold water
on them while using your fingers to gently rub away
any dirt. Cut the cleaned mushrooms into 1/4-inch
(6-mm) longitudinal slices.

2 Pour the oil into a medium saucepan and place
over medium heat. When the oil is heated, add the
onion. Sauté until the onion is golden brown, stirring frequently, about 5 minutes.

3 Reduce the heat to medium-low and add the
tomato. Cover the saucepan and cook until the
tomato becomes completely soft and mashed and
is combined with the onion to form a coarse paste,
stirring every minute or so and lightly mashing the
tomato, about 5 minutes.

4 Add the turmeric, red pepper, salt and black pepper. Stir to combine. Cook uncovered for 6 minutes,
stirring frequently. This is the *masala* (spice base).

5 Add the mushrooms and peas. Stir to combine.
Increase the heat to medium and cover the saucepan. Cook for 5 minutes, stirring occasionally. The
mushrooms will begin to release water and shrink
in size.

6 Remove the cover. Cook for 5 minutes, stirring
frequently. Add the yogurt and water. Bring to a rolling boil over high heat.

7 Reduce the heat to medium-low. Simmer uncovered for 5 minutes, stirring occasionally. Enjoy now
or let cool to room temperature and refrigerate or
freeze for later!

Mushroom and Pea Curry Khumb Matar Subzee

Mushrooms are one of my personal favorite vegetables, and this dish is one of my
favorite ways to cook mushrooms Indian style! My dad told me that when he was a
kid, his dad would occasionally go to the city to buy a variety of mushrooms, which
are considered a delicacy in India since they are not commonly available and they are
expensive. This dish can be eaten with Indian breads, such as Whole Wheat Flatbreads
(page 64), Oven Baked White Breads (page 66) or Oven Baked Whole Wheat Breads
(page 68), or with Plain Boiled Rice (page 79) or Rice with Cumin and Peas (page 78).

Serves 4
Prep time: 5 minutes (15 minutes if using whole
mushrooms
Cook time: 35 minutes
Refrigerator life: 3 days
Freezer life: 1 month
Reheating method: Place the refrigerated or
defrosted curry in a microwave, cover and stir
periodically. Or, place it in a saucepan over
medium-low heat and stir periodically. If the reheated curry seems too thick, you may add a bit
of water to it.

TIP: When cooking mushrooms, you will
see that they release a lot of liquid, which
is okay, because their liquid helps to create the curry base. Depending on the type
and freshness of the mushrooms you use,
some will release more or less liquid than
others. You may add a bit more or less
water than the suggested 1/2 cup (125 ml)
of water to create your desired consistency
of curry. You can then adjust the amount of
salt as desired.

Scrambled Breakfast Eggs Anda Bhurji

These Indian-style scrambled eggs are spiced and scrambled, though they are not fluffy like American-style scrambled eggs. This dish is eaten with soft and buttery Flaky Wheat Breads (page 70) and a small piece of Mango Pickle (page 41). You may top off this light, yet satisfying breakfast with a cup of Indian Tea (page 148). Another way to enjoy these eggs is to put them between two slices of toast, creating a tasty, toasted egg sandwich. You can even make a Mexican style breakfast burrito by placing the spiced eggs in a warm white flour tortilla, sprinkling on your favorite cheese, adding some salsa, and rolling it all up!

Serves 3 to 4
Prep time: 5 minutes
Cook time: 15 minutes
Refrigerator life: 2 days
Reheating method: Place the refrigerated eggs in a skillet over medium-low heat and stir periodically. A less preferred method is to place the eggs in a microwave and stir periodically.

2 tablespoons vegetable oil
1 small onion, diced
1 small fully ripe tomato, such as plum (Roma), diced
1 fresh finger-length green chili pepper, sliced into thin circles
2 pinches of ground turmeric
1/4 teaspoon ground red pepper (cayenne)
3/4 teaspoon salt
1/4 teaspoon ground black pepper
4 large eggs

1 Pour the oil into a medium nonstick skillet and place over medium heat. When the oil is heated, add the onion. Sauté until the onion is translucent, stirring frequently, about 3 minutes.
2 Add the tomato. Cook until the tomato pieces become soft, stirring frequently, about 5 minutes. Add the green chili pepper, turmeric, red pepper, salt and black pepper. Stir to combine.
3 Crack open each egg into the skillet. Cook until the eggs are opaque, stirring frequently so the eggs will break apart into small pieces, about 5 minutes. Enjoy now or let cool to room temperature and refrigerate for later!

Simple Egg Curry

Egg curry is a simple dish for an elegant breakfast or brunch meal. This dish goes best with soft and buttery Flaky Wheat Breads (page 70). Finish the meal off with a rich Indian Cappuccino (page 149) to get your day started off deliciously! You may even serve this at dinner, since it is a hearty dish and looks beautiful on the table.

Serves 3 to 4
Prep time: 5 minutes + 15 minutes to boil the eggs (can be done 1 day in advance)
Cook time: 25 minutes
Refrigerator life: 2 days

Reheating method: Place the refrigerated curry in a saucepan over medium-low heat and stir periodically. A less preferred method is to place the curry in a microwave, cover and stir periodically.

4 large hardboiled eggs (see tip below)
3 tablespoons vegetable oil
1/2 small onion, grated on the largest grating holes on a box grater or shredded in a food processor
1 small fully ripe tomato, such as plum (Roma), cut into 4 pieces
1/4 teaspoon ground turmeric
1/4 teaspoon ground red pepper (cayenne)
1/2 teaspoon salt
1/4 teaspoon ground black pepper
1 cup (250 ml) water

1 Peel the hardboiled eggs and slice each in half lengthwise.
2 Pour the oil into a medium saucepan and place over medium heat. When the oil is heated, add the onion. Sauté until the onion is golden brown, stirring frequently, about 5 minutes.
3 Reduce the heat to medium-low. Add the tomato and cover the saucepan. Cook until the tomato becomes completely soft and mashed and is combined with the onion to form a coarse paste, stirring every minute or so and lightly mashing the tomato, about 5 minutes.
4 Add the turmeric, red pepper, salt and black pepper. Stir to combine. Cook uncovered for 6 minutes, stirring frequently. This is the *masala* (spice base).
5 Add the water and stir. Bring to a rolling boil over high heat. Stir and reduce the heat to medium. Add the egg halves, yolk side up. Spoon some of the curry on the eggs. Simmer for 5 minutes. Enjoy now or let cool to room temperature and refrigerate for later!

> **TIPS ON HARD-BOILING EGGS:** Hard-boiling eggs is a fairly easy task. If you overcook the eggs, a gray-green ring will form around the yolks, but they are still okay to eat. To avoid the gray-green ring, I boil the eggs just for a few minutes, and then let them finish firming up as they sit in the hot water for a bit more.
>
> Place 4 large eggs (or however many you prefer) into a small saucepan. Add water to cover them, leaving about 2 inches (5 cm) of space from the top of the pan so that water does not boil over. Bring to a rolling boil over high heat. Boil for 3 minutes. Turn off the heat and let rest for 10 minutes in the hot water.
>
> Carefully pour the water out of the saucepan and into the sink. Use now to make desired dish, or cover and refrigerate the eggs, unpeeled, up to 1 day.

4 large hardboiled eggs (see page 138)
3 tablespoons vegetable oil
2 dried finger-length red chili peppers
1/2 teaspoon cumin seeds
1/2 teaspoon mustard seeds
1 onion, diced
1 tablespoon minced garlic
1 tablespoon peeled and finely grated fresh
   ginger
2 fresh finger-length green chili peppers, cut in
   half lengthwise
1/2 teaspoon tamarind concentrate (paste)
1 cup (250 ml) water
1/4 teaspoon ground turmeric
1/4 teaspoon ground red pepper (cayenne)
3/4 teaspoon salt
2 teaspoons Garam Masala (page 44)
Juice of 1 lime
1 handful fresh coriander leaves (cilantro)
   (about 1/4 cup/10 g packed leaves), rinsed and
   chopped

1 Peel the hardboiled eggs and cut them crosswise about three-quarters of the way through the egg, making sure not to cut the eggs in half.
2 Pour the oil into a medium saucepan and place over medium heat. When the oil is heated, tear each red chili pepper in half and add to the saucepan. Add the cumin seeds and mustard seeds. Sauté until the cumin seeds turn brown and you hear the mustard seeds pop, about 10 seconds. Do not let the cumin seeds burn and turn black.
3 Immediately add the onion, garlic, ginger and green chili peppers. Cook for 2 minutes, stirring frequently. Add the tamarind, water, turmeric, red pepper, salt and Garam Masala. Bring to a rolling boil over high heat.
4 Reduce the heat to medium. Cover and simmer until the onion is translucent, stirring occasionally, about 10 minutes. Some of the water will cook off.
5 Add the lime juice and coriander leaves. Stir to combine. Add the eggs, slit side up. Spoon some of the curry on the eggs. Cover the saucepan. Let rest for 30 minutes so the eggs can absorb the flavors. Enjoy now or refrigerate for later!

Tamarind Egg Curry Kodiguddu Pulusu

Pulusu describes a tamarind-based curry dish from the southern Indian state of Andhra Pradesh. In this dish, hardboiled eggs are slit to allow the tamarind-based curry flavors to be absorbed into the eggs. The curry is slightly thick and saucy, and has lots of diced onions in it. This egg dish can be served at lunch or dinner with an Indian bread, such as Flaky Wheat Breads (page 70), but it is typically served with Plain Boiled Rice (page 79). You can also add a side of Mango Pickle (page 41).

Serves 3 to 4
Prep time: 10 minutes + 15 minutes to boil the eggs (can be done 1 day in advance)
Cook time: 15 minutes + 30 minutes resting
Refrigerator life: 2 days

Reheating method: Place the refrigerated curry in a saucepan over medium-low heat and stir periodically. A less preferred method is to place the curry in a microwave, cover and stir periodically.

Creamed Spinach with Cheese Cubes Saag Paneer

This rich restaurant favorite is made from a firm style of Indian cheese that is cut into cubes and lightly pan-fried, and then simmered with spinach in heavy cream. This dish is accurately called *palak paneer*, since *palak* is spinach, and *paneer* is Indian cheese, but I have seen it more commonly called saag paneer. *Saag* actually refers to a dish made from mustard greens, spinach, or a mixture of both. This dish goes best with the Oven Baked White Breads (page 66), which is the bread commonly served with it in restaurants, but you can also serve it with Whole Wheat Flatbreads (page 64) or Oven Baked Whole Wheat Breads (page 68). I also eat it with Rice with Cumin and Peas (page 78) because its creamy consistency mixes easily with rice. Relatively speaking, I do not add a lot of heavy cream in this recipe (I find too much cream masks the bright taste of the spinach), but you can definitely add more if you prefer.

1 lb (500 g) fresh spinach (about 1 bunch) or 1/2 lb (250 g) frozen, chopped spinach

1 fully ripe tomato, cut into 4 pieces

1/2 cup (125 ml) water (if using frozen spinach only)

1/2 teaspoon ground turmeric

1/4 heaping teaspoon ground red pepper (cayenne)

1/2 teaspoon salt

1/2 teaspoon ground black pepper

3 tablespoons vegetable oil

1 1/2 teaspoons peeled and finely grated fresh ginger

1/2 small onion, diced

1 fresh finger-length green chili pepper, diced

1/2 to 1 recipe Indian Cheese Block, cubed and pan-fried (see page 44) (use the entire recipe if you prefer more cheese cubes)

1/2 cup (125 ml) heavy cream (add more cream as you desire to make it restaurant style!)

Serves 4

Prep time: 10 minutes + 1 hour, 50 minutes to make Indian Cheese Block, cubed and pan-fried

Cook time: 35 minutes

Refrigerator life: 3 days

Freezer life: 1 month

Reheating method: Place the refrigerated or defrosted spinach and cheese in a microwave, cover and stir periodically. Or, place it in a saucepan over medium-low heat and stir periodically.

1 If you're using frozen spinach, do not defrost. If you're using fresh spinach, thoroughly wash it and trim the bottom 1 inch (2.5 cm) off the stems and discard. Coarsely chop the leaves and remaining stems.

2 Place the spinach and tomato in a medium saucepan set over medium heat. If you're using frozen spinach, add 1/2 cup (125 ml) water to the saucepan and proceed to Step 3. If you're using fresh spinach, cook it for about 7 minutes, stirring occasionally. You will soon see the water released from the spinach, and the spinach will reduce in volume.

3 Add the turmeric, red pepper, salt and black pepper. Stir to combine and cover. Simmer for 15 minutes, stirring occasionally. The spinach will become soft and tender, and the tomato will be mushy, and everything will be mixed together well. Remove from the heat and transfer the contents to a blender.

4 Purée until smooth, but do not liquefy it, and then put the puréed spinach back in the saucepan. (Or, use an immersion blender and purée right in the saucepan.)

5 Pour the oil into a small skillet and place over medium heat. When the oil is heated, add the ginger, onion and green chili pepper. Sauté until the onion is browned, stirring frequently, about 4 minutes. Pour into the saucepan with the blended spinach.

6 Add the cheese cubes and heavy cream. Stir to combine. Simmer for 5 minutes over medium heat, stirring occasionally. Enjoy now or let cool to room temperature and refrigerate for later!

Indian Cheese and Pea Curry Matar Paneer

This dish is made with a firm style of Indian cheese that is cut into cubes, lightly pan-fried and then simmered with peas in a savory curry. Traditionally, the cheese cubes are deep-fried before putting them in the pea curry, but I lightly pan-fry the cubes instead so to make this recipe a tad bit easier and healthier! Matar paneer can be eaten with Indian breads, such as Whole Wheat Flatbreads (page 64), Oven Baked White Breads (page 66) or Oven Baked Whole Wheat Breads (page 68), or with Plain Boiled Rice (page 79) or Rice with Cumin and Peas (page 78). When serving this dish, keep an eye out to make sure everyone gets an equal amount of cheese cubes on their plate, instead of being taken all by one person!

Serves 4
Prep time: 10 minutes + 1 hour, 50 minutes to make Indian Cheese Block, cubed and pan-fried
Cook time: 25 minutes
Refrigerator life: 3 days
Freezer life: 1 month
Reheating method: Place the refrigerated or defrosted curry in a microwave, cover and stir periodically. Or, place it in a saucepan over medium-low heat and stir periodically.

3 tablespoons vegetable oil
1½ teaspoons peeled and finely grated fresh ginger
½ small onion, grated on the largest grating holes on a box grater or shredded in a food processor
1 fully ripe tomato, cut into 4 pieces
½ teaspoon ground turmeric
¼ teaspoon ground red pepper (cayenne)
½ teaspoon salt
½ teaspoon ground black pepper
½ cup (60 g) frozen or fresh parboiled green peas (see page 24)
1 recipe Indian Cheese Block, cubed and pan-fried (see page 44)
1¼ cups (300 ml) water

1 Pour the oil into a medium saucepan set over medium heat. When the oil is heated, add the ginger and onion. Sauté until the onion is golden brown, stirring frequently, about 5 minutes.
2 Reduce the heat to medium-low. Add the tomato and cover the saucepan. Cook until the tomato becomes completely soft and mashed and is combined with the onion to form a coarse paste, stirring every minute or so and lightly mashing the tomato, about 5 minutes.
3 Add the turmeric, red pepper, salt and black pepper. Stir to combine. Cook uncovered for 6 minutes, stirring frequently. This is the *masala* (spice base).
4 Add the peas, pan-fried cheese cubes and water. Stir to combine. Bring to a rolling boil over high heat. Stir and reduce the heat to medium. Simmer uncovered 5 minutes, stirring occasionally. Enjoy now or let cool to room temperature and refrigerate or freeze for later!

Crumbled Indian Cheese with Peas

Paneer Bhurji

This dish, made from homemade Indian cheese (*paneer*), is surprisingly easy to make, despite its elegant appearance. The soft, crumbled homemade cheese only takes minutes to make, and cooking this dish is even easier! This dish goes best with Indian breads such as Whole Wheat Flatbreads (page 64), Oven Baked White Breads (page 66) or Oven Baked Whole Wheat Breads (page 68). The only problem with this dish is that I can easily eat too much of it without keeping track!

Serves 3 to 4
Prep time: 5 minutes + 10 minutes to make Crumbled Indian Cheese
Cook time: 20 minutes
Refrigerator life: 3 days
Freezer life: 1 month
Reheating method: Place the refrigerated or defrosted cheese and peas in a skillet over medium-low heat and stir periodically. Or, place the cheese and peas in a microwave and stir periodically.

3 tablespoons vegetable oil
1/2 small onion, grated on the largest grating holes on a box grater or shredded in a food processor
1 small fully ripe tomato, such as plum (Roma), cut into 4 pieces
1 recipe Crumbled Indian Cheese (page 42)
1/2 cup (60 g) frozen or fresh parboiled green peas (see page 24)
1/2 teaspoon ground turmeric
1/2 teaspoon ground red pepper (cayenne)
1/2 teaspoon salt

1 Pour the oil into a medium nonstick skillet and place over medium heat. When the oil is heated, add the onion. Sauté until the onion is golden brown, stirring frequently, about 5 minutes.
2 Reduce the heat to medium-low. Add the tomato. Cover the skillet. Cook until the tomato becomes completely soft and mashed and is combined with the onion to form a coarse paste, stirring every minute or so and lightly mashing the tomato, about 5 minutes.
3 Add the cheese, peas, turmeric, red pepper and salt. Stir to combine. Increase the heat to medium. Cook until the cheese slightly darkens in color to a golden-yellow shade, stirring frequently and breaking apart the cheese into small pieces, about 7 minutes. Enjoy now or let cool to room temperature and refrigerate or freeze for later!

Chapter 7

Drinks and Desserts

This is my absolute favorite chapter. In this chapter, I hope to entice you with sugar, not spice! I have a sweet tooth, so planning, writing, making, and most importantly testing and tasting the desserts, or "sweets," as they say in India, was one of the most enjoyable parts of working on this book.

Desserts are made fresh daily by dessert makers called *halvai* and are sold in sweet shops found everywhere in India. Sweets are a must-have at weddings, festivities, grand events, or any celebration of good news, no matter how big or small. At weddings in India, people may hire a halvai, who comes to the wedding and makes fresh batches of sweets for all the guests.

Indian desserts come in a variety of tastes, textures and colors. I have chosen some of the most popular desserts that are served at restaurants and weddings, and are simply enjoyed every day. Coincidentally, all of these desserts are milk-based and, except for the instant powdered nonfat milk that is used to make Milk Balls in a Sweet Syrup (page 152), I use whole milk for desserts in order not to compromise any taste. Using reduced fat milk will not result in creamy desserts, and the taste and textures will not be ideal, so it is a good idea to use whole milk and just try to eat a small amount of the dessert instead!

In some desserts, such as Sweet Rice Pudding (page 155), Classic Indian Ice Cream (page 154) and Sweet Cheese Dessert (page 150) the milk is boiled until the water evaporates and it thickens, leaving thick and creamy evaporated milk that is sweetened with sugar to make homemade sweetened condensed milk. Although you can buy evaporated and condensed milk from the stores, I avoid them because I personally feel they have a metallic taste from the tin cans they are stored in. In other desserts, such as Sweet Cheese Dessert (page 150) and Sweet Cheese Ball Dessert (page 153), fresh *paneer* (Indian cheese), made from cow's milk, is the star ingredient.

The beverages in this chapter range from the comforting to the refreshing. The hot drinks such as Indian Tea (page 148) and Indian Cappuccino (page 149) can be soothing after a long, tiring day, and the chilled drinks such as Iced Coffee (page 148) and a variety of yogurt-based drinks, known as *lassi*, can be cooling on a hot day or simply enjoyed on a lazy Sunday afternoon.

And remember, a delicious way to calm your tummy after eating a spicy meal is to have a milky dessert or yogurt based beverage!

Sweet Yogurt Drink

Meethi Lassi

This thick and frothy yogurt drink is sweetened instead of salted like the Salted Yogurt Drink (recipe on left), but both drinks are delicious! Meethi lassi is a delight to drink on a hot day or as a refresher after being out in the heat.

Serves 2
Prep time: 5 minutes
Refrigerator life: 3 days

1 cup (250 g) store-bought or Homemade Plain Yogurt (page 36)
1/2 cup (100 g) sugar
10 ice cubes plus ice cubes to half fill 2 tall glasses

1 Place the yogurt, sugar and 10 ice cubes in a blender. Blend until the ice is all crushed. If you are making this drink for later, store in the refrigerator now and shake vigorously before serving.
2 Fill 2 tall glasses half-way with the ice cubes.
3 Pour the lassi into the glasses and enjoy!

Salted Yogurt Drink Namkeen Lassi

Lassi is a popular style of Indian drink made from Homemade Plain Yogurt (page 36) and served in tall steel glasses on hot summer afternoons, usually followed by a long nap! One of the most common Indian yogurt drinks is this thin salted one, called *namkeen lassi*. However, there are also popular sweet and fruity versions, such as Sweet Yogurt Drink (recipe on right), and Mango Lassi (page 147). Interestingly, namkeen lassi is also a very common drink in the country of Turkey, but the Turks call this drink *ayran*, and their lassi tends to be a bit thicker than the Indian one.

Serves 2
Prep time: 5 minutes   **Refrigerator life:** 3 days

1/2 cup (125 g) store-bought or Homemade Plain Yogurt (page 36)
1 1/2 cups (375 ml) water
3/4 teaspoon salt
Ice cubes to half fill 2 tall glasses

1 Whisk the yogurt in a medium bowl until it is smooth and there are no lumps.
2 Add the water and salt. Mix together. If you are making this drink for later, store in the refrigerator now.
3 Fill 2 tall glasses half-way with the ice cubes.
4 Pour the lassi into the glasses and enjoy! Have a nice siesta!

Mango Lassi

This mango-flavored yogurt drink could also be called a "mango smoothie," but it is commonly called "mango lassi," with the Hindi word *lassi* meaning "yogurt-based drink." Mango lassi can be found at almost any Indian restaurant where it is commonly made from canned mango pulp (which usually has added sugar), but now you are about to learn how to easily make them at home from fresh mangoes. This drink is ideal for the summer months, especially since that is when mangoes are in season. Here is my quick and easy version that will have you buying sweet, ripe mangos by the crate! This drink can be served along with appetizers and other cocktails, or anytime on a hot day for a refreshing drink.

Serves 2
Prep time: 5 minutes
Refrigerator life: 3 days

1 large fully ripe mango (about 1 lb/500 g)
1/2 cup (125 g) store-bought or Homemade Plain Yogurt (page 36)
1/2 cup (100 g) sugar
1/2 cup (125 ml) water
10 ice cubes plus ice cubes to half fill 2 tall glasses

1 Wash the mango. Insert a knife by the stem along the wide side of the mango. Slice the mango lengthwise, cutting as close to the pit as possible, to create a large oval-shaped piece. Repeat on the other side of the pit to create two pieces.

2 Place one piece, flesh side up, on the chopping board. Score the flesh into an approximately 1/2-inch (1.25-cm) grid or crisscross pattern. Do not cut through the through the skin.

3 Bend the scored piece of mango backward so that the cubes push upward. Using a small knife, slice across the base of the cubes to remove them from the mango skin. Repeat with the other piece. Cut off as much of the flesh as possible that still clings to the pit.

4 Place the cubed mango, yogurt, sugar, water and 10 ice cubes in a blender. Blend until the ice is all crushed. If you are making this drink for later, store in the refrigerator now and shake vigorously before serving.

5 Fill 2 tall glasses half-way with the ice cubes. Pour the lassi into the glasses and enjoy!

Indian Tea Chai

After tea became increasingly popular in Europe, the British established tea cultivation in India in the 1800s to satisfy the new European thirst. Since then, tea cultivation has flourished in India, and is probably the most popular drink in India and in Indian homes around the world. Hot tea is sold by street vendors all around India at bus and train stations, and is offered at fancy weddings and grand occasions. Tea may also be infused with spices such as ginger, cloves, and cardamoms. Chai is sipped first thing in the morning, after finishing lunch, with an afternoon snack, and finally after dinner. Even when traveling, my mom makes sure to pack her tea bags and sugar! I started making tea since I could first reach the stove because my mom would ask me to make it for her.

> **NOTE:** 1. If you're using reduced fat milk, use 1 cup (250 ml) of water and 1 cup (250 ml) of milk.
> 2. If you're using fat free milk, use 1/2 cup (125 ml) of water and 1 1/2 cups (375 ml) of milk.

Serves 2
Cook time: 5 minutes

1 1/2 cups (375 ml) water
2 bags black tea or 1 tablespoon loose black tea
2 whole green cardamom pods
1/2 cup (125 ml) whole milk (see note)
4 teaspoons sugar

1 Place the water and bagged or loose tea in a small saucepan. Open the cardamoms and add the seeds and the pods. Bring to a rolling boil over high heat.
2 Add the milk and bring to a rolling boil again. Don't let the milk boil over and out of the saucepan! Immediately reduce the heat to medium.
3 Simmer the tea for 2 1/2 minutes, stirring occasionally.
4 Pour the tea through a sieve evenly into 2 cups. Discard the cardamom seeds and pods, and the tea bags or loose tea collected in the sieve.
5 Add 2 teaspoons of sugar to each cup, stir and enjoy!

Iced Coffee

This drink, commonly called "cold coffee" in India, is a cooling way to enjoy the rich coffee that is grown in the southern region of India. On our frequent summer trips to India while growing up, my mother made it a point to visit her favorite coffee house for this invigorating drink and some snacks to go with it. The best way to enjoy this sweet and refreshing delight is with a straw in order to get through the creamy froth at the top of the glass!

Serves 2
Prep time: 5 minutes
Refrigerator life: 3 days

1 tablespoon instant coffee grains
2 tablespoons sugar
1/2 cup (125 ml) water
1 1/2 cups (375 ml) whole milk (see note)
10 ice cubes plus ice cubes to half fill 2 tall glasses

1 Place the coffee grains, sugar, water, milk and 10 ice cubes in a blender. Blend until the ice is all crushed. If you are making this drink for later, store in the refrigerator now and shake vigorously before serving.
2 Fill 2 tall glasses half-way with the ice cubes.
3 Pour the iced coffee into the glasses and serve with straws!

> **NOTE:** If using reduced fat or fat free milk, use 2 cups (500 ml) of milk and no water.

Indian Cappuccino

This is a signature drink my mother serves at the end of her dinner parties, and is always a hit. Because this coffee drink has milk in it, it is a cappuccino, though in India it's called "espresso coffee," or simply "espresso." This drink has a delicious creamy froth that is easy to get without using fancy milk-frothing machines. Simply pour the milk into the cup from as high a distance as you can, and watch the froth form! The prep work to make the cappuccino batter does require a bit of patience and a lot of arm strength to get it perfect and fluffy, but it can be made in advance and refrigerated. That way, whenever you are in the mood for this drink or you have company coming over, you just have to boil the milk and water and use a dollop of the pre-made cappuccino batter!

NOTE: 1. If using reduced fat milk, use 1¹/₂ cups (375 ml) of milk and ¹/₂ cup (125 ml) of water.
2. If using fat free milk, use 2 cups (500 ml) of milk and no water.

Serves 2
Prep time: 10 minutes (Cappuccino Batter can be made 3 days in advance and refrigerated)
Cook time: 5 minutes

1 cup (250 ml) whole milk (see note)
1 cup (250 ml) water
For garnish: 2 pinches of either coffee granules, cocoa powder, ground cinnamon or ground nutmeg

Cappuccino Batter
2 teaspoons instant coffee granules
4 teaspoons sugar
2 teaspoons water

1 To make the Cappuccino Batter: Thoroughly mix together the instant coffee granules, sugar and ¹/₂ teaspoon of the water in a small bowl for 2 minutes.
2 Add another ¹/₂ teaspoon of the water. Beat vigorously for 2 minutes with a spoon. The color will become light brown and the mixture will start to become creamy. It is important to add the water a little bit at time, and then beat vigorously so the water is absorbed and air is beaten in, allowing the batter to become light and fluffy, which leads to more froth when making the cappuccino.
3 Add another ¹/₂ teaspoon of the water. Beat vigorously for 3 minutes with a spoon.
4 Add the remaining ¹/₂ teaspoon of the water. Beat vigorously for 3 minutes with a spoon. The mixture will become light brown and creamy like a thick pudding. It should not be watery. Place the batter aside for use now or cover and refrigerate up to 3 days.
5 To make Indian Cappuccino: Put 1 heaping tablespoon of the cappuccino batter into each of the 2 cups.
6 Pour the milk and water into a small saucepan. Bring to a rolling boil over high heat, stirring occasionally as it comes to a boil. Don't let the milk boil over and out of the saucepan! Immediately turn off the heat.
7 Put 2 tablespoons of the boiled milk in each cup. Stir to mix the batter and the milk. Pour the remainder of the boiled milk evenly into each cup from at least 6 inches (15 cm) above the cup to allow the froth to form. Sprinkle a pinch of coffee granules, cocoa, cinnamon or nutmeg on top of the froth for garnish. Enjoy!

Sweet Cheese Dessert Ras Malai

This luscious Indian dessert, known as *ras malai* in Hindi, is typically served at weddings and parties. It consists of discs of soft Indian cheese (*paneer*) that are soaked in a sugar syrup, and then placed in a cardamom-hinted milk base, which is my husband's favorite part! This dessert is served chilled in a bowl, with lots of the milky base to slurp up afterwards!

Serves 4
Prep time: 5 minutes + 1 hour refrigerating + 10 minutes to make Crumbled Indian Cheese
Cook time: 45 minutes + 20 minutes cooling time + 2 hours to chill in the refrigerator
Refrigerator life: 3 days
Freezer life: 1 month
Serving method: Gently stir the refrigerated or defrosted ras malai and serve chilled.

> **TIP ON CRUSHING PISTACHIOS**
> Use a mortar and pestle to coarsely crush the pistachios. Alternatively, put the nuts in a plastic bag. Put the bag on a cutting board and hit with a rolling pin until the nuts are crushed. *Note:* If you only have salted pistachios handy, you can rinse them and pat dry with a paper towel, and then crush them.

1 recipe Crumbled Indian Cheese (page 42), chilled for 30 minutes in the refrigerator
1¼ cups (250 g) sugar
2 cups (500 ml) water
2 cups (500 ml) whole milk
5 whole green cardamom pods
¼ cup (65 ml) half-and-half
2 drops kewra essence (optional)
2 tablespoons coarsely crushed, unsalted pistachios (see tip)

1 Blend the chilled cheese in a mini food processor until smooth and creamy. At first the cheese may seem as if it's crumbling even further in the food processor, but soon it will come together in a ball. Add any few loose bits of cheese, to the ball with your hand.

2 Divide the cheese into 4 equal pieces. Wash your hands so they are clean and it is easier to continue working with the cheese.

3 Using your hands, gently roll each piece into a smooth ball. Flatten each ball between your palms to make a 2-inch (5-cm) disc. Cover and refrigerate for 30 minutes to allow the cheese discs to set.

4 To make the syrup, bring 1 cup (200 g) of the sugar and 2 cups (500 ml) of the water to a rolling boil, in a medium saucepan, over high heat.

5 Add the cheese discs to the boiling syrup. Cook for 2 minutes while boiling. Reduce the heat to medium. Simmer for 15 minutes, undisturbed. The cheese discs will slightly fluff up.

6 Meanwhile, bring the milk to a rolling boil, in a heavy bottomed, large-sized saucepan, over high heat, stirring frequently as it comes to a boil. Don't let the milk boil over and out of the saucepan! Immediately reduce the heat to medium.

7 Open the cardamoms and add the seeds and the pods. Simmer the milk until it is half reduced to 1 cup (250 ml), stirring frequently, about 15 minutes. If any skim forms, simply stir it back in. If there is any scorched milk at the bottom of the saucepan, do not scrape it.

8 Add the half-and-half. Simmer for 3 minutes, stirring frequently. Add the remaining ¼ cup (50 g) sugar and stir until it has all dissolved. Remove the cardamom pods and discard. You may leave the seeds in.

9 Gently remove the cheese discs from the syrup, and place in a serving dish without overlapping them. Discard the excess syrup or use as desired.

10 Pour the milk from the saucepan over the cheese discs. Let rest undisturbed as the milk cools to room temperature (about 20 minutes). Sprinkle on the kewra essence, if using, and gently stir. Cover and place in the refrigerator until chilled. Before serving, sprinkle the pistachios on top of the cheese discs. Enjoy now or keep refrigerated or freeze for later!

Creamy Sweet Carrot Dessert Gajar ka Halwa

This delicious dessert, known throughout India as *gajar ka halwa*, is from the northern Indian state of Punjab, where it is called *gajrela* in the Indian dialect Punjabi. Gajar ka halwa is made with shredded carrots cooked in sweetened milk, resulting in a rich and creamy dessert. And because this dessert is made with milk and vegetables, you can justify going back for a second serving! It is usually warmed before serving, but I actually prefer it chilled, straight from the refrigerator. I like my mother's version of this recipe, which I share with you below, because her version is creamier and milkier than what I have seen typically served at restaurants.

Serves 4
Prep time: 10 minutes   **Cook time**: 55 minutes
Refrigerator life: 5 days   **Freezer life**: 1 month
Reheating method: Gajar ka kalwa might harden a bit in the refrigerator, but will soften when heated. To heat, place the refrigerated or defrosted gajar ka halwa in a microwave and stir periodically. Or, place it in a saucepan over medium-low heat and stir periodically.

1 large carrot, peeled
4 cups (1 liter) whole milk
1/4 cup (65 ml) half-and-half
1 tablespoon slivered almonds or 5 whole
    almonds, blanched and slivered (see page 24)
1/2 cup (100 g) sugar
Seeds from 2 green cardamom pods, crushed (see
    below)

1 Using a box grater, shred the carrot on the small grating holes. You should get about 1 cup (100 g) shredded carrots.
2 Bring the milk and shredded carrot to a rolling boil, in a heavy bottomed, medium-sized stockpot, over high heat, stirring frequently as it comes to a boil. Reduce the heat to medium.
3 Simmer the milk until it has all cooked off, leaving the carrots in a mushy consistency, stirring occasionally, about 45 minutes. If any skin forms, simply stir it back in. If there is any scorched milk at the bottom of the pot, do not scrape it.
4 Add the half-and-half and 1/2 tablespoon of the almonds. Simmer until all the half-and-half has cooked off, leaving the carrots in a mushy consistency, stirring occasionally, about 5 minutes. Add the sugar and stir until it has all dissolved.
5 Enjoy now or let cool to room temperature and refrigerate or freeze for later! Before serving, sprinkle the remaining 1/2 tablespoon almonds and the crushed cardamom seeds on top. This dish will further thicken as it cools, so if you like it extra thick, serve it chilled. If you prefer it a little less thick, serve it warm or reheat it before serving.

Crushing Cardamom Seeds

1 Open 2 whole green cardamoms and remove the seeds.
2 Use a mortar and pestle to coarsely crush the seeds. Alternatively, put the seeds in a plastic bag. Put the bag on a cutting board and hit with a rolling pin until the seeds are crushed.

Milk Balls in Sweet Syrup Gulab Jamun

My husband describes this popular Indian dessert as donuts in pancake syrup! Since desserts are readily available at markets everywhere in India, it is not that common to make them at home, but after my mother came to the United Stated, she tried her hand at making desserts at home, including gulab jamun. She had picked up a tip from another Indian American friend wanting to make desserts which was that Bisquick, which is a pancake and baking mix, can be used to easily make gulab jamun! Although gulab jamun are usually served warm, I prefer to eat them chilled, but sometimes, I cannot wait for them to chill in the refrigerator, and I eat them up warm! I also add a few drops of rose essence to this dish, which is why this dish is called "gulab jamun," since *gulab* means "rose" in Hindi and a "jamun" is a dark purple fruit popular in India, but the dessert is actually dark golden brown. If you do not have rose essence, this dessert still tastes sweet, juicy and delicious!

Makes 8 Gulab Jamun

Prep time: 10 minutes + 10 minutes resting

Cook time: 50 minutes + 3 minutes to deep fry + 3 hours sitting

Refrigerator life: 2 weeks

Reheating method: Gulab Jamun might harden a bit in the refrigerator, but will soften when heated. To heat, place the refrigerated gulab jamun in a microwave and stir periodically. Or, place the gulab jamun in a saucepan over medium-low heat and stir periodically.

Syrup

2 cups (400 g) sugar

4 cups (1 liter) water plus 6 tablespoons warm water

4 whole green cardamom pods

Dough

1 cup (70 g) instant nonfat dry milk
  (see note)

1/2 cup (60 g) Bisquick mix or
  homemade substitute (recipe
  follows)

1 1/2 tablespoons vegetable oil
  plus extra for deep frying

2 drops rose essence (optional)

1 To make the Syrup: Place the sugar and 4 cups (1 liter) of the water in a medium saucepan. Open the cardamoms and add the seeds and the pods. Bring to a rolling boil over high heat. Reduce the heat to medium. Simmer until the syrup is half reduced to 2 cups (500 ml), about 45 minutes. The syrup will be and be sticky and may develop a light yellowish tinge to it. Turn off the heat.

2 To make the Dough: Mix together the dry milk and Bisquick or home-made substitute in a medium bowl. Add 1 1/2 tablespoons of the vegetable oil and 6 tablespoons of the warm water. Using one hand, thoroughly knead together to make a soft and sticky dough. Since the dough is sticky, it can be tricky to manage, but the softer the dough, the softer the Gulab Jamun will be. Let rest uncovered at room temperature for 10 minutes so the dough can further absorb the water and become more manageable and not as sticky.

3 Knead the rested dough for 1 minute. Divide the dough into 8 equal pieces, leaving a pinch of dough aside to test the oil. Using your hands, gently roll each piece into a smooth

> **NOTE:** Dry milk is a powdered milk product that results when most of the moisture has been removed from liquid milk. I use instant nonfat dry milk, which can be stored at room temperature. It is usually found in the baking section of the grocery store.

ball. If you hands get too sticky with the dough, you may wash them and keep them slightly wet, and then continue to roll the balls.

4 Pour 2 inches (5 cm) of oil into a medium wok or deep stockpot, and place over medium heat. Test the oil's heat by dropping a pinch of the dough into the oil. If the dough immediately turns dark brown, the oil is too hot, and will cause the balls to burn on the outside, and the center of the balls will be raw, so you will need to reduce the heat a bit. The oil should just be warm and bubble around the balls, so the balls can gradually cook on the inside. When the oil is properly heated, slide all the dough balls into the wok. Fry until the balls have turned golden brown, turning frequently, about 3 minutes. The balls will turn crisp and will expand a bit. Using a slotted spoon, remove the cooked balls and place on paper towels to allow the excess oil to drain.

5 Add the rose essence, if using, to the warm syrup. Stir to combine. Add the cooked balls to the warm syrup, making sure they are not on top of each other. The balls will float in the syrup. Cover and let sit for 3 hours at room temp, turning every 30 minutes so they can evenly fluff up and soften as they absorb the syrup. Enjoy now or refrigerate for later! Serve each Gulab Jamun with extra sugar syrup poured on top.

Homemade Bisquick Substitute
1/2 cup (60 g) all-purpose flour
3/4 teaspoon baking powder
1/4 teaspoon salt

To make a substitute for Bisquick powder, in a small bowl, mix together the flour, baking powder and salt.

Sweet Cheese Ball Dessert Rasgoola

Rasgoola is one of my favorite Indian desserts and every time I visit India, I gobble up a bunch of them! They are sweet and juicy cheese balls from the eastern Indian state of Bengal. Soft Indian cheese (*paneer*) is shaped into small circles that are then simmered in a simple sugar syrup. Rasgoola are served chilled, so after you've cooked them, you do have to wait while they chill in the refrigerator! I like to sprinkle a few drops of kewra essence to give a traditional flavor, but this is optional.

Serves 5
Prep time: 5 minutes + 1 hour refrigerating + 10 minutes to make Crumbled Indian Cheese
Cook time: 20 minutes + 20 minutes cooling time + 2 hours to chill in the refrigerator
Refrigerator life: 3 days
Reheating method: None! Serve chilled.

1 recipe Crumbled Indian Cheese (page 42), chilled for 30 minutes in the refrigerator
1 cup (200 g) sugar
2 cups (500 ml) water
2 drops kewra essence (optional)

1 Blend the chilled cheese in a mini food processor until smooth and creamy. At first the cheese may seem as if it's crumbling even further in the food processor, but soon it will come together in a ball. Add any loose bits of cheese to the ball with your hand.

2 Divide the cheese into 10 equal pieces. Wash your hands so they are clean and it is easier to continue working with the cheese.

3 Using your hands, gently roll each piece into a smooth ball. Cover and refrigerate for 30 minutes to allow the cheese balls to set.

4 To make the syrup, bring the sugar and water to a rolling boil in a medium saucepan over high heat.

5 Add the cheese balls to the boiling syrup. Cook for 2 minutes while boiling. Reduce the heat to medium. Simmer for 15 minutes, undisturbed. The cheese balls will slightly fluff up. Remove from the heat and let rest undisturbed as the syrup cools to room temperature (about 20 minutes).

6 Sprinkle on the kewra essence, if using, and gently stir. Cover and place in the refrigerator until chilled. When serving, place 2 Rasgoola per person in a dessert bowl, and add plenty of the syrup. Enjoy now or keep refrigerated for later!

Classic Indian Ice Cream Malai ki Kulfi

Kulfi is a delicious treat commonly sold as ice cream bars on thin wooden sticks in the streets of India. When I visit India in the hot summer, I am always happy to hear the loud holler of the kulfi vendor "kool-feeeeee, malai walee!" which means ice cream of sweetened and thickened boiled milk. He comes down the streets pushing his big cart loaded with kulfi bars. This ice cream has a sweet milky flavor with a hint of cardamom. Kulfi is not churned during the freezing process, so it has a solid, dense texture rather than a soft and creamy texture of a typical ice cream. No ice cream machine is needed for this easy to make cooling treat!

> **TIP:** This recipe may be doubled, but if you were to triple it or quadruple it for a large party, it's best to make it in single or double batches. The time needed to bring very large amounts of milk to a boil and then to reduce the milk by half increases the chances of scorching the milk and turning it a yellowish color, which is not as desirable as creamy white milk. Smaller batches will cook faster and give you tastier and prettier results.

Serves 4
Prep work: 5 minutes
Cook time: 20 minutes + 20 minutes cooling time + 3 hours to set in the freezer
Freezer life: 1 month

2 cups (500 ml) whole milk
5 whole green cardamom pods
1/4 cup (50 g) sugar
2 tablespoons coarsely crushed, unsalted pistachios (see "Tip on Crushing Pistachios," page 150) (optional)

1 Pour the milk into a heavy bottomed, medium-sized saucepan. Bring to a rolling boil over high heat, stirring frequently as it comes to a boil. Don't let the milk boil over and out of the saucepan! Immediately reduce the heat to medium.
2 Open the cardamoms and place the seeds and pods in a tea infuser and place in the saucepan. (Or you can place the seeds and pods in a small cheesecloth pouch tied with a string.)
3 Simmer the milk until it is half reduced to 1 cup (250 ml), stirring frequently, about 15 minutes. If any skin forms on the surface, simply stir it back in. If there is any scorched milk at the bottom of the saucepan, do not scrape it.
4 Add the sugar and stir until it has all dissolved. Remove from heat and let cool to room temperature (about 20 minutes) to avoid transferring very hot milk into plastic molds.
5 Remove the cardamom pods and seeds and discard. Pour the milk (and any thick skin) into ice cream bar molds or an ice cube tray or any shape mold you prefer. Put in freezer until frozen, about 3 hours.
6 Remove the frozen ice cream from the molds by tilting the molds sideways and running under hot water until the ice cream loosens and you can take it out. Sprinkle pistachios on top if desired. Enjoy!

Serves 4 to 6
Prep time: 5 minutes   **Cook time:** 30 minutes
Refrigerator life: 5 days   **Freezer life:** 1 month
Reheating method: Stir and serve either chilled or
heated. To heat, place the refrigerated or defrosted
kheer in a microwave, cover and stir periodically. Or,
place it in a saucepan over medium-low heat and stir
periodically.

1/4 cup (45 g) uncooked white Basmati rice
1/2 cup (125 ml) water
2 1/4 cups (565 ml) whole milk
4 whole green cardamom pods
3/4 cup (185 ml) half-and-half
2 tablespoons blanched and slivered almonds
    or 10 whole almonds, blanched and slivered
    (see page 24)
1/2 cup (100 g) sugar

1 Place the rice in a small bowl and wash with cold
water until the water runs clear, carefully draining the
water out of the bowl after each rinsing. Pour the rice
into a sieve to drain.
2 Place the rice and the water in a heavy bottomed,
medium-sized saucepan. Bring to a rolling boil over
high heat. Cook uncovered until the rice has absorbed
all the water, stirring occasionally, about 3 minutes.
3 Add the milk and stir. Bring to a rolling boil, stirring
frequently as it comes to a boil. Don't let the milk boil
over and out of the saucepan! Immediately reduce the
heat to medium.
4 Open the cardamoms and add the seeds and the
pods. Simmer the milk for about 15 minutes for it to
thicken and blend with the rice, stirring frequently.
If any skin forms, simply stir it back in. If there is any
scorched milk at the bottom of the saucepan, do not
scrape it.
5 Add the half-and-half and almonds. Reduce the
heat to medium-low. Simmer for 10 minutes, stirring
frequently.
6 Add the sugar and stir until it has all dissolved.
Remove the cardamom pods and discard. You may
leave the seeds in. Enjoy now or let cool to room
temperature and refrigerate or freeze for later! The
kheer will further thicken as it cools, so if you like it
extra thick and creamy, serve it chilled. If you prefer
it a little less thick, serve it warm.

Sweet Rice Pudding Kheer

Kheer, or rice pudding, is a popular dessert that is found around the world in different variations such as *arroz con leche* (rice with milk) from Mexico and *rizogalo* (rice milk) from Greece. In India, kheer is a much loved dessert served at weddings, temples, or at any festive occasion. Kheer can be made with different consistencies from very thin to a thicker, porridge consistency, which is what I personally prefer as this recipe reflects. You may serve this dessert in small bowls. Kheer is usually served warm, but I enjoy eating it chilled!

Resource Guide

To make things convenient for both you and me, I have tried my best to cook with ingredients and spices that can be easily found at a local grocery store, without having to make any special trips to ethnic markets. However, there are a few ingredients such as fresh curry leaves and the different varieties of Indian lentils that might require a trip to an Indian market or require you to place an order from an online market or a store that ships goods.

I have compiled a list of online Indian grocers and some brick-and-mortar stores throughout the United States, and also some in Canada and London, that you can visit and, in some cases, order food and spices from to be shipped to your home. Some of the bigger Indian grocery stores have more than just spices, lentils, burlap bags filled with Basmati rice, flours, and varieties of *pappadum* ready to be cooked, but they also have fresh produce such as juicy mangoes and vegetables, fresh herbs, Indian frozen foods, refrigerated pre-made *paneer* (Indian cheese), packaged snack mixes, and snack foods such as *samosa*. Stores also have chilled Indian beverages, my favorite being bottled mango juice! And some Indian grocery stores have beautiful Indian cooking tools, utensils and serving dishes made from copper, brass, or stainless steel. You might even find organic health and beauty products such as fragrant sandalwood soap, herbal skin creams made with turmeric, natural hair dyes made from the henna plant and perfumed incense sticks for aromatherapy relaxation. At some grocery stores, you might even be able to rent a Bollywood movie (most come with subtitles!) and buy an Indian music CD.

In large cities, Indian markets are often located in an Indian shopping district—a "Little India"—where you can find a range of types of stores and services, and, depending on its size, multiple grocers. You might find stores that sell Indian jewelry made of gold, diamond, precious stones and even costume jewelry, or traditional men and women's clothing (kurta pajama and sari). There are likely to be snack shops selling Indian street food or hole-in the wall cafes, which offer food from the different regions of India. If you like, you may step into an Indian beauty salon to get your eyebrows neatly shaped by the threading technique. Just as in done in the markets in India, bargaining (or haggling as I see it!) is common at most of these shops (other than for food, groceries, cafes and salons). Don't be afraid to try out your negotiating skills. If you pay the asking price for bangles or a sari you will have definitely made the shopkeeper's day!

ONLINE STORES

If you do not have an Indian store nearby, you can order your Indian dry groceries online from one of these grocers. Some online stores will also ship fresh produce and other fresh groceries.

www.ishopindian.com (United States, Hawaii and Alaska; international) This online Indian grocery store has pictures for its products, and that is helpful when ordering. You can get all your spices, fresh curry leaves, and also Indian cooking utensils such as a *karahi* or spice box, Indian movies and music, and also herbal health and beauty products. The distribution is from Wisconsin. The website itself has limited fresh produce such as fresh curry leaves, fresh ginger and fresh garlic, but if you would like to order some fresh produce that is not on their website such as green or yellow mangoes or Indian eggplants, you may contact them (see website for contact info) to find out what weekly fresh produce they have in stock, since it changes week to week, and also season to season.

www.indianblend.com (United States, Hawaii and Alaska; Canada; Mexico and other countries upon request) This website has pictures of each item, and if you click on each item, it gives you a description of the product. In addition to buying your spices from here, you can even browse the Indian jewelry and choose some to wear at your next Indian dinner party or as a gift for a friend! The distribution is from Atlanta, Georgia. Fresh produce, such as green and yellow mangoes, are available only when in season.

www.patelbrothersusa.com (United States, not Hawaii or Alaska) This is the online component of the Patel Brothers store in Flushing, NY, that you may also physically shop at. (Patel Brothers is a franchise with retail stores all throughout the United States.) If you do not see an item on their website, such as green mangoes, give them a call or email them (contact info on website). They might able to send it to you.

www.spicesofindia.co.uk (UK) This online store serves the UK. Along with a large variety of Indian groceries and spices, this online store has an amazing variety of fresh fruits and vegetables ready to ship, and there is even the option to buy the Indian *tandoor* oven!

INDIAN MARKETS

If you're new to shopping at Indian markets, I can understand that the exotic sights and aromas may be intimidating, but just ask for help if you need it. I hope you enjoy yourself, discover new ingredients and save a buck, since I have found shopping for ingredients at Indian grocery stores is more economical than shopping at my local American grocery store. Just remember to call before going to see if the stores have fresh curry leaves or green and yellow mangoes, as these are seasonal, and to make sure they are open and the address is the same.

NORTHEAST (Boston, NY, Philadelphia)

Patel Brothers
425 Moody St, Waltham, MA 02453
(781) 893-1003
This store, located in Boston's Little India, has every ingredient you will need. Patel Brothers has a website that you can order Indian groceries from (see the online section for more details).

Kalustyans
123 Lexington Avenue, New York, NY 10016
1-800-352-3451 (toll free only in the US)
(212) 685-3451

www.kalustyans.com. Just a few blocks south of Murray Hill in Manhattan is a concentrated area of Indian shops and restaurants, which is Little India, but also cleverly called Curry Hill! The Indian shops are centered around the intersection of 28th Street and Lexington Avenue. Kalustyans is a well-stocked international grocery store that has everything Indian also. This store is never-ending! It just keeps going and going and I enjoy perusing the aisles there. You wouldn't imagine from the small exterior how big and stocked the inside is. The only items I could not find at this store were green and yellow mangoes, but there are other Indian grocery stores in the same area, and you should be able to find them there.

Patel Brothers
37-27, 74th St, Queens, NY 11372
(718) 898-3445
This Patel Brothers store is located in the Jackson Heights neighborhood of Queens, which is the main Indian shopping area in New York. I visited this area once and was surprised at the number of Indian shops crammed against each other on the street. This area definitely has to be called Little India, with Indian restaurants, businesses, travel agents, music and video stores, clothing, jewelry, and of course Indian grocery stores! If for some odd reason you do not find what you are looking for at Patel Brothers, I am sure you can look around and spot another Indian grocery store nearby. Patel Brothers has a website that you can order Indian groceries from (see the online section for more details).

International Foods and Spices
4203 Walnut St, Philadelphia, PA 19104
(215) 222-4480
In west Philadelphia, you will find this Indian grocery store that has fresh curry leaves, spices, lentils, and Indian flours in different varieties.

MID-ATLANTIC (D.C.)

Daily Spices
8424 Lee Hwy, Fairfax, VA 22031
(703) 752-2314
If you are in the D.C. area, you can stop by this store to get your supply of Indian groceries. While you are here, if you would like to get a taste of Indian cinema, you can rent an Indian Bollywood movie to take home and enjoy!

SOUTHEAST (Atlanta, Charlotte, NC, Miami)

Patel Brothers
1711 Church Street, Decatur, GA 30033
(404) 296-2696
My mother-in-law's choice store for Indian spices and ingredients is the ubiquitous Patel Brothers store. This Atlanta area store is located in the Little India shopping area in the city of Decatur, so after shopping, step into an Indian café for a cup of Indian tea. Patel Brothers has a website that you can order Indian groceries from (see the online section for more details).

Payal Indian Grocery & Spices
6400 Old Pineville Rd, Charlotte, NC 28217
(704) 521-9680
This shop has the basic Indian spices and ingredients, and fresh produce such as green pickling mangoes and curry leaves. Pickling mangoes are not always available, so perhaps a quick call to the store to make sure they have them before you go will be helpful.

Indo American Grocery
13760 SW 84th St, Miami, FL 33183
(305) 382-7570

This Indian market in Miami offers a bounty of ingredients for you to make a delicious Indian meal at home. Bags of spices, fresh curry leaves, lentils, flours, rice and more are available at this store.

MID-WEST (Chicago, Kansas City, Detroit)

Patel Brothers,
2610 W Devon Ave, Chicago, IL 60659
(773) 262-7777
If you live in the Chicago area and you want to go to an area where Indian stores, cafes, and boutiques are lined up against each other, Devon Avenue is the place to be. It is the Little India of Chicago, and is where the Patel Brothers franchise first started and their headquarters still remains. This grocery store should have everything you could possibly think of when wanting to cook Indian food! Patel Brothers has a website that you can order Indian groceries from (see the online section for more details).

KC India Mart
8542 W 133rd St, Overland Park, KS 66213
(913) 681-0808

For the Kansas City area, this store will have the basics for Indian grocery shopping. Fresh curry leaves might not always be readily available, so call them before you go.

India Town
34714 Dequindre Rd, Sterling Heights, MI 48310
(586)-264-6200
Fill your shopping bag with fresh vegetables, numerous spices, and a variety of *pappadums* varying in spiciness at this Detroit-area Indian grocery store. Pick out some spiced snack mixes to enjoy with your afternoon tea or coffee break!

SOUTHWEST (Houston, Dallas, Las Vegas, Phoenix)

India Grocers
6606 Southwest Freeway, Houston, TX 77074
(713) 266-7717
This is my favorite Indian grocery store in Houston. It is in the Little India of Houston, also simply called "Hillcroft" after the name of the street where the Indian shops are concentrated on. (India Grocers is located on the freeway that runs next to Hillcroft.) India Grocers is a one-stop shopping place for Indian spices, kitchen ware, fresh curry leaves and great prices on fresh mint and coriander leaves (cilantro). Will ship small orders upon request.

Indian Supermarket
9400 N Macarthur Blvd, #114, Irving, TX 75063
(972) 444-0020
This shop offers a good selection of spices, lentils, flours, and other Indian ingredients for residents of the Dallas and Fortworth area.

India Market
5006 S Maryland Pkwy # 7, Las Vegas
NV 89119-4710
(702) 736-6677
In this Las Vegas Indian grocery store you will find a variety of lentils, flours, spices, and other ingredients for your Indian cooking needs. You can also buy some Indian mixed snacks and biscuits to munch on while you watch a Bollywood movie, which you can also buy from here! Will ship small orders upon request.

India Plaza
1874 E Apache Blvd, Tempe, AZ 85281
(480) 557-8800
India Plaza is a big grocery store in the India Plaza

Shopping Center near Phoenix. In the plaza, there are all types of items available from Indian music, jewelry, kitchen utensils and more. There is also a beauty salon for you to stop in for some pampering after you are finished shopping!

ROCKY MOUNTAIN (Denver)

My India's
1000 Depot Hill, Unit E, Broomfield, CO 80020
(303) 466-0800
If you live in the Denver area, this store can provide you with your basic Indian cooking ingredients. Choose from a variety of colorful whole and ground spices, legumes and lentils and everything else to prepare a fabulous, yet easy, Indian meal at home!

WEST (San Francisco, Los Angeles)

New India Bazzar
1107 Polk St. San Francisco, CA 94109
(415) 928-4553
This shop near the Tenderloin neighborhood of the city will not only fulfill your basic needs for Indian spices and ingredients, but you can also buy an Indian Bollywood movie!

New India Sweets & Spices
1245 S Fairfax Ave, Los Angeles, CA 90019
(323) 936-6736
This store is actually a combination grocery shop and café, although the café part is just a small seating area with a table or two! You can shop here for all of your Indian groceries, and then sit down for a *samosa* snack or get a quick lunch to go! They also have a small selection of freshly made Indian desserts. Last time I was there, along with getting a cool and refreshing guava drink, I got tempted to buy a Cadbury's chocolate bar with fruits and nuts in it, just as I used to enjoy them in India on my trips there as a child.

NORTHWEST (Seattle, Oregon)

Apna Bazar, 2245 148th Ave NE
Bellevue, WA 98007
(425) 644-6887
You should be able to find a variety of spices, dry ingredients, and fresh produce at this store, so it is worth the traffic to drive here from Seattle!

The Souk
1916 Pike Place Market, Seattle, WA 98101
(206) 441-1666

This is an international spice shop that has dry spices and grains. It is located in Seattle's Pike Place Market, which is a fun and bustling outdoor area lined with shops and restaurants, and places to get fresh seafood, so you can pick up your spices and some fish to make a fish curry for dinner! This shop does not have any fresh produce, but they may sometimes have fresh curry leaves. You could go to Apna Bazar in Bellevue to get fresh mangoes and other produce. Will ship small orders upon request.

Fiji Emporium
7814 N Interstate Ave, Portland, Oregon, 97222
(503) 240-2768
In addition to offering basic Indian groceries, including goat meat, this store also sells Indian musical instruments, fragrant incense sticks and rents Indian movies. This store also has foods from Australia, New Zealand and, as the name suggests, Fiji. Will ship small orders upon request.

CANADA

Punjab Food Centre
6635 Main Street, Vancouver, B.C V5X 3H3
(604) 322-5502
The central Indian shopping area in Vancouver is the Punjabi Market which consists of a few blocks of Indian stores and businesses on Main Street between 49th and 51st Avenues. The Punjab Food Centre is the place where you can buy spices, ingredients and beautiful metal kitchenware.

BJ Super Market
1449 Gerrard Street, East Toronto, ON. M4L 1Z9
(416) 469-3712
In Toronto, there is a Little India neighborhood on Gerrard Street between Coxwell and Greenwood. This small strip is also known as the Gerrard Indian Bazaar. Here you can find BJ Super Market and a variety of other Indian shops and restaurants.

Marché Priyanka
808 Rue Jean Talon West, Montreal, Quebec
(514) 278-5757
In Montreal, there are many Indian stores on Jean Talon between Parc and L'Acadie. Marché Priyanka is located on that strip, and there you can do your Indian grocery shopping.

LONDON

The Indian Spice Shop
115-117 Drummond Street,
Camden London NW1 2HL
020 7916 1831
Drummond Street is home to a number of Indian stores and restaurants. The Indian Spice Shop sells numerous Indian spices and groceries, and you can look around Drummond Street for other shops as well to buy vegetables, lentils, flours and other groceries.

Bristol Sweet Mart
80 St. Marks Road, Bristol BS5 6JH
0117 951 2257
www.sweetmart.co.uk
You can do your Indian grocery shopping at this store by going into the store, or simply by ordering online from the comfort of your home.

Quality Foods
47-61, South Road, Southall - UB1 1SQ, Middlesex
020 8917 9188
This store is located in a large, yet highly concentrated area of Indian shops and outdoor stalls filled with fresh vegetables for sale. It is hard to pick which shops to go into especially when you are shot of time, but you can get started with your Indian grocery shopping at Quality Foods.

V B & Sons
147 Ealing Road, Wembley, Middlesex HA0 4BU
020 8795 0387

This Indian supermarket is one of the most popular in London. It is in the Wembley area, which is a very popular Little India shopping center in North London. There are also outdoor stalls with vegetables for sale.

Index

AFGHANISTAN

JAMMU AND KASHMIR

Indus

CHINA

My dad was born in Buttar Sivia Village, District Amritsar

Rice

HIMACHAL PRADESH

I was born here

My mom was born in Jalandhar

PUNJAB

Chandigarh
UTTARAKHAND

PAKISTAN

Indus

HARYANA

Wheat

DELHI ★

Taj Mahal

HIMALAYAN MOUNTAINS

NEPAL

Mount Everest
29,029 ft
(8,848 m)

SIKKIM

BHUTAN

ARUNACHAL PRADESH

Brahmaputra

ASSAM

Tea

NAGALAND

RAJASTHAN

• Jaipur

UTTAR PRADESH

Yamuna   *Ganga*

BIHAR

Ganga

MEGHALAYA

BANGLADESH

MANIPUR

TRIPURA

MIZORAM

MYANMAR

GUJARAT

MADHYA PRADESH

Narmada

CHHATTISGARH

JHARKHAND

WEST BENGAL

Kolkata
(Calcutta)

Tapti

MAHARASHTRA

India Gate

Mumbai •
(Bombay)

• Pune

ORISSA

Mahanadi

Godavari

Fish

Bay of Bengal

My husband's birthplace

Krishna

• Hyderabad

Prawn

Krishna

ANDHRA PRADESH

Chili peppers

Coconut

My father-in-law was born in Pasumarru Village, District Krishna

Arabian Sea

Panaji •
GOA

Fish

My mother-in-law was born in Repalli

Fish

Banana

KARNATAKA

Rice

Bangalore •

• Chennai
(Madras)

Fish

Fish

LAKSHADWEEP

TAMIL NADU

Coffee

Kaveri

Coconut

KERALA

ANDAMAN & NICOBAR ISLANDS

N

W   E

S

Coconut

MALDIVES

SRI LANKA

0   300km

scale 1 : 12 300 000

INDIAN OCEAN